The Battle for Yellowstone

PRINCETON STUDIES IN
CULTURAL SOCIOLOGY

Paul J. DiMaggio, Michèle Lamont,
Robert J. Wuthnow, and Viviana A. Zelizer,
Series Editors

A list of titles in this series appears at the back of the book

The Battle for Yellowstone

Morality and the Sacred Roots of Environmental Conflict

Justin Farrell

PRINCETON UNIVERSITY PRESS
Princeton and Oxford

Requests for permission to reproduce material from this work should be sent
    to Permissions, Princeton University Press
Published by Princeton University Press, 41 William Street, Princeton,
    New Jersey 08540
In the United Kingdom: Princeton University Press, 6 Oxford Street,
    Woodstock, Oxfordshire OX20 1TW

press.princeton.edu

Cover photograph by Jared White, The Wilderness Society
Cover design by Jason Alejandro

First paperback printing, 2017
Paper ISBN: 978-0-691-17630-7

The Library of Congress has cataloged the cloth edition as follows

Farrell, Justin, 1984–
The Battle for Yellowstone : morality and the sacred roots of environmental conflict / Justin
Farrell.
pages cm. — (Princeton studies in cultural sociology)
Includes bibliographical references and index.
ISBN 978-0-691-16434-2 (hardcover : alkaline paper) 1. Environmentalism—Moral and
ethical aspects—Yellowstone National Park.   2. Environmental ethics—Yellowstone National
Park.   3. Environmental policy—Yellowstone National Park.   4. Yellowstone National Park—
Environmental conditions. 5. Social conflict—West (U.S.) 6. Environmentalism—Moral
and ethical aspects—West (U.S.) 7. Environmental ethics—West (U.S.) 8. Environmental
policy—West (U.S.) 9. West (U.S.)—Environmental conditions.   10. West (U.S.)—Social conditions. I. Title.
GE198.Y45F37 2015
333.78′30978752—dc23
                          2014046237

British Library Cataloging-in-Publication Data is available

This book has been composed in Minion Pro and Clarendon

Printed on acid-free paper. ∞

Typeset by S R Nova Pvt Ltd, Bangalore, India
Printed in the United States of America

For Ashley, my love.

CONTENTS

ILLUSTRATIONS

TABLES

ACKNOWLEDGMENTS

One of my most vivid childhood memories of the Yellowstone area was watching one summer—with my late brother Joshua—as a resort company built a small hotel next to my grandfather's aged cabin. My curiosity about the deeper meaning of this relatively minor construction project would stay with me for many years. As time passed, and with each summer spent in the area, it seemed that while so much within Yellowstone National Park stayed the same, so much just outside its borders changed. As part of an extended family deeply attached to this area, I listened over the years as relatives lamented these changes brought on by expanding tourism and land development, while at the same time—and somewhat paradoxically—opposing government interference or increased environmental regulation aimed to slow the very changes they bemoaned. At its most basic level, this book is my own attempt to reconcile these family experiences with the cultural, moral, and political puzzles that came in their wake.

Of course, the name printed on the front of this book obscures the fact that this is the product of countless people. I am indebted to many women and men who graciously guided me on my academic journey. My earliest experiences in Princeton working for Robert Wuthnow conducting interviews with farmers in the rural midwest opened my eyes to the study of culture, and with his help, I applied to graduate programs in sociology. Since that time, Bob has been a steady and invaluable resource, including reading and commenting on a full draft of the manuscript.

I owe my biggest debt of gratitude to Chris Smith and Omar Lizardo. Chris's direct and incisive advice kept me grounded and on track as I struggled to bring the Yellowstone conflict into conversation with sociology of culture, environment, morality, and religion. Omar gave me the confidence to follow my instincts, to think outside of the box, even in the face of disciplinary norms and boundaries. Fortunately, too, Omar's guidance happened most often with the assistance of a good microbrew. I know that at times I pushed the limits of the idiom "not all who wander are lost," but nevertheless, Chris especially continued to believe in the project during its most difficult seasons. With a spirit of patience, he invested in the idea by asking difficult questions, giving blunt feedback, and pushing me to continually make the project better. Indeed, Chris and Omar's critical eyes and valuable insight were matched only by their consistent generosity. I am also indebted to Kraig Beyerlein, for our early morning conversations that kept my eye on the methodological ball, especially in the early stages as I planned my research strategy. Rory McVeigh influenced the project more than he may realize, with his continual push for me to focus on the broader structures of moral culture. In addition to commenting on various stages of the project, Jessica Collett and Terence McDonnell were a constant source of positive encouragement. My fellow graduate students Daniel Escher, Peter Barwis, and David Everson helped in many different ways. I am thankful for their friendship. Last, I want to thank Eric Schwartz, Meagan Levinson, Ryan Mulligan, and Leslie Grundfest at Princeton University Press for their support and expertise during the publishing process. Additionally, I am indebted to the series editors, Paul DiMaggio, Michèle Lamont, Robert Wuthnow, and Viviana Zelizer, for their initial enthusiasm about the project.

I am extraordinarily grateful to the people in the Greater Yellowstone area who let me into their lives. From the miners, farmers, and ranchers, to the new-west transplants, anti-wolf activists, and conservationists, I hope that in what follows I have rewarded your trust and faithfully told your stories in all of their fascinating complexity.

Support for research and writing of the book was provided by a three-year STAR Graduate Fellowship from the Environmental Protection Agency, as well as various grants and fellowships from the graduate school at Notre Dame, the Center for the Study of Religion and Society at Notre Dame, the Louisville Institute, the National Science Foundation, the Society for the Scientific Study of Religion, and the Religious Research Association. After collecting the data, I wrote a good portion of the manuscript at Blue Line Coffee in Omaha, Nebraska, and am grateful to Chris and the baristas for pouring out such a rich source of community.

As I reflect upon the years that it took me to write this book, it becomes harder and harder to separate the manuscript from the priceless memories spent with family during its various stages. In reading the various data, sections, and chapters, I see the life-sustaining love during holiday celebrations, family dinners, spirited political discussions, Frisbee with sweet-boy-Norman, festive parties, tailgate BBQs, and the like. The Renshaw clan were always the first to celebrate even the smallest achievement, and the exuberance with which they pour out their love still astounds me to this day. My brother Jordan offered constant encouragement, in addition to his own academic expertise, reading and insightfully commenting on every chapter. My parents, Mike and JoAnn, my biggest fans, have been by my side since I decided on a life in academics. They have been especially supportive of this project and, with their knowledge of the Yellowstone area, have been indispensable discussion partners. As a first-generation college student, my foray into the academic world was as new to them as it was to me, but that did not stop them from offering their unconditional support, and even participating with me in this new life of learning. It is readily apparent how proud they are of me, but as I grow older, I find myself reflecting on how proud I am of them.

This book was written in memory of my older brother Joshua, whom I lost to a car accident in 2001. I thought of him often as I traveled, researched, and wrote about all of these Yellowstone areas we explored together as we were growing up. No doubt, I have written with him heavy on my mind, fighting recurrent bouts of deep heartache, but sometimes disrupted by bursts of joy when I came across something that reminded me of the unforgettable times we shared in this place called Yellowstone.

Finally, this book is for no one else but Ashley, my love. She came into my life as Joshua left it, and I simply cannot imagine life without her. She patiently endured the itinerant, uncertain, and self-absorbed nature of academic life, while still managing to build a successful career for the greater good in nonprofit development. She was my rock and my strength throughout the project, always by my side, and always willing to share this long journey with me. For so many more reasons, I dedicate this book only to her.

The Battle for Yellowstone

Introduction: Bringing Moral Culture into the Fray

Yellowstone holds a special place in America's heart—a young nation's Eden and the crown jewel of modern preservation. As the world's first national park, it is globally recognized as the prototype of natural purity and goodness. But in recent decades, Yellowstone and its surrounding areas have become a lightningrod for environmental controversy, an area plagued by social disunity and intractable political struggle. The unyielding battle for Yellowstone—the topic of this book— has become one of the most symbolically and substantively important examples of modern environmental conflict. The significance of this case is heightened by the growing set of interrelated and intensifying environmental conflicts facing human societies around the world: climate change, energy constraints, toxic waste, food and water shortages, genetic engineering, population growth, public land management, pollution, and decreasing biodiversity. In recent decades, these environmental problems have come to intersect with, and rival in importance, other social problems and conflicts in modern societies. More and more attention has been devoted to understanding environmental problems, as demonstrated by the growth in public concern, expanding laws, the emergence of new institutions, international (dis)agreements, and an explosion in the volume of research in the natural and social sciences about the causes, consequences, and solutions to environmental problems.

Nestled at the feet of the towering Teton Range, just off the shore of the picturesque Jackson Lake, and within minutes of the southern border of Yellowstone National Park, is the University of Wyoming–National Park Service research center. The center buzzes with teams of biologists, ecologists, and other natural scientists from around the world conducting research on myriad problems facing the Greater Yellowstone Ecosystem (GYE). Seeking affordable housing during my fieldwork, I was fortunate to stay on this beautiful campus, which provided me not only a temporary base for my own research, but also close contact with some of the world's preeminent natural scientists. From my discussions with these experts, I quickly learned how deeply committed they were to solving the most urgent threats facing the ecosystem. Equally captivating was the depth and complexity of their technical tools and the capabilities they applied to this effort. This research center is only one small example of the massive endeavor, both inside and outside the GYE, by armies of natural scientists to supply vast technical expertise about this ecosystem. Alongside natural scientists are equally large groups of economists, lawyers, policy specialists, and other technical experts who work diligently on contentious issues in the GYE—creating a flurry of biological research, economic valuation, legal scrutiny, policy programs, city planning, cost-benefit analysis, and the like, in the hopes of providing enough scientific empirical analyses and evidence to resolve the many intractable conflicts that plague the area.

Accordingly, management decisions in the GYE rely on a hyperrationalized form of governance that privileges technical facts, scientific analysis of nature, bureaucratic administration, and legal formalism. Decision makers such as state agents (e.g., National Park Service workers, forest rangers, etc.), interest group members (e.g., environmentalists and cattle industry, tourism, and oil and gas groups), elected officials (e.g., judges, governors, representatives), and scientists are caught up in a world of prediction and world mastery—where, as Max Weber describes, "one can, in principle, master all things by calculation" (2009, p. 139). For example, when faced with an environmental problem, managers follow a long line of formal scientific procedures, deciding first whether a given "problem" is in fact a problem, examining potential causes, solutions, alternative solutions, long-term ecological effects, how to balance economic impacts, how to strategically push solutions through institutional channels (e.g., through litigation or legislation); and later analyzing whether solutions worked and how to improve upon them in the future. Decision makers in the GYE often "get stuck in one of these activities, such as calling for ever more research or endlessly debating potential solutions" (Clark, 2008, p. 23). These science and policy efforts are especially protracted in the GYE, involving hundreds of diverse interest organizations, dozens of state agencies, three separate state governments, hundreds of thousands of local residents, and millions of concerned Americans.

Scholars studying such problems—as well as the stakeholders in the thick of the struggle—rely on well-worn theories to explain this conflict: as simply a clash between experts and an ignorant, illiterate, or ill-informed public; or as the lack of sufficient ecological and biological knowledge; or as the need to simply reshape individual stakeholders' "attitudes"; or they turn to social movement explanations relating to resource mobilization; or to an innate struggle over political power; or more simply, to economic self-interest. To be sure, these theories matter a great deal. Yet, I found that they do little to fully explain the Yellowstone conflict. They tell us more about the *how* of conflict than the *why*. We are then left with the following puzzle: Why, with the flood of expert scientific, legal, economic, and political efforts to resolve disagreements over Yellowstone, are matters not improving? Despite all of these efforts, why do even the most minor issues still recurrently erupt into impassioned and long-lasting disputes? It became clear that we need a better theoretical approach if we are to fully understand why this American icon of peace became, and continues to be, the site of intractable acrimony and toxic polarization.

Put in its broadest terms, my argument is that this modern obsession with scientific, legal, and economic reasoning misses out on deeper cultural mechanisms driving the conflict in the first place. Put more specifically, my argument is this: *any sociological account of this conflict should be built upon a more empirically accurate and philosophically sophisticated model of human persons and cultures, which does not presuppose narrow or deterministic motivational frameworks but understands that the "why," in the end, is a question of morality—perhaps even spirituality—stemming from our lived experiences as part of human cultures, shaped by narratives and moral orders that tell us most fundamentally who we are, why we are, what we should do, and why it all matters.* Drawing on work in cultural sociology and moral theory to make this argument,[1] I reorient our attention to the sorts of "whys" that make life meaningful for different cultures, and propel them forward toward particular ends, and not other ends. These are the sorts of answers to the "why" questions that we need to incorporate into our theories and methods if we hope to improve our understanding of the human-environment relationship more generally.

Thus, environmental conflict in Yellowstone is not—as it would appear on the surface—ultimately all about scientific, economic, legal, or other technical evidence and arguments, but an underlying struggle over deeply held "faith" commitments, feelings, and desires that define what people find sacred, good, and meaningful in life at a most basic level. The current and allegedly most important resources relied upon by actors and observers of the conflict do not, and cannot, ultimately define for different people why one *should* care about Yellowstone *in the first place*, why an intact ecosystem is better than a fragmented one, why aesthetic beauty should or should not be protected, why some animals should be venerated while others are considered pests, why some land is "too special" to drill while other land is drilled with indifference, or why people might view their old-west labor, recreation, and heritage as profoundly meaningful, perhaps even sacred. Answers to these questions are only possible and made meaningful in the context of larger moral orders and spiritual narratives that shared human cultures are built upon.

To be clear, my sociological approach in this book focuses less on the individuals themselves, and more on the cultural, moral, and spiritual contexts in which stakeholders are embedded, shaping their beliefs and desires. Somewhat implicit in my argument is that, for a variety of reasons, these deeper moral and spiritual meanings are often *ignored, muted,* and *misunderstood.* But only as we engage these sorts of questions at a much deeper level can we begin to understand

---

1 I draw primarily from Smith (2003). As I describe below, other influences include Jasper (1997), Taylor (1989), and Wuthnow (1989).

why the mountains of technical evidence marshaled in the Yellowstone conflict have done little to solve disputes that are, finally, not about the facts themselves, but about what make the facts meaningful. Further, this book shows that when we glimpse beneath the cultural context of the Yellowstone conflict, and bring these deeper moral and spiritual dimensions to the surface, we often learn what conflict is really about—and in some cases discover roadmaps leading beyond the thick pines of technorational policy stalemate.

More concretely, where does such an approach lead us? It leads us to the more peculiar cultural influences that structure life in the American West. It leads us to the more subtle, but ever-powerful, narratives informing what the "good life" looks like, and how one might go about living it. It leads us to investigate what it means to be a "good" person, and the larger contexts and practices that shape such commitments. It leads us to examine changing ideas about the natural environment, particularly with regard to what it is "good" for. Such narratives and commitments influence, and are influenced by, larger socioeconomic forces at work in American life during the 19th and 20th centuries. In examining the historical sources and contemporary effects of such commitments, my approach engages narratives about manifest destiny, rugged individualism, human dominionism, and other cultural ingredients making up what I call an "old-west" way of life. At the same time, we can shed light on environmental disputes by uncovering competing narratives and moral commitments that have taken hold in the American West, about the romantic vision for the spiritual redemption of nature, the intrinsic value of nonhuman animals, and the promise and progress of environmental science.

Beyond the specifics of the conflict, my cultural approach yielded a handful of important, and related, theoretical puzzles that are investigated along the way. How do aspects of social life that are thought to be about instrumental value or material preferences become infused with moral and religious meaning? How are habits of talk about morality and spirituality organized and patterned by larger social structures in American life? Why do individuals who are embedded within strong moral and religious cultures still struggle to recognize or coherently articulate their reasons for their behavior? Where, and how, does spirituality show up in "secular" contexts, and does it operate differently here than in traditionally religious contexts academics have tended to study? How are moral and spiritual claims used *in conjunction* with technical, scientific, and economic claims? What are the social and political conditions under which moral and spiritual factors can actually influence collective action? How do stakeholders engage in "moral boundary work" to mark their work, and their identities, as more virtuous than others?

In what follows in this introduction, I briefly present the conflict in Yellowstone, elaborate on my theoretical argument, and specify my substantive and theoretical contributions to the social scientific study of environment, culture, religion, and morality. I conclude with a roadmap outlining how these

Figure I.1: The Greater Yellowstone Ecosystem, approximate area shaded in gray. Yellowstone National Park is at the center, in white.

contributions unfold in the chapters that follow. Chapters 1 and 2 trace in historical detail the social organization of competing moral orders, providing the larger cultural and institutional context in which to understand the emergence of the conflict, and setting the backdrop for the finer-grained case studies that follow. Chapters 3, 4, and 5 pick up here and dig down into the inner workings of three of the most contentious conflicts in the GYE today, showing more concretely how morality and spirituality are tangled up in, and exert considerable influence on, conflicts that appear to be about rational, economic, secular, and scientific life.

Introducing the Greater Yellowstone Ecosystem

Yellowstone National Park (YNP) is part of a larger social and ecological system referred to since the mid-1980s as the "Greater Yellowstone Ecosystem." The GYE is a powerful symbol of the American West, and its natural and cultural resources occupy a privileged place in the American imagination. It is comprised of 20 million acres of diverse biological and topographic resources, and is one of the last large, intact temperate ecosystem in the world. It contains 60 percent of the world's geothermal regions. The headwaters of the Missouri-Mississippi, Columbia, and Colorado rivers are all located within the GYE. Spread over three states (Figure I.1), about 32 percent of the area is privately owned, while the rest of the GYE lands are under control of the United States Forest Service (seven national forests comprise 32 percent of GYE), the Bureau of Land Management (19 percent), the National Park Service (Yellowstone and Grand Teton National Park, 7 percent), indigenous tribes (5 percent), and other state and federal agencies (5 percent). Private lands are integral to the health of the ecosystem because they tend to be located in lower-elevation valleys and floodplains, meaning that many species in the GYE rely heavily on private lands for survival. Thus, even though only 32 percent of the GYE is privately owned, private landowners are especially critical in decision making about the health of the ecosystem.

In addition to vast wildlife populations, the GYE is also home to many small and midsize rural communities scattered throughout its 20 counties. Today, the population has grown to about half a million people. Unlike other rural counties across the United States, many of these 20 counties have experienced extraordinary population growth over the past few decades. Census data show that between 1970 and 2000, the counties making up the GYE experienced a 62 percent aggregate increase in population. Five of the counties within the GYE were in the top 10th percentile of overall population growth in the United States. From 2000 to 2010, counties like Sublette County, Wyoming (increased 73 percent), and Teton County, Idaho, ranked 10th and 12th, respectively, out of all 3,080 counties in the United States in percentage population growth. As a result of this population explosion, rural land development in these 20 counties increased more than 350 percent from 1970 to 2000, placing some parts of the GYE in the top five fastest growing land development areas in all of the United States.

The demographic, economic, and cultural changes that swept over the GYE region since 1970 are central to my story about the moral dimensions of conflict. I refer to this new social reality as the "new-west," a term describing a shift away from the "old-west" heritage of utilitarian extraction toward a new culture of natural amenity–minded transplants, influenced by new ideas about nature and motivated to both enjoy and protect its natural amenities.[2] The rise of the new-west was motivated in part by new moral and spiritual ideas about the natural environment that flourished during the mid-20th century. As I will show, these new ideas, and the growth that followed, would have major consequences on the old-west way of life. The hardworking, rugged rancher and dusty cattle drive were replaced with "cappuccino cowboys," college-educated telecommuters, wealthy retirees, and others seeking outdoor adventure lifestyles. New-west hubs, like Bozeman, MT, and Jackson Hole, WY, were transformed into premier destinations for a burgeoning cultural and environmental elite. Some came to enjoy the area, others came to protect it, but many came to do both. These dramatic changes redefined in the GYE what it meant to be a "good"

2 For more see Jones et al. (2003); Krannich et al. (2011); Rasker et al. (2003); Shumway and Otterstrom (2001).

person in relation to nature, simultaneously rejecting ecologically harmful old-west heritage and practices as ecologically evil and morally wrong. This led to the institutionalizing of an alternative moral order, rooted in new moral and spiritual values and ecological science.

In one sense, the current conflict is nothing new, as Yellowstone has always been roiled in some sort of controversy. As the world's first national park, its development during the 19th century required the violent removal of indigenous tribes and was a cash cow for the railroad industry. People have passionately debated for nearly 150 years how Yellowstone should be enjoyed, how much development is too much, and whether it could or should be more "natural." But in recent years the conflict has escalated and expanded to unforeseen levels. A main reason why the arena of conflict expanded was the decision by natural resource managers to expand the physical bounds of land management to include private and public areas far outside YNP. New research in ecology and biology showed that if Yellowstone was to remain in its "natural" state, managers would need to expand the area of protection from 4 million acres to the 20 million acres that make up the GYE today. Expanding the footprint of protection meant increasing opportunities for conflict, and in recent decades the GYE has been ensnared in intense struggles over wolf reintroduction, grizzly bear and bison management, oil extraction, natural gas "fracking," the viability of ranching, the explosion of tourism, and motorized (e.g., snowmobile) recreation in and around the park. These conflicts cycle in and out of the courts, often over decades, consuming millions of private and public dollars for scientific research, legal costs, and political lobbying. More often than not, when policy decisions are finally made, they are short-lived, as competing interest groups incessantly appeal for more technical knowledge, political favor, or public input in hopes of stalling administrative rulings or reversing policy.

For example, the highly contentious reintroduction of wolves to the GYE in 1995 followed a long process of nearly two decades of social conflict involving executive directives from six U.S. presidents, debates by dozens of congressional committees, 120 rancorous public hearings, bomb threats, more than 160,000 public letters written to the U.S. Fish and Wildlife Service, incurring over $12 million in scientific research costs alone (USFWS, 1994; Wilson, 1997). Since their controversial reintroduction, this conflict over wolves has not subsided but has become more rancorous and technically focused, as anti-wolf and pro-wolf groups continue to battle about the effect of wolves on the ecosystem, their endangered-species status, hunting and trapping, and state control over species management. Or consider another issue, recreational winter use in Yellowstone, which has been tied up in research and litigation since 1998 in circuitous fashion: a 1998 lawsuit over snowmobiling successful in a D.C. court; a 2000 plan vacated by a Wyoming court; a 2003 plan vacated by a D.C. court; a 2004 plan upheld by a Wyoming court; a 2007 plan vacated by a D.C. court; and a 2008 plan upheld in a Wyoming court. In this tortuous process, new research and political lobbying has caused a dizzying, lurching legal process costing millions for all involved. These two examples are merely the tip of the iceberg.

These ongoing struggles have five sets of stakeholders in common: interest groups, citizens, bureaucratic agencies, elected officials, and technical experts. Beginning with interests groups, there are 243 nonprofit organizations participating in environmental issues in the GYE; many are conservation organizations, but some are "wise-use" groups that are at loggerheads with many of the practices and ideals of conservation organizations.[3] Millions of citizens are also involved in the conflict, at a local, national, and international level. These include citizens who live in the GYE, those who visit on vacation, and many who have never been to the area but nevertheless treasure and seek to defend it from afar. By bureaucratic agencies I mean the collection of 28 different local, state, and federal institutions that are charged with managing natural resources in the region. Elected officials include members of presidential administrations, which have been especially hands-on in some of the most contentious issues, as well as governors, judges, congresspersons, state legislators, county leaders, and local town officials. Because the GYE is the ideal setting for natural-science research, scores of technical experts also exert an important authoritative voice in the region, supplying piles of important biological and ecological evidence that frame many of the hot-button debates. Technical experts also include economists and various other social scientific and political professionals working in the region.

With so much attention focused on Yellowstone, experts are scrambling to understand why, in the Yellowstone area, so "many issues are highly contentious and not easily resolvable"—and why interactions between people in the region are so "politicized and conflict-ridden as rigid ideologies crash against one another" (Clark, 2008). Famed naturalist Jack Turner (2009) describes the Yellowstone area as a "battleground that in years to come will make the conflict over drilling in the Arctic National Wildlife Refuge seem like child's play." Other experts have used the metaphor of a "battleground" to describe the "heated controversy" over Yellowstone (Keiter and Boyce, 1994), while others wonder why the area and the handling of its issues "looks more like a bar room brawl than a professional, scientific undertaking" (Cherney, 2011).

Toward a Theory of Morality and Environment

As I described above, the attempt at mastery by observation and calculation and the resulting mountains of scientific evidence have brought little consensus and done little to reduce the intensity and intractability of conflict. In fact, as I will show in Chapter 2, conflicts have progressively gotten worse over time. But why

3 Building on data from Northern Rockies Conservation Cooperative (2012) I constructed a new database of all interest groups working in the GYE. See Chapter 2 for more.

has this area become a hotbed of bitter and emotional contestation? Why, with all of the expert technical efforts to solve issues in the area, does just about every one of them nonetheless turn into a vehement and malignant struggle? Indeed, these struggles involve good old-fashioned economic self-interest, the mobilization of resources, and the pursuit of political power. Certainly, they also involve earnest (and much needed) debates over environmental science and the need to inform an "ill-informed" public about the biological and ecological foundations of preferred policies. But I quickly learned, and as I show throughout this project, there is something much deeper and more profound going on here. Drawing on Smith's (2003) theory about the inescapable moral makeup of human persons and culture, my goal is to show the deep moral and spiritual underpinnings of what appears to be rational and scientific life.[4] I wish here to push back against theories and explanations that do not take into account the deeper moral forces that structure human culture and pattern human behavior.

Thus, as I scratched in my research beneath the surface of the flurry of natural science, legal disputes, and economic analysis, I found that below and behind all of this technical evidence and debate lay deeper moral and spiritual commitments that are sometimes unacknowledged, and rarely articulated, yet which ultimately propel these endeavors. The most basic scientific decisions about what is worth knowing in the first place and what evidence is important, are driven by normative commitments and the belief that analytical, rational, and other empirical facts about the world matter in some way, toward some good (e.g., "healthier" ecosystems; the preservation of a cherished way of life). Thus, even ostensibly purely rational or analytical research is first and more basically shaped by what people see as good and meaningful: Are biologically intact ecosystems better than disrupted or fragmented ones? Do animals have intrinsic rights apart from their instrumental value to humans? Are humans only one small part of nature, or are they sovereign over it? Why should we care about Yellowstone in the first place? Basic questions like these are, in the end, not resolved by natural science or economic valuation because they are, by their very nature, meaningful only in the context of larger moral commitments about nature and humanity. They are, at their root, moral, philosophical, and spiritual questions.

I claim that to explain the intensity and intractability of this GYE conflict we must recognize that—more than scientific disagreements and rational self-interest—at stake here are fundamental moral beliefs, feelings, commitments, and desires, so deeply held and so dear to those who hold them that they are often taken for granted as fundamental to reality. So to understand the conflict, we need to bring to the surface what people deeply care about in the first place. We need to know what identity-shaping stories, large and small, they tell to make sense of their world and their place in it. We need to know about their innermost sense of

---

4 My theoretical approach is also influenced by Jasper (1997), MacIntyre (1988), Taylor (1989) and Wuthnow (1989).

who they are, why they and the world exist, and how they believe they should act. We need to know what it is about nature that they find meaningful, and sacred, that they put their faith in as scientifically nonverifiable presuppositions and commitments, and believe worthy of defending. Answers to these questions help uncover the moral commitments that motivate and make meaningful the mountains of scientific, technical evidence marshaled in the conflict. Without these deeper beliefs, desires, and commitments about nature and humanity, this evidence would itself be meaningless, existing only in a social vacuum. In other words, this GYE conflict is not ultimately a struggle over facts (true and false), but a struggle over moral truths (good and bad). Of course, technorational facts are not lost in this struggle—they are all that seem to exist to many combatants involved—but such facts, I will show, are actually merely tools in the deeper cultural struggle over the moral and spiritual connections between nature and human culture and the broader attempt by different groups to realize and protect their respective moral orders.

To be clear, by "moral" I mean an orientation toward what is right and wrong, good and bad, worthy and unworthy, just and unjust—not established by our own actual desires, decisions, or preferences but instead believed to exist apart from them, providing standards by which our desires, decisions, and preferences themselves can be judged.[5] Moral commitments shape basic practices ranging from how to treat friends, family, and coworkers, to public and political practices relating to civil rights, poverty, the "culture wars," biomedical ethics, corporate ethics, art conflict, gender, identity, and—for our purposes—the natural environment. Social actors more or less internalize moral commitments unconsciously (Haidt, 2001; Vaisey, 2009) and consciously from meaningful narratives, face-to-face interactions (Blumer, 1969; Collins, 2005; Goffman, 1959), external structures and boundaries (Alexander, 2003; Douglas, 1966; Geertz, 1973; Wuthnow, 1989), and through our experiences as physical bodies in the social world, as the recent explosion of work in moral psychology, linguistics, and neuroscience have shown (Cerulo, 2010; Damasio, 1994; Lakoff and Johnson, 1999). The discipline of sociology in large part began as a quest to analyze the sources, varieties, and consequences of these moral questions, which first had their origin in philosophical and theological communities. Indeed, Durkheim himself considered the discipline of sociology to be the "science of morality" (Durkheim, 1997) and Weber described some of his most important work as the study of "the motives of moral action" (Campbell, 2006).

What I mean by "moral order" here is an interpersonally and institutionally shared structure of moral beliefs, desires, feelings, and boundaries that are derived from larger narratives and rituals (Wuthnow, 1989). Friendly to this definition

---

5 This definition derives from Taylor (1989), and is also adapted by Smith (2003). For a broad sociological discussion about the question "What is morality?" see Abend (2011); Tavory (2011); Porpora et al. (2013).

(although a bit too strong, completely collapsing the social with the moral) is Durkheim's claim that "the morality of each people is directly related to the social structure of people practicing it" (Durkheim, 1973, p. 87). People act "morally," as I mean it here, when their action affirms and fulfills the shared beliefs and commitments of what is understood to be good, right, and just (and not merely a personal preference, taste, or desire)—whether or not those actions are normally considered "moral" per se. A few simple examples are worth offering: the environmentalist acts morally when she sells her car and begins cycling to work (believing that pollution is harmful and wrong); the U.S. citizen acts morally when he goes out to vote (believing in democracy and self-governance); in certain contexts a woman acts morally when she submits herself to—what she understands to be—naturally given gender roles (believing in communal duty and obligation). But of course the very same acts that are defined as right and just in some moral orders are deemed wrong in others. A woman who abandons her community's "naturally" given gender expectations is demonized and perhaps killed in one context, yet in another context she would be lauded as a pioneering hero. Thus, more important than the individual actions themselves are the social institutions, cultural systems, practices, and narratives in which actors and their actions are embedded and which define for them what is good, right, and just.

How does all this relate to conflict? A fundamental motivation for human behavior, and social conflict, is, I suggest, the struggle to enact and sustain moral order.[6] I argue that conflict can become especially intense and intractable when groups compete to enact and sustain moral orders that are incommensurable. By incommensurable, I mean instances when there is no common standard or metric by which we can compare the moral orders to each other to adjudicate which one is more worthy of being chosen or realized. In other words, conflict is intense and unending because the deeper narratives and moral commitments at the heart of the conflict cannot be resolved by recourse to some external, objective, equally applicable standard. They are more like faith commitments that are "true" only within their larger frameworks of cultural belief and practice. In the GYE, the current standards that are used (e.g., law, ecology, economic valuation) are themselves influenced by these presuppositional commitments that are first *believed* to be true and right: endangered species should not go extinct; nonhuman animals have rights to exist; biodiversity and wilderness have worth; aesthetic beauty has worth; humans have more rights than nonhuman

---

6 I draw heavily from Smith (2003) to elaborate this point. I want to caution, though, that this claim should not be mistaken for a commitment to hard structural-functionalism, because humans do not, of course, always act in ways that are consistent with their own and others' moral standards. But inconsistency in individual behavior does not itself dismiss the fact that humans are part of much larger systems of cultural and moral meaning that guide "good" and "bad" behavior. In fact, as Smith claims, inconsistency in moral behavior can actually reveal the influence of larger moral orders at work: a husband stays late at the office and violates his obligation to be at family dinner because he is motivated by larger gender expectations about being the breadwinner.

animals; individuals should have control of their private property without federal interference; the culture of utilitarian work and recreation is sacred. This issue of incommensurability raises deep questions about the effectiveness of practical rationality in GYE management, because, if the standards themselves derive from deeper stories and moral commitments, how, we might ask, can we rationally decide which deeply held moral order should be realized? Meanwhile, most social actors involved simply miss the fact that they are fighting tooth and nail to promote and defend incommensurable moral orders, obsessively marshaling evidence that is itself meaningless when abstracted from their larger narratives and moral commitments, all the while in so doing obscuring what the debate is ultimately about. My purpose here is to reduce the level of obscurity that clouds these arguments and conflicts.

Human Believers, Narrative Structure, and Enacting Moral Orders

Shifting the analytical focus of the conflict toward these deeper incommensurate and conflicting moral orders raises basic theoretical questions that need to be addressed: What are humans, that they construct shared belief systems? Where do these moral systems of meaning come from? And how are humans propelled forward by these commitments, influencing—and being influenced by—social structures and institutions? It is important to unpack the details of this theoretical approach here because it guides the logic underlying this book. I focus narrowly on three related claims: (1) *Humans are believers*, by which I mean that instead of having some universal or indubitable foundation of knowledge, we as social beings must place our faith and trust in unverifiable starting points that we socially construct to define our worlds, (2) *Narratives structure moral orders*, by which I mean that humans are believers embedded in stories big and small that separate sacred from profane and tell us who we are, why we are, what we are doing, and why it all matters. Moral orders are thus not static sets of individually formed analytical propositions about right and wrong, but are part of larger creative stories that direct our lives and make what we do significant, (3) *People strive to enact and sustain moral orders*, meaning that moral orders have real-life consequences—especially for social conflict—and that humans, often together through morally animated institutions and social structures, seek to realize and perpetuate their moral order. Thus, when groups in the GYE challenge—and are challenged by—one another, it is not simply about politics or money, but about who they are as a moral people.

My aim in this book is not to set up a false dichotomy between rationality and morality, between science and religion, or any other clumsy dichotomy that can be too easily assumed. Indeed, morality can be very rational in thought and practice, and rationality, as I argue here, is meaningless without underlying moral commitments. There is no need to choose one or the other, and in fact, the case of GYE conflict shows most clearly the interpenetration of fact (what is) and value (what ought to be). In other words, people often weave together into a mutually supportive whole what they think ought to be (e.g., Healthy ecosystems are good) with facts about the world (e.g., Yellowstone needs wolves to be ecologically healthy). Moreover, the lines between rationality and morality are blurred because they depend on the institutional setting in which they are performed. For example, the scientific "fact" that Yellowstone wolves improve ecological health is perfectly rational to pro-wolf advocates and ecologists, yet when viewed through the lens of an anti-wolf perspective it is seen as irrational, and even immoral, because wolves symbolize the intrusion of the federal government and a threat to human dominion over nature.

HUMANS AS BELIEVERS

Humans are necessarily believers because there is no indubitable foundation for knowledge other than the knowledge people acquire as participants in specific human cultures. While myriad thinkers since the Enlightenment have sought such indubitable foundations, they have no doubt come up short.[7] Instead, we enter into human cultures that are founded upon beliefs and commitments that could be very different (a visit to other cultures quickly proves this point). We have only what has been believed in and constructed. It is paradoxically a world of seemingly predetermined built-up social structures for those born into it, yet a world still open to immense creativity and change. The one thing we cannot escape is that we place our trust in beliefs that are not certain, and cannot be empirically verified as True.

Of course, to say that people put their faith in unverifiable commitments can sound awkward and preachy to some modern people. Consider a few basic examples of how different human cultures and moral orders are built up from very different starting-point moral commitments: some people believed, and still do, that whites are born free and blacks are born to be slaves. Some believe that humans are innately evil, and others believe that they are innately good. Some believe that a purposeful God created the world in six days, while others believe a random explosion 13 billion years ago was responsible. Some people believe that women are innately inferior to men, while others believe that they are equal. Some people believe that the struggle against oppression, injustice, and inequality is a moral obligation, while others believe that our only obligation is to improve the human race through domination and exploitation of the inherently weak. Some believe that the natural environment is a harmonious and spiritual balance of interdependent relationships, while others believe that the natural world is

---

7 For more on this see Berger and Luckmann (1966); Smith (2003); Taylor (1989); Jasper (1997); MacIntyre (1990); Rorty (2009). The massive and fragmented body of work characterized as "postmodern" also begins from this larger claim against strong foundationalism.

a material storehouse for conquering and consumption. The point here is that because we have no objective set of given knowledge—and no objective way to verify our beliefs as irrefutably true—we necessarily build our lives upon these sorts of deeply held moral commitments.

Even this short list of examples reveals the radical diversity of fundamental starting-point assumptions that have guided the course of human history. The radical openness of human cultures to socially construct meaningful moral orders has been obscured by our modern commitments to our own moral projects that posit indubitable foundations of knowledge and motivation, such as neoclassical economics, behaviorism, or social Darwinism. Not only do ostensibly rational projects like these begin with their own set of moral commitments that cannot be empirically verified, but they can completely miss the creative ways that human cultures socially construct their lives from deeply held moral beliefs about themselves and the world around them.

The fact that human cultures are at their root about deeply held moral beliefs explains why, following Durkheim, cultures persistently sacralize physical and mental objects. Thus, people do not believe in a detached, abstract, emotionless sense, but instead their believing impels them to set aside objects that are especially powerful, worthy, and important—deserving of honor, protection, and devotion. Deeply held assumptions at the center of a moral order (e.g., humans have rights; nature has intrinsic value; Jews are an inferior people; manifest destiny demands Indian removal) incline people to erect moral boundaries to protect what they believe to be sacred, explaining "the extreme strictness of the prohibitions that separate the sacred from the profane" (Durkheim, 2001, p. 237). We see this most clearly in the visceral emotional reactions to the breaching of sacred boundaries—people get angry, impassioned, and defensive. Various examples of the sacred include the environment, the nation-state, individual freedom, the burial site, the sporting event, animals, heritage, work, or private property rights—and post-Enlightenment moderns are no less inclined toward sacralizing and defending these than are "traditional" or primitive societies.

Because those involved in the GYE conflict are believers in socially constructed stories that give them meaning and direct their lives, they too sacralize aspects of the physical and mental world. Thus, explanations of the conflict that attempt to wholly reduce it to technical disagreements or the need for more scientific evidence or the pursuit of self-interest badly miss out on deeper cultural (and emotional) mechanisms that are continually operative. Of course, that does not mean we should disregard science and self-interest—because both are very real mechanisms in the conflict—but my claim here is that we need to contextualize each within its own moral story (e.g., Enlightenment rationality, *homo economicus*, objective science, empirical prediction), and examine their influence alongside other socially constructed moral orders about nature that I argue give meaning to the conflict in the first place.

NARRATIVES STRUCTURE MORAL ORDERS

Moral codes are not socially constructed in a vacuum, but are linked to larger narratives that creatively tell us who we are, where we are, what we are, why we are here, what we should do, and why it all matters. In other words, humans "are symbol-making creatures, who spin webs of meaning around ourselves. We proliferate metaphors and language for describing the world...and we tell each other story after story. Into this roiling cognitive activity we mix emotions and moral evaluations...attaching new moral values to existing ones...[creating] interpretive frameworks through which we filter all our experience" (Jasper, 1997, p. 10). The very basis of human communication is, and has been since the beginning, storytelling. We live within, tell, and retell narratives big and small. For our purposes, it is important to know that "narratives"—understood here as *meaningful* accounts of human actions arranged into connected events— are much more than historical recountings of factual events, but contain actors and a plot (middle, beginning, end) and are intended to convey meaningful points about the world.[8] Narratives have told of the origins of the cosmos, of different tribes and peoples, of heroic leaders, of evil villains, of lessons learned, of (re)interpreted pasts, and of futures promised. Today we moderns may not paint on cave walls to tell our stories, but we rely as heavily on narratives to convey normative insights about our experiences, how we should act, and what is real and significant.

People's understandings of the environment in the GYE are learned and acquired through day-to-day socialization experiences, much of which, I argue, is influenced by these larger narratives. To be clear, these narratives should not be mistaken as strong structures existing in every person's mind, but are general ways to understand and describe the cultural logic of different groups. Oftentimes they are not fully articulated by actors. Uncovering such narratives thus requires the researcher to construct them from sometimes piecemeal scripts, arguments, and observations. Guiding moral narratives I explore throughout the following chapters include manifest destiny, rugged individualism, human dominionism, old-western heritage, the rise of ecological science, place attachment to physical settings, and various environmentalist subnarratives about the spiritual redemption of nature. People "pick up" moral lessons in their day-to-day experiences as participants in these orienting stories: your grandfather did it this way and we should revere and respect our ancestors; we are in a battle against instrumental utilitarianism and should continue to fight for the spiritual redemption of nature; environmental laws are part of an ongoing attack from the federal government on our innate private property and states' rights; for decades we stumbled through the dark but now have scientific tools to precisely measure and predict ecosystem harm and ethics; this land has become part of who we are as old-westerners and

---

8 For more, see MacIntyre (1981); Ricoeur (1984).

we must defend against attempts to destroy our identity and culture. We make these stories, and they make us. I am suggesting, in a strong sense, that "the stories we tell are not mere entertainment. Nor do they simply suggest for us some general sense of our heritage. Our stories fully encompass and define our lives" (Smith, 2003, p. 78). They elaborate the contours of the sacred and profane in deeply personal, *narrative* form.

ENACTING AND SUSTAINING MORAL ORDERS

Humans strive to enact and sustain moral orders, most often through morally infused institutions and social structures. They propel behavior toward certain moral ends, even though sometimes these ends are anything but singular, clear, consistent, or well-articulated. When there are competing moral orders, the issue of incommensurability becomes especially important. If, as in the GYE, no amount of empirical evidence can adjudicate, or make commensurate, different moral visions about what nature is good for, then conflict becomes especially intense and intractable. In some cases it is impossible to reduce opposing values to a common metric.

For example, in the midst of the conflict over abortion, opposing groups fight about how to weigh, measure, and assess scientific facts about the fetus, yet in the end it is not about the facts, but what the facts mean within an "internally coherent and mutually shared view of the world that is tacit, never fully articulated, and, most importantly, completely at odds with the world view held by their opponents" (Luker, 1984, p. 159). In the same way that science cannot ultimately determine the value of the fetus (or the proper role of women in American society), the value of "nature" in the GYE cannot ultimately be determined by ecology, instrumental cost-benefit analysis, or any other commensurable technique, because the "True" value of nature is first determined by deeper belief commitments, narratives, and practices of competing groups.

In the struggle between competing moral orders, groups attempt to transform their opponent's sacred stories and core intrinsic values from right to wrong, good to bad. I refer to this as "moral devaluation" and describe this process in more detail below. In the GYE, environmentalists have by and large devalued the old-western moral order by redrawing the boundaries about what is sacred and profane vis-à-vis nature, rejecting the utilitarian relationship with the land that was once the pinnacle of the good life in the GYE. Old-western cowboys represented the best of American exceptionalism, romantic nationalism, and material promise. God favored their work, and God favored the spread of liberty and self-government across the American West. Their labor institutions were a bearer of these values, incarnating their moral relationship to the land and making them morally worthy people. But in today's moral battle for the GYE, these ideals are no longer desirable or "good," but in a radical reversal, they are considered by many to be harmful and morally wrong. The utilitarian moral vision of old-westerners did not simply lose authority in the area, but, more important, their sacred stories were completely rejected, and their role in history was redefined as immoral. Moral devaluation is intensely personal and elicits such a strong emotional reaction because it involves the condemnation of one's very self. This process of moral devaluation is made "objective" through scientific research about the harmful effects of traditional ways of life, and it is institutionalized through the establishment of environmental laws making these practices unethical and illegal.

Theoretical Contributions

It is my hope that this theoretical approach offers tools to improve knowledge and research in the study of culture, rationality, and conflict—in addition to more field-specific contributions in environmental sociology, sociology of culture, and sociology of religion. Moreover, even in the discipline of sociology more broadly, scholars have noted the surprising shortage of studies of morality "as it is actually lived" (Porpora et al., 2013), beyond the useful, but nevertheless limited, fMRI laboratories, abstract philosophical theories, large-scale surveys, or game theory experiments that accompany the reemergence of interest in morality from sociology, psychology, linguistics, and neurosciences. Drawing on these insights, but moving beyond them, this book provides a case-study account of morality "in the wild" (Hitlin and Vaisey, 2010) that is both in-depth and comprehensive, rooted in the historical development of a particular place and particular peoples.

Turning to work in environmental sociology, I take a more critical and constructive approach, arguing that the "science of morality" has largely been ignored by environmental sociologists, and make the case that our theories about the human–environment connection would be greatly improved by a more rigorous focus on the moral dimensions underpinning human cultures. With regard to sociology of religion, I claim that, in contrast to the overemphasis on individual-level data and religious organizations (e.g., congregations and denominations), we have a lot to learn by searching for the influence of the sacred in "secular" places we might least expect it. In other words, I aim to demonstrate that despite endless debates about secularization, we should move forward by paying special attention to explosions of the sacred within, and across, institutions that we have not traditionally thought of as "religious"—especially highly bureaucratic, scientific, or rational institutions, such as those in the GYE. I elaborate why this is the case, drawing on recent work to show how this book offers a more fruitful direction of research for scholars interested in how religion impacts social and political life.

I end by bringing this introduction full circle, returning to the theoretical counterarguments posed at the beginning of this chapter about conflict, rationality, and self-interest. I further engage these competing arguments and show how they offer incomplete explanations. Instead of a complete rejection of these counterarguments, I incorporate them into my theory by further drawing on conflict theory. In particular, I argue, consistent with my theory, that the moral and spiritual dimensions of conflict become entwined with—influencing and being influenced by—changes in the structure of economic, political, and status-based exchange markets.

BRINGING CLASSICAL QUESTIONS INTO ENVIRONMENTAL SOCIOLOGY

I view this project as contributing to a much-needed focus on the moral bases of environmental problems. In this section I want to briefly reflect on the state of environmental sociology as it pertains to the theory I have elaborated throughout this chapter. My main goal is to provide a constructive critique of the field, arguing that while the moral dimension of the environment has flourished in other fields, it has by and large been ignored in environmental sociology's theories and empirical analyses. In doing so, I hope to point out blind spots that hinder the field from moving forward toward a more comprehensive, culturally informed, and accurate understanding of the human–environment relationship.

A science of morality has been neglected, in part, because Weber and Durkheim themselves, found less traction in environmental sociology than in other subfields. Another primary reason has to do with how environmental sociologists have operationalized "nature" as a resource—primarily as a material good for human survival (Van Koppen, 2000). Since the emergence of environmental sociology in the early 1960 to the 1970s, this definition of nature has been successfully used to examine the myriad threats human societies pose to the natural resources we depend on for our survival. The field itself is organized around material problems that arise in the interaction between humans and the environment on various issues such as ozone depletion, water scarcity, biodiversity, pollution, energy crises, food and hunger, globalization, and population growth. The social constructionism movement in environmental sociology brought some cultural (and moral) issues to the fore, but sustained attention to the moral dimensions of nature have largely occurred outside of the bounds of sociology, in history (e.g., Hays 1989; Nash 1989, 2001), law (e.g., Nagle 2005), religion (e.g., Albanese 1991; Tucker and Grim 2013) anthropology (e.g. Kempton et al. 1996) and environmental ethics.

An early hallmark of the field was its apt criticism of mainstream sociology that it had privileged "social facts" over biophysical ones. Thus, since the early 1960s, environmental sociologists have made a concerted effort to bind the material to the social. In this successful effort, much more attention has been given to the material aspects of nature, in the effort to point out the myriad threats human societies pose to the natural resources we depend on for our survival. As a consequence, the predominant theories in environmental sociology have—for good reason—favored material-based theories and models. For example, early human ecology theories (Duncan, 1959; Park, 1952), Catton and Dunlap's model of the general functions of the environment (supply depot, living space, waste repository), Luhmann's system theory (1989), treadmill of production and other neo-Marxist theories (Dickens, 2002; Pepper, 1993; Schnaiberg, 1980), Beck's risk society theory (1992), and ecological modernization theory (Spaargaren and Mol, 1992). These theories have, in different ways, been extremely beneficial to the growth of what is still a relatively young field of research. Moreover, many environmental sociologists are aware of the moral, aesthetic, and spiritual dimensions of humanity's relationship to the natural environment, despite the fact that a significant blind spot still remains with regard to any sort of deep theoretical account or rigorous empirical analysis of those dimensions.

While environmental sociology as a whole has focused on material problems rather than the cultural structures that produce them, there are examples of work that has, to some extent, engaged moral phenomena, albeit in indirect ways. The most well-known are the ubiquitous public opinion studies that measure environmental attitudes about environmental domination and environmental concern. Researchers use surveys to gather information on percentages of the population who agree or disagree about a variety of statements about values, justifications, and policy preferences (e.g., Dunlap et al. 2000, Dunlap et al. 2001; for similar work outside sociology see Kellert 1996). This valuable line of work correlates these attitudes with various demographic characteristics, often finding that the younger, well-educated, and politically liberal are most concerned about the environment. Others in the social-psychological tradition use similar survey methods to argue that in addition to demographic factors, we should pay close attention to social-psychological survey constructs that predict environmental concern (Dietz et al., 1998). These early studies formed the "value-belief-norm" theory of environmental behavior (Stern 2000). In addition to the aforementioned work, Ronald Inglehart (1971, 2008) uses surveys to identify broader intergenerational shifts in what he calls "postmaterialist" values, arguing that younger generations who are not strapped with material concerns about health and survival are freer to focus on postmaterialists concerns like aesthetics and quality of life, thus explaining their higher rates environmental concern. While it has come under widespread attack, the theory makes interesting theoretical claims about the relationship between moral concepts, like the "good life," and environmental concern. Nevertheless, this short analysis shows that the small amount of work on moral phenomena in environmental sociology has largely been relegated to this tradition of attitudinal survey work, which itself has traditionally ignored any sort of deep analysis of human culture.[9]

9 But see Bell (1994) and Feinberg and Willer (2013) for alternative examples. This body of work I describe above on environmental values, as measured through attitudinal surveys, operates with four implicit and questionable assumptions: First, surveys tend to include closed-ended questions and

The strong influence of the natural sciences within the discipline is an additional reason why morality has, unfortunately, remained on the sidelines. Because environmental sociology is the study of how social systems interact with ecosystems, environmental sociologists rely heavily on natural scientists for knowledge about ecosystems. The natural sciences provide environmental sociologists concrete metrics by which to understand the actual impact of individuals, institutions, and societies on material ecosystems. These measurement tools and metrics, which again emphasize nature as a *material resource* for human health and survival, are critical for environmental sociologists who strive to build useful knowledge about how we might organize society in more sustainable ways. Thus, in this sense, it is quite easy to see how moral dimensions of nature rooted in emotion, aesthetics, expressive symbolism, or spirituality might seem out of touch to environmental sociologists, especially those working closely with natural sciences that find little professional value in these domains of experience, and may view morality as distracting from the material problems we face.

This has hindered the larger impact of environmental sociology. In a recent reflection on the state of environmental sociology, Gould and Lewis (2009, p. 295) conclude that "environmental sociology has largely remained a subdiscipline unto itself" and call for a renewed emphasis to integrate and "extend it into all aspects of sociology as a whole." I argue here that one important way that we might extend it into the larger discipline of sociology is to link the environment to the concerns of the founders of the discipline, who themselves were deeply committed to the "science of morality" (e.g., Durkheim, Weber) and paid particular attention to culture and the ways moral orders have political and material repercussions.

But the irony is that all projects—even modern academic projects like environmental sociology—are, finally, propelled by deeper moral beliefs and commitments, such as equality, justice, empathy, and concern for worsening environmental disruption. Thus, to recover a moral imagination in the discipline we do not have to look far beyond ourselves and our work, for it is fundamentally built into much of what we strive for through our research. Along these lines, Gould and Lewis (2009, p.295) again conclude that to solve environmental problems—which for many environmental sociologists is the ultimate end—we must "question our goals. What do we want? What's the desired end?...how we proceed will depend on what we value. We ask our students to define 'the

therefore restrict respondents to a set of answers that are biased from the outset. Kempton et al. (1996, p. 88) argue that the influence of religion on environmental concern has been neglected for this very reason—namely, the environmental literature has largely ignored the topic and thus researchers have not included measures of religion on their survey questionnaires, and this only reinforces the original assumption that it doesn't matter. Second, that individual attitudes are relatively stable. Third, that attitudes measured outside a real-life social context are meaningful. Fourth, that attitudes, as indicated on a survey, actually determine subsequent behavior.

good life.'" These are the deeper questions of moral worth and value that I argue are critical for sociological analysis. Thus, one contribution of the present project is to bring these questions to the surface of the discipline. We must link these meanings to the material environmental consequences we care so much about. We must bring morality into the center of our analyses because it is an inescapable part of human culture to begin with, and our theories will suffer until we rigorously account for it. This project is but one small attempt to contribute to the field of environmental sociology a concrete and systematic analysis of morality that takes into account the complexity of moral orders, situates them in the historical development of institutions and social structures, and shows how they actively influence an important, and long-lasting, environmental conflict.

A SOCIOLOGICAL ACCOUNT OF "SPIRITUALITY" IN "SECULAR" CONTEXTS

Throughout this introduction I have invoked the concept of "spirituality" in service of my argument about the cultural dimensions of conflict. I have resisted defining the concept because definitions of "spirituality," or the "spiritual," tend to confound more than they illuminate.[10] Spirituality is a fuzzy notion that eschews any box or pigeonhole in which researchers have have sought to place it. I sidestep these unnecessary lacunae, and instead favor something more akin to Supreme Court Justice Potter Stewart's famous definition of obscenity—we tend to know it when we see it. Admittedly, we can say that "spirituality" conveys meaning, in a broad sense, about that which cultures experience as sacred, mystical, other, or set apart from everyday life. Hardly an all-encompassing definition, this general understanding can help us examine how spirituality shapes environmental issues in the GYE.

Like morality, the concept of spirituality (and religion more generally) has largely been left out of sociological conversations about the environment. We therefore know relatively little about the social and political influence of spirituality on environmental conflict. This can be partially attributed to the critiques noted above about the neglect of morality, but something larger is also going on here with respect to spirituality and religion. In most fields of research, and in social life more generally, popular understandings of spirituality have conceptualized it as an *individual* phenomenon. This is akin to Bellah and colleagues' (2008) appraisal in *Habits of the Heart* of "Sheila-ism," a now-famous term used as shorthand to describe religious individualism in American life, denoting how Sheila created her own individualized spirituality using self-determination, and relying on her own personal experiences. For me, then, it became clear that much of the popular and scholarly work about spirituality and environment understood spirituality to be something confined to the individual,

10 For more, see Bender (2010).

not something socially produced through larger narratives and structures of social life. For example, a popular representation of spirituality in nature is the romantic soul-seeking of "patron saints" of environmentalism, such as John Muir and Henry David Thoreau. Spirituality is produced (and reproduced) through highly individualized experiences of divine beauty and splendor out in the natural world. Moral principles about how one ought to relate to nature flowed from self-directed individuals and their highly personalized experiences with nature. The problem with such popular stereotypes—and the subsequent modeling of these conceptions in what has largely been individual-level research—is that they often obscure the larger historical, cultural, political, and economic structures in which people like Thoreau, or Sheila, are embedded, ultimately coming to shape their spiritual feelings and commitments.

In addition to the view of spirituality as something that separate individuals do, is another, and perhaps more important, reason why it has been ignored in sociological analyses of the environment. This has to do with the *perceived* fate of spirituality and religion in contexts deemed to be "secular." Such contexts can be all-encompassing—as big as Weber's claims about *Entzauberung* (disenchantment) of Western civilization, but they can also be smaller bounded "secular" contexts, such as the GYE, dominated by science and technorationality. The post-Enlightenment differentiation of the sacred from the secular in Western society, along with the rise of an industrialized society, led most social critics (e.g., Weber, Marx, Spencer, Comte, Freud, Mills) to assume that the spiritual was being stamped out by post-Enlightenment forces of bureaucratization, modern science, industrialization, rationalization, and urbanization. Indeed, C. Wright Mills represents well these widespread beliefs about the fate of the sacred in this new world:

> Once the world was filled with the sacred—in thought, practice, and in-stitutional form. After the Reformation and the Renaissance, the forces of modernization swept across the globe and secularization, a corollary historical process, loosened the dominance of the sacred. In due course, the sacred shall disappear altogether except, possibly, in the private realm. (Mills, 1959, pp. 32–33)

In recent decades this strong version of the secularization thesis has come under serious question, given the vitality and growth of religion around the world. But one thing is still clear: in our modern situation in the West, the spiritual and sacred dimensions of life have undergone considerable change with the rise of modernity, scientific rationality, humanistic education, technology, capitalism, bureaucratic life, and so on. This has, in large part, to do with institutional differentiation—namely, the modern separation of church, state, education, science, health, and law from one another. What does this mean for the study of spirituality, especially within these distinct "secular" institutions that make up social contexts like the GYE?

Within a context like the GYE, this might lead us to believe that we will not find spirituality and religion within its institutions that are, by all accounts, highly bureaucratic and rationalizing. Or we might expect the sacred to be confined to traditional institutions, such as religious congregations. *But I claim here, and demonstrate throughout this book, that spirituality in the GYE has not been dealt a death blow by such rationalizing forces, but that it has become deeply entwined within scientific and rational institutions that we take to be "secular."* In other words, spirituality and religion are still inescapably present in modern life, even though they have become more difficult to observe. With this in mind, Courtney Bender's (2010, p. 286) recent sociological analysis of spirituality contends that researchers have two choices: "We can continue to be surprised and perplexed at the irruptions of the sacred into daily life" or, alternatively, we can accept this reality and resign ourselves to "investigate how those irruptions take place and work to locate the institutions and practices that contribute both to their occlusion and to their continuation." This makes it all the more important to approach the fuzzy concept of "spirituality" not as something individualistic or confined only to religious institutions, but as something deeply intertwined with, and expressed through different collective histories, practices, and social structures.

Thus, one of the underlying arguments of this book is that we should search for spirituality in secular contexts, rather than the typical locations scholars have sought out. With the contemporary shift away from identifying with organized religion (e.g., "I'm spiritual, but not religious"), we will do well to move our focus away from traditional institutional locales (e.g., mosques, churches, synagogues) and toward more "institutionally diverse" aspects of the sacred (Luckmann, 1967). This does not mean that we will find "religion" everywhere we look. Nor does it mean that spiritual and sacred factors, when present, will always trump secular factors like science, law, or economics. In most cases they won't. But sometimes the surprising eruptions of the sacred can have unexpected and profound consequences. Thus, as I demonstrate throughout this book, we should not assume a false dichotomy of the sacred *or* the technoscientific, and this need not be an inherently conflictual relationship. Instead, it is a complex configuration that is part and parcel of the entanglement of the sacred in modern life. And finding explosions of spiritual fervor in (secular) contexts that we tend to not view as religious challenges simplistic linkages between the secular and the spiritual, between secularization and modernity, between the mystical and the scientific, and between the religious and the political

These sacred elements of social life have clear political repercussions that are rarely acknowledged in environmental research. This is true of observers and participants in the GYE conflict, and equally true of the research in environmental sociology. Stretching our definitions of the "spiritual" beyond popular and scholarly perceptions of self-determining individualists like John Muir or Sheila-ism, and away from traditional religious institutions, might open up new doors for social scientists to engage sacred realities and narratives that have real-world material consequences for the natural environment.

RETURNING TO SOME COUNTERARGUMENTS: CULTURE, RATIONALITY, SELF-INTEREST, AND VALUATION

In one sense it is not entirely surprising that a region like the GYE, full of rational bureaucracies (government agencies, environmental organizations, and businesses) rooted in political and legal procedure, natural science, and cost-benefit analysis, would favor what Weber called formal-procedural rationality (*Zweckrationalität*), and either fail to notice or overtly ignore substantive-value rationality (*Wertrationalität*). But work in cultural and economic sociology has shown that social life is much more complex, and there is more to the modern narrative that moral, spiritual, and other deeply meaningful aspects of social life are simply crowded out by rationality. In fact, this is where the story begins, and where things start to get interesting. To end here would be to accept a model of rationality that is oversimplified and disconnected from the ways in which environmental conflict is hardly "rational" in the classical sense of the word, but is deeply influenced by identity and culture.

We must therefore attend to the different ways rationality is practiced, resisted, and institutionalized. We should move beyond conventional approaches to rationality that assume actors pursue universalized and transparent self-interests, somehow putting culture and identity aside to make political decisions.[11] Frank Dobbin (1999, p. 237) notes that this model of rationality has unfortunately become "conventional wisdom about political conflict." It is a model that wrongly assumes rational actors pursue these interests, "calculating their expenditures of political capital using a universal arithmetic of cost and benefit." Thus, a more accurate model proposed in this book focuses on how cultural experiences and identities shape for people what is both rational *and* moral.

But this means decision making is more complicated. How are we to adjudicate between different groups' opposing visions of what is rational and moral? How do we attribute a commensurable metric of worth to these cultural practices and identities? Economists answer this question using the market—that is, measuring value through consumer behavior, for example, how much people are willing to pay to tolerate wolves on GYE public and private lands, or the determination of costs and benefits of drilling for natural gas near the border of Yellowstone. But economic strategies, while useful for determining the value of most tangible commodities, pose limits for goods and exchanges that people may view as morally objectionable, such as endangered species or sacred land—or more intangible goods such as love, emotions, personhood, cultural heritage, or aesthetic beauty.

11 See Espeland (1998) for an in-depth analysis of rationality and identity.

One way forward is to link different valuations of nature to the human variety of "sociohistorical experiences with particular natural sites, landscapes, or wildlife" (Fourcade, 2011, p. 1725). Over the past century, sociohistorical developments in the GYE have led to different moral visions of nature, especially the "cultural tension between the 'useful' and the 'beautiful'" (Fourcade, 2011, p. 1737). These different cultural formations of nature—and in my case what it is "good for"—are more than just descriptive, but exert real causal power in the social, political, and legal process. These causal mechanisms are often masked by material influences that prevail in bureaucratic processes (e.g., the National Environmental Policy Act (NEPA)), economic valuation, and other rational and "commensurable" techniques.

Thus, the metric of money is only one axis by which we can assess what things are "worth" and other justifications, or "economies of worth," are also relevant.[12] These other justifications for valuing the natural environment have come under some sociological consideration, but we have much, much more to learn. Some have explored more biologically based values inherent to humankind that shape different values of nature (Kellert, 1996), but these fail to capture the cultural contingencies that shape this process. Whatever our approach, it is clear that individuals and institutions—from the most "technical" and "rational" to the most "unskilled" and "irrational"—rely on different interpretations of nature and its value to define their relationship to it. For thinkers like Muir and Thoreau it was rooted in aesthetic beauty and immanentist spirituality; for many conservation biologists, values exist in evolutionary processes and biodiversity; and for many ethicists and philosophers, it is about nonhuman rights, the moral value of biodiversity, and the health of the biological community for future generations.

How moral meanings of nature *change over time* is also important. One approach to this question, which I take in the first section of this book, is to examine the historical and institutional processes by which nature acquires moral and spiritual value. We can observe the "cultural process of sacralization" to understand how utilitarian aspects of social life become "invested with moral and religious meaning" (Zelizer, 2010, p. 41). Like the organization of cultural meaning around life insurance, children, blood, or organs,[13] I uncover the institutional process leading to the moralization and sacralization of nature (and Yellowstone). And, as I have argued, these processes have, unfortunately, been neglected in prior attempts to explain environmental conflict in the region. Of course, these sorts of moral dimensions are difficult to detect amid the procedural rationality of NEPA, legal formalism, commensurability techniques, scientific analysis of nature, and bureaucratic administration. But with this cultural approach in mind, we have a roadmap to probe more deeply beneath

---

12 See Boltanski and Thévenot (2006) for more on the economies of worth perspective.
13 Zelizer (1979, 1985); Healy (2006).

the surface, pointing us toward the thick webs of meaning that structure our lives and propel our behavior.

ENTANGLING THE MORAL WITH CONFLICT OVER ECONOMICS, POLITICS, AND STATUS

I have said a lot about the importance of moral orders, but under what circumstances are people's deeply held commitments more likely to come into overt conflict? With this question, we return to where we began the chapter, focusing on the conditions that result in conflict. Like the study of morality, the study of social conflict is perhaps as old as sociology itself. Conflict, or competition between groups, continues to be of central importance to topics at the heart of the discipline—race, gender, class, social movements, religion, politics, and so on. Sociologists, especially those shaped by Karl Marx, have investigated social conflict from the perspective of material and economic competition. For Marx, moral meanings and other cultural values were a mask used strategically to hide material pursuits. This approach has taught us a great deal about social conflict, yet it is incomplete. I agree with Nicola Beisel (1997) that moral conflict— competition between groups about "right" and "wrong"—itself has consequences for class reproduction. Moreover, like Beisel, and others who have studied moral politics,[14] I believe that conflict can bring to the surface new insights about how morality actually matters in social life, and how seemingly benign symbolic competition over moral meanings can have real consequences for economic well-being, political power, and status hierarchies.

As I have argued, a full account of social conflict in the GYE must simultaneously address how moral-symbolic concerns influence—and are influenced by— struggles for political and economic power. It is not my aim to explain in depth every dimension of this conflict, as I have instead chosen to focus on its deeper root causes—namely, moral and spiritual commitments and the struggle to enact and sustain incommensurable moral orders. Nevertheless, our moral orders sit beneath excruciatingly complex political, economic, and status-based systems. Rory McVeigh's (2009) "power devaluation" theory is especially useful here to explain when conflict might be more likely because he focuses on how structural change can result in "power devaluation" in some groups, providing incentive for conflict. Drawing on microeconomic logic, McVeigh argues that three distinct social "markets" of exchange are particularly important: *economic, political,* and *status-based.* Macro-level structural changes can alter these exchange markets in ways that devalue some groups and award advantages to others. McVeigh applies his theory to explain why the 1920s Ku Klux Klan grew in some areas, but not others, and how the moral politics of the Klan was motivated by broader economic, political, and status devaluation in American society. But at the same

14 Gusfield (1963); Hunter (1991); Luker (1984); Tepper (2011).

time McVeigh carefully avoids "economic reductionism" and takes seriously the ways "economic grievances articulated by the movement were intertwined with cultural identities" (McVeigh, 2009, p. 50).

Structural, rather than individual-level, change is integral to the power devaluation model, and I build on this approach here to gain insight into the structure of moral order, arguing that economic, political, and status-based shifts from old-west to new-west created the necessary conditions for a struggle between opposing moral visions of nature. In recent decades this dramatic political, economic, and status-market change has challenged the sacred rights, privileges, and practices long enjoyed by old-westerners. There are new people, new economic markets, new ideas about nature, and, most important for our purposes, new moral boundaries around what is sacred and profane. Old-western towns filled with rugged farmers and ranchers transformed into premier destinations for outdoor enthusiasts, environmentalists, and America's mega-elite. While I argue that these changes were motivated by new beliefs about what land was "good" for (e.g., preservation/amenities vs. extraction), it is useful here to understand how *economic, political*, and *status-based* devaluation interacted with the prevailing moral order, to provide incentives for conflict. I consider each of these in turn, focusing on a few examples that illustrate how moral culture is deeply intertwined with these factors—as both a cause and consequence of these structural changes.

In terms of *economic devaluation*, between 1970 and 2010 the once dominant traditional economic industries declined, dwarfed by the explosion of new-west nonlabor (e.g., dividends from investments, rent, transfer payments), services (e.g., tourism related), and government industries. A new economy emerged that emphasized the enjoyment of natural and cultural amenities. Many old-westerners experienced devaluation in the economic exchange market because of the decline in demand for family ranching and farming in the GYE during the 20th century, combined with the increase in the supply of new industries. The increase in the supply of new-west jobs originated from the belief that traditional practices were objectively harmful to the ecosystem and that a new economy should be built that reconnects humans in nonconsumptive ways with the beauty of natural amenities in the GYE. These new jobs not only required new skills, but they required a new worldview and the rejection of the utilitarian moral vision and its practices as no longer viable and morally wrong. Old-westerners have been able to sustain and even reassert their moral and cultural identity by participating in the natural amenities economy in ways that are consistent with their utilitarian moral vision, for example, in tourism industries as outfitters for hunting, fishing, or motorized recreation. Thus, debates about economic livelihood have largely shifted away from the appropriateness of ranching and farming to what constitutes morally appropriate recreation—namely, how should the land be enjoyed?

Political devaluation occurred in the wake of the most significant political change in the region since the establishment of YNP in 1872. This was the realization—based on the moral commitment to the intrinsic value of intact ecosystems—that to protect Yellowstone, managers would need to expand the bounds of protection to include private lands far beyond the park's border. With the urging of environmentalists and scientists, federal land managers gradually recognized by the mid-1980s that they needed to expand the zone of protection from 4 million acres to about 20 million acres, which now makes up the invisible boundaries of what is referred to as the "Greater Yellowstone Ecosystem." This large-scale implementation of new moral beliefs onto 20 million acres of public and private land led to a significant devaluation of political purchasing power among private landowners living within these new bounds. Perhaps even worse, Americans living outside the GYE, from New York City to California, began to gain more political power over the area. In the minds of many old-westerners, this—symbolic and literal—expansion of the federal government into their lives through the inscription of new moral value onto their private lands provided incentive for conflict in the struggle to regain political control—a type of control firmly rooted in their deep commitment to private property rights and local autonomy.

Last, old-westerners experienced *status devaluation* as all of this structural change reconfigured social hierarchies in the GYE. Within a status market, individuals and groups offer certain practices and cultural knowledge in exchange for prestige and esteem from others. In the old-west the display of hard work, practical knowledge, and the successful transformation of land for resource acquisition was exchanged for admiration and respect from others. The demand for these traits declined in the late 20th century, and new practices were now valued: new-west elites engaged in conspicuous leisure in the GYE and supported "green" policies as a way to distinguish themselves from the immoral utilitarian practices upon which old-west culture was founded. Ironically, many elites in the new-west transcend the old-west cultural markers of hard work, while at the same time reappropriating dominant symbols of the cowboy into their life of leisure, whether that is wearing expensive cowboy hats and boots, enjoying dude ranches and guided hunting, or spending millions to fashion their second home into a luxurious log cabin of yesteryear. They begin to acquire a stake in the health of the local land and believe more and more that they know what is good for the future health of the area. By supporting these more restrictive environmental policies they attempt to stop further growth in the GYE, thus ensuring that new-west status markers remain relatively scarce. A second prominent group contributing to new status-based relationships are GYE environmentalists. Old-west markers of esteem were linked to practical knowledge gained through experience working with the land, and through various family traditions, such as hunting and fishing. With the expansion of ecological science into all areas of GYE life, practical markers of prestige have been devalued in favor of traits and behaviors that display political, legal, and scientific expertise.

A Roadmap

As I have argued, only when we shift our attention to investigating what it is about nature that people find meaningful, that they find sacred, that they put their faith in and believe worthy of defending, will we start to understand what all the fighting over the environment is really about. Indeed, a host of interrelated and important economic, legal, and technoscientific factors are at work, but at bottom, the origins of the GYE conflict are about meaning. Such differences of meaning are especially difficult to resolve because there exists no external objective standard upon which to adjudicate between claims that are only "True" within larger narratives and moral orders that cultures use to make sense of the world and define their reality. Here I will provide a quick roadmap outlining how this argument unfolds throughout the rest of the book.

APPROACH TO RESEARCH

My analytical approach in this book is broad in that I seek to reconstruct the cultural context—in sociohistorical detail and institutional complexity—within which different moral and spiritual ideas about Yellowstone emerged. But my approach is also in-depth, in that it uses detailed case-study examinations of specific contemporary conflicts to demonstrate how deeply held moral commitments influence, in different ways, the ongoing political struggles. Because our human moral orders come largely from socialization into life-defining narratives, I pay particular attention to the historical development and influence of the following narrative elements that are relevant for explaining my case: manifest destiny, rugged individualism, human dominionism, old-western heritage, wildness and wilderness, the rise of ecological science, indigenous tribal religion, place attachment to physical settings, American imperialism, and environmentalists' redemption of the natural world.

   To accomplish this, I rely on three different sources of data: (1) *Quantitative indicators of broader social and moral change in the region.* These longitudinal data, culled from various sources (e.g., U.S. Census Bureau, Internal Revenue Service, Bureau of Economic Analysis) describe socioeconomic shifts, marking significant institutional change in the region from "old-west" to "new-west." These data provide the necessary historical and cultural scaffolding for understanding more recent moral change in the region. (2) *A profusion of discourse texts,* including "big data" corpora. These text corpora are both historical and current; examples include material discourse like scientific reports, social media, public letters written to the National Park Service, culturally important images, written histories of communities, meeting transcripts, protest-event transcripts, social movement newsletters, documentary films, news articles, and legal materials such as laws, lawsuits, and court opinions. By "big data" I refer to the hundreds of thousands of public comments letters I collected and organized for computational content analysis. I make use of emerging computational methods in sociology adapted from the computer sciences, made possible by the growing availability of digital texts. On the whole, this large collection of discourse (e.g., spoken, written, produced with media), from multiple arenas of social life, complements my quantitative data and provides great insight into social practices. (3) *Two years of ethnographic participant observation and interviews in the GYE.* These rich data come from living full-time with communal activist groups, routinely attending public meetings, observing environmental protests, taking part in the bureaucratic activities of the National Park Service, participating with both old-westerners and new-westerners in practices that are culturally meaningful in this area (e.g., recreation, labor, environmental service trips), conducting over 100 formal and informal interviews, observing ranchers, farmers, environmentalists, park managers, and the myriad routines of day-to-day life in the GYE.

The concurrent focus on these three sources of data allows me to uncover the historical, narratological, and structural patterns of meaning and morality, as well as to get at—as best one can—moral meanings through more grounded techniques of participant observation and micro-interaction. Following the recent explosion of interest in morality in psychology, law, philosophy, and neuroscience, Hitlin and Vaisey (2010, p. 11) argue that sociologists' "main contribution in this vein is the determination to investigate moral phenomena 'in the wild' as far as possible." My case of GYE conflict provides an excellent social laboratory to do just that—namely, to examine in concrete ways how moral commitments emerge and are put to use in a specific context, through particular identities, and in the midst of major social-structural change. Thus, not only does this conflict elicit an abundance of competing claims to investigate, but because Yellowstone is such a symbolically important and even sacred place for so many Americans, it serves as an emotional lightning rod that reveals in stark terms our nation's moral boundaries around nature.

THE LANDSCAPE OF WHAT FOLLOWS

This book unfolds in two symbiotic parts. The first is largely sociohistorical. I focus on the development of cultural contexts and social structures in which stakeholders now find themselves. The goal here is to present, in historical detail, how through various institutional currents and channels, competing moral orders and spiritual narratives took hold in the GYE. Chapters 1 and 2 are essential for understanding the case studies of modern-day conflict presented in later chapters.

Beginning with Chapter 1, I show how materially instrumental or utilitarian aspects of social life can acquire moral and religious meanings. I argue that the use of natural resources in Yellowstone underwent a process of "moralization" that had important institutional effects on the area (e.g., more government attention, scientific research, censuring, public sentiment, emotional disgust). As a sort of scaffolding for explaining this process of moralization, I document the emergence and interaction of three "moral visions" (utilitarian, spiritual, biocentric) in Yellowstone in the 19th and 20th centuries. To demonstrate the effects of this process, and how the meaning of Yellowstone changed from its early years, the chapter ends with an analysis of how new moral visions were institutionalized into new laws and policies, both nationally and locally, culminating in the creation of the Greater Yellowstone Ecosystem—thus creating the social conditions for eventual intractable contemporary conflict that would soon follow.

Chapter 2 keeps with this macro-level focus on GYE institutions, picking up where Chapter 1 leaves off, and examines how dramatic social change in the GYE after 1970 ramped up competing moral commitments. I draw on a wealth of longitudinal data about demographic, economic, and cultural rearrangement to show how the area transitioned, in striking fashion, from old-west to new-west. I make two arguments: First, that this large-scale social change has important *moral* causes and consequences, as competing groups erect and protect new moral boundaries in the fight for nature. Second, that this new social and moral arrangement fostered protracted environmental conflict. I present the cast of characters involved in GYE conflicts, and then document the rise of conflict using a host of original time-series indicators, across a variety of institutional fields (e.g., lawsuits, voting segregation, congressional attention, scientific disputes, public responses, interest group conflict, carrying capacity conflict).

In the remaining chapters I build on this sociohistorical approach, descending from the birds-eye-view level down into the inner workings of some of the most contentious and intractable conflicts in the GYE. In doing so, I am able to show specifically and concretely how morality and spirituality actually influence the day-to-day practices of environmental conflict. Each fine-grained case study shows the *different* ways in which these cultural elements are tangled up in—and come to influence—disputes that, on the face of it, appear to be purely rational, secular, scientific, legal, or economic.

Chapter 3 goes inside a bitter, long-lasting, and sometimes violent dispute over the Yellowstone bison herd—America's only remaining genetically pure and free-roaming herd, which once numbered more than 30 million but was exterminated down to a mere 23 single animals. This intractable issue hinges on current scientific disagreements about the biology and ecology of the disease brucellosis (*Brucella abortus*). But in recent years, a more radical, grassroots, and direct-action activist group called the Buffalo Field Campaign (BFC) has found success by shifting the focus of the debate away from science, toward the deeper religious dimensions of the issue. Drawing on full-time ethnographic participation, as well as computational content analysis of all organizational literature, I show how the infusion of the conflict with moral and spiritual feeling has brought to the fore deeper questions that ultimately needed to be answered, thus making this a public religious conflict as much as a scientific one, sidestepping rabbit holes of intractability. I focus particular attention on meanings related to genetic purity, species "wildness," and native spirituality. In making this argument, I observe the ways in which BFC activists engaged in a phenomenon I call moral and religious "muting." This has theoretical implications for understanding how certain elements of culture (e.g., individualism and moral relativism) can organize and pattern others—especially in post hoc explanations of religiously motivated activism.

Chapter 4 examines perhaps the most well-known, and most controversial, conflict in the history of Yellowstone: the reintroduction of wolves in 1995, after they had been exterminated from the Rocky Mountains just six decades earlier. Hundreds of popular and scholarly books and articles have been written about the reintroduction, nearly all of which focus on the biology, ecology, and economic impact of the wolf's return. But the eventual restoration of wolves brought little resolution, even despite such scientific and economic certainty. This is because, as I argue, the ongoing war over the wolf is not ultimately about wolf science, about ecosystem dynamics, or about economic costs and benefits. Instead, I show that deeper cultural commitments are knowingly, and unknowingly, pushed beneath the surface of rational policy debate, and the failure to acknowledge them hinders opportunities for conflict resolution. My goal in this chapter is to demonstrate this point and to empirically uncover, and rigorously examine, the competing moral orders that motivate this ongoing war over the wolf in Yellowstone. In my research I found that two polarized sides rely on contrasting narratives to draw moral boundaries around the animal, and they bring these boundaries to bear in sustaining the conflict. This analysis draws on a wide variety of data to make this case, including discourse analysis, in-person interviews, observation, and computational content analysis of thousands of public letters written to the U.S. Fish and Wildlife Service. This chapter not only demonstrates the importance of deeply held moral and spiritual commitments in the conflict, but more specifically shows how different moral arguments tend to cluster together, and how geographical proximity influences the types of moral and spiritual arguments people make.

Chapter 5 investigates an "outlier" case of environmental conflict, where things did not follow the same social patterns I observed elsewhere in the GYE. I view this counterexample case as an important analytical alternative to what has been presented thus far, in hopes of learning something new and unexpected about my larger argument. The case study involves conflict over a plan to drill 136 natural gas wells just to the south of Yellowstone, in Sublette County, WY. This plan is not unusual, given that this county includes two of the largest gas fields in the United States and that most residents of this county and state support this economically beneficial activity. But in a radical reversal, a large group of miners, outfitters, ranchers, and other old-westerners acted against their own economic and cultural traditions, starting an environmental movement to oppose drilling in this particular area. But why oppose drilling here, and virtually nowhere else? In other words, why are some parts of nature treated as more special than others, more deserving of strong moral boundaries and protection? And what leads old-westerners, who tend to have a deep-seated hatred for environmental regulation and to rely on mineral extraction for their economic well-being, to become environmental activists? Common theories about economic self-interest, resource mobilization, and NIMBY movements fail to adequately explain this ironic turn of events. Instead, I find that the intense negative reaction to drilling in this area, as opposed to other areas, is caused by a violation of strong moral boundaries linked to old-west place attachment. These deep emotional, and sometimes spiritual, bonds, which shape one's sense of self, community, and connectedness with the natural world, sparked an unlikely movement to shut down drilling. I conclude the analysis with a reflection on how old-west activists make sense of this new identity as environmental activists, and the perceived moral baggage that comes along with it. I show how they engage in moral "boundary work" to assert their old-west identity over and against "tree-hugger" groups, who do not share "Wyoming values" and are thus regarded as less virtuous.

1. Believing in Yellowstone: The Moralization of Nature and the Creation of America's Eden

As the ice on the Yellowstone Plateau began to melt from thousands of years of deep glaciation, new life emerged, and humans followed the retreating ice in search of animal and plant sustenance. Archaeologists, paleontologists, and historians trace the melting ice and the existence of human life in Yellowstone back at least 11,000 years (Cannon, 1993; Haines, 1977). Yet most popular knowledge, and our most powerful American myths about the brave "discovery" of Yellowstone by white Euro-American mountain men, reach back a short 200 years, only 1.2 percent of the span of time that humans have been known to inhabit the region. During these 200 years—as more groups came to inhabit the Yellowstone area—its natural resources took on new meaning. Deep moral and spiritual disagreements formed then are the bedrock upon which contemporary conflict in the area takes place.

This chapter recounts America's early relationship with Yellowstone. How did the meaning of Yellowstone change from the time it was "discovered" and made a national park? More specifically, how, over the course of the late 19th and early 20th centuries, was Yellowstone sacralized and moralized? In sociology, this relates more generally to how aspects of social life that are thought to be about instrumental or material preferences become invested with moral and religious meaning (Zelizer, 2010). Similarly, work in psychology has theorized the processes of "moralization," whereby utilitarian preferences are converted into values (Rozin, 1999; Rozin and Singh, 1999). For example, the act of smoking in American society underwent a process of moralization beginning in the late 1960s. What was once a behavioral preference, a mere taste or personal choice, is now a morally laden act, something viewed by many as disgusting and wrong. When a practice such as smoking—or in this case, the use of Yellowstone— becomes moralized, it is more likely to receive "attention from governments and institutions, to encourage supportive scientific research, to license censure [and] to recruit the emotion of disgust" (Rozin, 1999, p. 218). This process of institutionalization through science, law, and public sentiment legitimizes a new moral order about aspects of life that were before thought to be about material preferences or mere taste.

What does this mean for the historical development of Yellowstone, and the recent rise of conflict? In this chapter I make the historical argument that the use of natural resources in Yellowstone underwent a process of "moralization," whereby instrumental and material relationships with nature were invested with moral and spiritual meaning. This process had important institutional effects on politics in the area (e.g., more government attention, scientific research, censuring, public sentiment, emotional disgust). As a sort of scaffolding for explaining this process of moralization, I document the emergence and inter-action of three "moral visions" of Yellowstone. By moral vision I mean a bundle of practices, beliefs, and feelings groups (and individuals) use to discern right and wrong, good and bad, desirable and undesirable, just and unjust about the natural environment.[1] Using these three ideal types to structure my historical and analytical framework, I begin with the early days in the Yellowstone area as my starting point for this moralization process. New ideas began to emerge in the Yellowstone area and throughout the nation about the meaning of nature, its economic and noneconomic value, and how humans ought to relate to it. This moral upheaval was paired with large-scale social and economic change in the United States that created a context of opportunity to institutionalize these new moral visions into daily life. I focus on these historical contingencies throughout, drawing on larger developments in American life, as well as local developments in Yellowstone itself.

Before jumping into the story of moralization in the area, a brief introduction to the utilitarian, spiritual, and biocentric moral visions will be useful. *I define the utilitarian moral vision as a bundle of practices, beliefs, and feelings oriented toward the physical transformation of nature for useful purposes.* The utilitarian vision is not simply a crass materialism, amoral greed, or purely economic approach to nature. It moralizes nature by defining what it is good for (e.g., resources, practical use), but it also moralizes the work one does in nature, as well as the workers themselves. Making utilitarian use of the land not only provided material gain, but it satisfied deeper narratives about the self-made man, manifest destiny, rugged individual will, inevitable progress, and the traditional (Protestant) valuation of hard work. Land is seen as a resource for consumption, but that does not negate the deeper relationships with the land that go far beyond economic dependence. There are deeper affective bonds rooted in physical

---

1 My use of the term moral "vision" is akin to similar concepts in sociology and psychology, such as moral "worldview" (Bellah et al., 2008), moral "repertoire" (Swidler, 2001), moral "ethic" (Shweder, 2003), moral "schema" (Narvaez and Bock, 2002), or moral "model" (Strauss, 2005). Vision denotes a sense of forward-looking that I think describes well these concepts, such as the utilitarian vision looking toward "progress" or the spiritual vision looking toward creating an eventual "Eden."

interaction and interpersonal, community, and cultural experiences in particular spaces that transcend economic valuation and inform what it means to live a "good" life and be a "good" person.

The spiritual moral vision refers to a bundle of practices, beliefs, and feelings oriented toward nature that emphasize aesthetic beauty, "living" nature, personal experience, and theological obligation. This approach is influenced by religious impulses in 19th-century transcendentalist thought that emphasized emotion, intuition, aesthetics, wildness, and immanent divinity. It represents attempts by thinkers like Henry David Thoreau and John Muir to (re)sacralize nature in response to materialist and consumerist pressures of American life. This vision is also a reaction against the tendency in Western culture that renders the divine as "transcending" the world, separating the divine from a disenchanted nature. But this moral vision finds goodness in this world, because the earth is not "a dead, inert mass" but "has a spirit" (Nash, 1989, p. 37). The romantic wilderness ideals of Thoreau and Muir play a large role in the GYE, especially because of symbolism of Yellowstone as America's "Eden." But this moral vision also taps into more everyday experiences such as kinship with animals, gardening, going on walks, or feeding birds. Thus, to live the good life is to be in communion with nature, and a good person is one who not only experiences this community but, according to Muir, also values and protects its least "practical" members because even "poor creatures, loved only by their Maker" are "beautiful in the eyes of God and deserve our love and protection" (Muir quoted in Nash 1989, p. 39). Many people situate these ethical obligations within religious frameworks, as recent work on the relationship between religion and ecology has shown.[2] Of course, one does not need to be traditionally religious or participate in a religious congregation to exhibit characteristics of the spiritual moral vision.

The biocentric moral vision describes a bundle of practices, beliefs, and feelings oriented toward the inherent health of biotic communities and the moral obligation to the interdependence of all members of such communities. This approach is heavily indebted to scientific observation and measurement, especially evolutionary theory, ecology, and conservation biology. Thus, this moral vision is ostensibly the most "rational," but it too has deeper moral and cultural commitments. The fundamental moral commitment of this vision is that healthy ecosystems are intrinsically (and extrinsically) *better* than unhealthy ecosystems, and that humans should not place themselves above other members of the biotic community. These deeply held moral commitments were heavily influenced by scientific research in ecology that revealed the interdependence of all species in a larger web of life. Aldo Leopold describes the moral dimensions of this vision best in his famous land ethic, stating that "a thing is *right* when it tends to preserve the integrity, stability, and beauty of the biotic community. It is *wrong* when it tends

---

2 Tucker and Grim (2013) provide a nice overview of this line of work.

otherwise" (1986, p. 262; emphasis added). According to the technical expertise of the natural sciences, a healthy ecosystem functions best when there is equality among its members. Equality implies intrinsic rights of all biotic members, not just the most powerful (e.g., humans). Because the GYE is one of the last large intact ecosystems in the world, many of the intractable debates in the GYE are about equality and the rights of nonhuman animals in the ecosystem versus human rights, such as buffalo, elk, and wolves. Table 1 lays out these moral visions in considerably more theoretical, historical, and illustrative detail.

How does the moralization of nature, demonstrated by the interaction of these broad moral visions, relate to social conflict? Historically speaking, the emergence of the spiritual and biocentric moral visions developed in response to the long-held utilitarian ideals and practices of early Americans. Up until the emergence of these alternative visions, conflict was largely motivated by clashing economic interests (e.g., among trappers, traders, and railroaders) or clashes with indigenous Indian residents who were perceived as threatening the development of the tourism industry. The chapter begins by tracing the origins, manifestations, and consequences of the utilitarian worldview in the Yellowstone area. With the "discovery" of Yellowstone by Euro-Americans, it became a target for resource extraction by fur-trading companies, railroad conglomerates, and politicians who viewed areas like Yellowstone as a "wonderland" of natural resources. The formation of Yellowstone as a national park was heavily influenced by a complex utilitarianism that was a peculiar mixture of a deep ethical-utilitarian relationship with the land and crass attempts at material gain. Yet at the same time, Yellowstone was the product of a fledgling spiritual vision of nature in the United States that challenged the quasi-religious quest of limitless progress and unbridled American individualism. But the spiritual alternative to the utilitarian ethic could only go so far toward protecting Yellowstone in a political, economic, and legal context in which appeals to intrinsic value or spiritual experience held very little authority. The biocentric vision, with its scientific evidence, would provide a much-needed moral yardstick about the impacts of human activity in the GYE.

To demonstrate the effects of this process of moralization, the chapter concludes with an analysis of how these moral visions were actually institutionalized into American culture and politics. The moralization of smoking led not only to feelings of disgust and condemnation about the immorality of such a practice, but it led to the passing of new laws that prohibit smoking in public places. Similarly, the moralization of nature, assisted by changing socioeconomic conditions after World War II, led to the institutionalization of spiritual and biocentric visions into new laws and policies. Most notably, as I explain, Yellowstone National Park would come to be part of a "Greater Yellowstone Ecosystem"—a biological community that science showed expanded far beyond the borders of the park to include private land in Montana, Wyoming, and Idaho. These events brought utilitarian resource extraction culture into closer proximity with the competing

Table 1.1: Summary of Moral Visions

	Utilitarian	Spiritual	Biocentric
Theoretical Factors			
What is nature good for?	Resources, identity	Inspiration, sacredness	Life-support community, source of rights
Experience of nature	Physical transformation, attachment	Subjective, divine, purer realm	Observation, scientific management
Embodied practices	Meaningful work, ranching, farming, mining	Sensual experiences in nature and of nature (e.g., paintings, photography)	Hands-on field research (e.g., collaring wolves, sampling water quality)
Epistemology	Practical experience, tradition	Senses, emotion, religious influence	Scientific consensus
Teleology	Survival	Reenchantment	Ecological sustainability
Economic valuation of nature?	Yes	No	Yes
Instrumental value of nature	Economic gain, recreation	Quality of life, recreation, spiritual renewal, well-being, divine rewards	Survival of life-support systems, institutional incentives for research (status, economic gain)
Noninstrumental value of nature	Cultural significance, heritage, place attachment	Intrinsic value independent of human experience	Future generations, education
Historical Factors			
Emergence in GYE	Early 1800s Manifest destiny, individualism, sacralizing work	Nascent in late 1800s, institutionalized mid-1900s	Early 1900s
Influential American narratives	Private property rights	Reaction to materialism, Post-WWII quality of life	Decentering humanity, Rise of ecological sciences
Larger social group	Old-west	New-west	New-west
Specific individuals	Long-time residents, ranchers, farmers, other extraction industry individuals	Tourists, elite transplants, Americans outside of GYE, photographers, grassroots environmental groups	Researchers, environmental groups, government officials
Recreation patterns	Hunting, fishing, motorized recreation	Nonconsumptive hiking, camping, birding, fishing	Generally nonconsumptive
Popular stereotypes	Greedy, backward, exploitative	Misanthropic, tree-huggers	Power hungry, hiding interests behind science

Sample quotes from GYE

"They [environmentalists] are feasting on our savings accounts, our culture, our way of life, in order to impose their own culture of wolves. They, too, like the wolves, were foreigners, people who grew up in cities." —Old Westerner

"The real magic of Yellowstone may be in people going beyond the idea of personal gain and thinking of the common good. This place has been sacred to people throughout the ages" —Yellowstone National Park, park ranger

"Removal of the gray wolf from the federal list of endangered species is ecologically unsound. Gray wolves are apex predators and as we kill off the majority of these creatures whole ecosystems suffer. These animals live on land that belongs to all of the US, not just farmers and hunters. It is important to keep in mind that ecosystems are interconnected and the more that are destroyed, the more impoverished the entire US becomes."

"Management should be left up to individual states and not controlled by groups whose only real mission is to continue their war against sportsmen and the agricultural industries..let Wyoming manage their own resources, not people from a thousand miles away that have no clue what's best for the Rockies!" —Quote from public letter written to U.S. Fish and Wildlife Service

"My core value systems have always centered on those experiences of my childhood of backpacking, fishing, and traveling in Montana's mountains, and a sense of freedom I was not able to obtain in the midwest. I remember like yesterday the first time I saw a wild grizzly bear, and from that point on it was no looking back. To me, that bear was a magical presence, something I was awed by." —Prominent GYE environmentalist

"The parks are about preservation of unique natural features and ecosystems, not about recreation and personal gain of those who benefit from the visitors." —Quote from public letter written to National Park Service

interest of Americans who valued and used Yellowstone for its spiritual resources, and they led to endeavors to protect it from biological disruption—thus creating the conditions for eventual intractable contemporary conflict that would soon follow.

Early Utilitarian Use and the Formation of Yellowstone National Park

THE FIRST HUMANS IN YELLOWSTONE

For 11,000 years the Yellowstone area was a "busy place at times, what with all the hunters, gatherers, fishers, miners, and assorted travelers who came and went over the millennia before white people came along and tacked a couple of centuries of 'history' onto the story" (Schullery, 2004, p. 9). What kind of "land ethic" did early humans in Yellowstone practice? As hunter-gatherers, early Yellowstone residents made aggressive use of natural resources by establishing strategic migration patterns through the area so as to be in the right place at the right seasonal time for hunting mammals and gathering plants. The harsh winters on the Yellowstone plateau prevented early groups from living in the area year round. As the seasons changed they crisscrossed the area, carving well-worn trails, clearing brush and forests for campsites, excavating obsidian for weapons, and herding and hunting animals. Popular ideas about indigenous peoples, especially more recent American Indians, are imbued with romantic ideals about living off the land in simple ways, while exerting little to no influence on local ecological processes. Yet recent work has demonstrated that early humans in Yellowstone aggressively managed natural resources, using their own forms of technology and altering landscapes and animal populations that later Euro-American explorers would interpret as untouched and purely "natural" (Kay, 1994; Pyne, 1982; Spence, 2000; Wagner et al., 1995). Indeed, the management of natural resources by native peoples would not compare to the severity and scope of ecological disruption introduced by European-Americans, but the notion that Yellowstone has always been a pure Eden of untrammeled wilderness is more a product of anachronistic imagining than historical reality.

Thus, in trying to understand the land ethic of native peoples in Yellowstone, we would do well to move beyond romantic ideals about pure harmony, or untrammeled "nature," that assume no ecological disruption, and pursue a richer, more complicated blending of two ethics we tend to keep at a distance: utilitarian and spiritual. *These were blended for Yellowstone's first residents because the utilitarian use of the area's resources held profound spiritual meaning.* The spewing geysers, hot springs, bubbling mudpots, and other geothermal wonders were a source of sacred power, providing medicine and healing for the Blackfeet, Crow, Sioux, Nez Perce, Bannock, and Shoshone tribes, among others. Like the flora and fauna, these wonders were spiritually meaningful but were also practically useful. Because these groups held in common the spiritual power of these sacred resources, the Yellowstone area was viewed as neutral ground, thus there was very little intergroup conflict between tribes (Weixelman, 1992). In contrast to future generations, where the battle lines of protracted conflict would be drawn between a utilitarian versus a spiritual value of Yellowstone, the early tribes could not separate these values, thus Yellowstone was not a point of sacred dissension, but quite the opposite.

THE "DISCOVERY" OF YELLOWSTONE AND THE ROOTS OF THE OLD-WEST

For those first human populations who inhabited the Yellowstone area for 11,000 years, the prospect of Yellowstone being "discovered" would make little sense. Indeed, the Yellowstone area was never lost and certainly did not need to be discovered. Nevertheless, to the rest of the world it was "discovered" shortly after 1806 when the Lewis and Clark expedition passed just north of the area. One member of the party, John Colter, returned to the area to expand the Missouri Fur Trading Company's business opportunities. Colter is the first documented white person to have visited Yellowstone, where over the course of the next few years he sought out fur-trading opportunities with local tribes.

The roots of the Yellowstone old-west were planted with the arrival of Colter, and the thousands of fur-trapping "mountain men" who would soon follow. The Yellowstone area, and its treacherous geothermal features, would soon acquire a reputation in the American East as a sort of dangerous "hell" that was as exciting as it was frightening. Later writers would refer to Yellowstone as "Colter's Hell."[3] These early attitudes about Yellowstone reflected prevailing American sentiments about wilderness, stirring up feelings of fear and isolation.

At the base of this fear were cultural commitments to human exceptionalism and Western progress. The unknown and uncontrollable elements of this new land—especially its mysterious geothermal features—threatened this worldview. For European-Americans influenced by Enlightenment thinking, the descriptions and hand-drawn sketches of this untamed area challenged their deepest cultural narratives about the advancement of science and new technological tools to wrestle nature into submission. Indigenous groups possessed a cultural tool kit that enabled them to explain these wonders and make them meaningful through folk beliefs, sacralization, superstition, reverence, and ritual. But enlightened 19th-century Americans had, in their view, ostensibly moved beyond these sorts of superstitions. Nevertheless, of course, they had their own folk beliefs and rituals, rooted in a reverence for Progress and the conquering spirit of humanity

---

3 Despite the fact that "Colter's Hell" was actually a hot spring east of Yellowstone near Cody, WY. See Schullery (2004) for more.

in the pursuit of prosperity—their own moral and spiritual lens through which they would eventually develop new explanations, and new uses, for the "hell" that was Yellowstone.

Heroic legends about the courage of white mountain men who dared to conquer this far off and dangerous land in the spirit of Progress quickly secured a prominent place in the American imagination. These men, and the adventures on which they bravely went, became the stuff of campfire legends, embodying sacred American ideals about manifest destiny and the thrill of conquering untamed wilderness. Theodore Roosevelt would later praise the mountain man for his "self-command and patience, his daring, restless love of adventure, and, in time of danger, his absolute trust in his own powers and resources" (Schullery, 2004, p. 35). On the other hand, some have questioned just how unconstrained, undomesticated, and self-commanding these men really were. Paul Schullery continues, describing the complex and ironic history that these old-west mountain men came to represent:

> We see them as exemplifying a wild, free life, unfettered by social constraints, yet it was commerce and industry that paid their way and drove most of them to the wilderness in the first place ... the irony is that the very wildness they represented—both in themselves and in the western landscape—was doomed, in good part by their own activities. As they "explored" the West (a region already explored quite thoroughly by Native Americans), they were preparing the way for generations of people whose primary goal was to domesticate it beyond recognition.

These Yellowstone mountain men were indeed rugged and capable individualists on thrilling adventures, but by the 1820s these adventures became more and more about monetizing Yellowstone's natural resources. Between 1822 and 1840 trappers came in search of beaver pelts, which were in high demand in the East, most commonly used for felted hats, such as the one worn by Abraham Lincoln. Beavers became nearly extinct in the region, and with many of the "valuable" animal populations plundered, a new wave of Americans came to the area in search of minerals. Increases in the number of mining camps led to growing populations and settlements in Idaho and Montana. The future area of Yellowstone National Park was still relatively unexplored, and like the pelt trappers, the miners collected stories about their own adventures and returned home to captivate sold-out audiences with tales about Yellowstone's wonders. In Montana, and eventually in the rest of the nation, popular interest began to grow, and several official expeditions were launched to determine Yellowstone's true "value."

THE FORMATION OF YELLOWSTONE NATIONAL PARK

What value was Yellowstone? Three major expeditions sought to answer this question. Both excited by, and doubtful of, the far-fetched stories of trappers and miners, the American public wanted to know if these mountain men were telling tall tales, or if there really was a place where geysers erupted hundreds of feet into the air, mudpots boiled over, where kaleidoscopic pools would cook a fish and swallow a man, and canyons and waterfalls rivaled Niagara. The accounts that came from three major expeditions met and exceeded the hyperbole of the first mountain men. Beginning with the first expedition in 1869, Yellowstone opened its doors to its first group of tourists—a small party of privately funded Montana men. Their most important accomplishment was to record trusted accounts and tell stories that provided inspiration for a second larger, and more "official" expedition. In 1870, along with an escort from the U.S. Army to protect them from "Indian trouble," the Washburn party of 15 prominent politicians, attorneys, and businessmen from Montana set out to investigate the Yellowstone plateau area. Their accounts were published in the *Helena Daily Herald* and the *New York Times*. These men, and their expedition, are most famously remembered as exemplars of the national park creation myth—which still powerfully shapes Americans' collective ideas about protected lands like Yellowstone. One of the leaders of the expedition, Nathaniel Langford, tells the creation story that emerged the last night as they camped at the junction of the Gibbon and Firehole rivers, noting in his journal the proposed plan by some members of the expedition to privatize the park for selfish gain and the subsequent objection by Cornelius Hedges, who, as the story goes, altruistically suggested that instead of sectioning off for private gain, the area might be made into a national park:

> Last night, and also this morning in camp, the entire party had a rather unusual discussion. The proposition was made by some members that we utilize the result of our exploration by taking up quarter sections of land at the most prominent points of interest, and a general discussion followed ... Mr. Hedges then said that he did not approve of any of these plans—that there ought to be no private ownership of any portion of that region, but that the whole of it ought to be set apart as a great National Park.[4]

The story goes that this land was just *too special*. That against all odds in this American period of greed and growth moving westward, the nation had a moral duty to set this land aside to protect it from privatization and exploitation. The men at the campfire that night were heroes—conservation saints with the moral foresight and fortitude to do the right thing in the midst of extraordinary economic pressure. They vowed to give everything they had to ensure Yellowstone's protection. But this creation myth—part fact and part fiction—is much more complex, and perhaps less public-minded, when seen in the light of these individuals' personal, political, and economic motivations

---

4 For more on this creation myth see Schullery and Whittlesey (2003).

Figure 1.1: Thomas Moran, *The Grand Canyon of the Yellowstone*, 1872. Smithsonian Institution.

(Barringer, 2002). The construction—and subsequent deconstruction—of this story provides insight into changing ideas about what Yellowstone was good for.

Following this expedition, and funded by Jay Cooke of the Northern Pacific Railroad, Langford traveled throughout the United States, speaking in major cities like New York, Washington and Minneapolis, telling the public and government officials about what the Washburn party had seen. Langford's presentation caught the eye of Ferdinand Hayden of the U.S. Geological Survey and inspired him to conduct his own geological survey in the Yellowstone region the next year in 1871. This third major expedition was the first government-funded exploration of the area (Congress apportioned $40,000), and was the most influential expedition leading to the establishment of a national park. Hayden sought to provide an educated appraisal of Yellowstone's wonders, based on science, and with the help of two of the nation's best landscape photographers and painters, William Henry Jackson and Thomas Moran. Landscape photos and paintings of the imagined frontier, of a rough-hewn western paradise, and measureless wilderness were already powerful symbols in the American imagination, and Hayden knew this type of evidence was needed to substantiate rumors about the grandeur of Yellowstone. He knew this would be an effective strategy to elicit public emotion and drum up political support for a public park (Figures 1.1 and 1.2). Upon his return, and armed with the evidence he needed, Hayden joined the Washburn party lobbying effort, and by December 18, 1871 congress considered bills to keep the Yellowstone area from falling into private hands. On March 1, 1872, President Grant signed the Yellowstone Act, creating

Figure 1.2: William Henry Jackson, *Castle Geyser and Crested Pool*, Upper Geyser Basin, 1871. National Park Services Yellowstone Photo Collection, http://www.nps.gov/features/yell/slidefile/history/jacksonphotos/Images/14832.jpg

the first national park in the world. With the nation still picking up the pieces from the Civil War, the fact that the government set aside a remote parcel of land was odd to some, and legislators and the public certainly did not grasp at the time the magnitude of the decision.

A COMPLEX UTILITARIANISM

But what sorts of moral intentions were behind this bill, and the establishment of Yellowstone more generally? That is, what *good* were all these natural wonders? What purpose did they serve, and upon what values did Congress appeal to protect them? Hayden, Langford, and others made overt appeals that drew on traditional utilitarian as well as emerging spiritual justifications. They told the story about that night at the campfire, about courageous men refusing to make a personal profit on such profound wonders. Stepping back a bit, it is useful to consider two primary modes of thought in these debates over why something is or isn't worth protecting—competing moral logics still drive the conflict today, in very similar ways, as I will demonstrate in later chapters. First, with regard to utilitarian values, Schullery (2004) argues that in the end the establishment of YNP "all came down to cash." Proponents of Yellowstone may have had cash on their mind, yet their political arguments rarely appealed to the bottom line, and instead they shrouded their economic interests in language about the usefulness (or uselessness) of the land. For example, supporters of the Yellowstone Act continually pressed the argument to Congress that because the plateau had extreme winters and could not support any type of agriculture, it would *not be good* for anything else. When it came to traditional extractive uses, Yellowstone was useless, and to protect it the nation would not be forfeiting much. More explicit utilitarian arguments appeared elsewhere in the media. For example, a local Helena, MT, paper rejected the idea of a park on the grounds that a designated wilderness would dampen tourism revenue; similarly, a different Montana paper lauded the idea because of the potential economic benefits it would bring by shining a light on a region that had thus far been ignored by most Americans.

These utilitarian arguments rang true to an American public and a Congress who supported westward expansion and the popular view of the West as a storehouse of natural resources. Behind the rhetoric, and behind its most ardent lobbyists—including Nathaniel Langford—was the powerful railroad industry, which was in the midst of planning future stops along its soon-to-be completed transcontinental line. The American financier and railroad mogul Jay Cooke envisioned future profits and cunningly funded new expeditions to the area, and he underwrote Langford's speaking engagements across the United States. Cooke's strategy paid off by convincing the public and Congress of the value of the park and the need to ostensibly protect it from private interests. The role of the railroad in the establishment of the park is fitting, given that the railroad itself had become an American icon of progress. It allowed Americans to mass transport nature into cities by hauling extracted resources such as ore, lumber, and buffalo hides. Popular iconic lithographs (Figure 1.3) showed enormous black locomotives barreling down the tracks, through the sides of mountains, moving "relentlessly into the wilderness, sweeping away forests, Indians, and gloomy skies, spreading in its wake fertile fields, solid farmhouses, and great cities under a shining sun" (Dunlap, 2005, p. 22).

Yet it would be unfair and inaccurate to suggest that the establishment of Yellowstone rested completely on the powerful tourism interests of the railroad or concerns about the uselessness of the Yellowstone plateau for agriculture. Another angle from which to understand the story, and the development of environmental values in the region, is to see this as indicative of a broader moral shift (albeit a slow one) in how Americans understood their relationship to the West and to nature more generally. In this sense, the extraordinary features of Yellowstone, including its scenic vistas and waterfalls, as well as its unique geothermal features, had spiritual value. For a small few, this was reason enough to protect it, over and above any utilitarian reason. Moreover, the protection of such beauty was something Americans could be proud about and as years passed, Yellowstone Park could become for Americans something akin to Europe's grand cathedrals and historic castles—a feeling born from what Alfred Runte (1987)

Figure 1.3: Gustav Krollman, Northern Pacific poster series, 1930–1931.

described as "cultural insecurity" and the desire to create objects of national pride that would rival their European ancestors.

It is also important to remember that while the establishment of Yellowstone was influenced by utilitarian interests, it was a product of a growing window of political opportunity initiated by a small movement in Europe and the United States concerned with setting aside tracts of land that offered serenity or were exceptionally beautiful. The first in the American West was Yosemite Valley in 1864. Making Yellowstone a national park was a bold new step beyond just protecting a valley and was a dramatic turn of events whereby the federal government protected a massive tract of land larger than the states of Delaware and Rhode Island combined. This act, while soiled by greed, still represented a fledgling interest from the American public in the noninstrumental and spiritual value of wild places. Yellowstone came to embody this new way of relating to nature. Photographs and paintings from the early Yellowstone expeditions stirred emotions within a growing number of American people and helped reinforce the idea that deep down in the American heart, the value of Yellowstone might exist outside the realm of utilitarian interests.

Thus, Yellowstone is the product of people who were both saints and sinners. There were those—albeit a small bunch at this time in history—who were motivated by their spiritual attachment to undisturbed nature, who were tired of the endless materialism in America, and who saw preservation as a moral obligation. A larger number were committed to economic progress, nationalism, and the human exploitation of Yellowstone as a commodity through commercial tourism. Indeed, Yellowstone is a product of both of these ideals, and many of the people responsible for its establishment held both in simultaneous tension. Men like Langford devoted their lives to keeping Yellowstone out of private hands, yet, ironically, his environmental accomplishments were in large part influenced by the benefits he would gain from a supremely powerful railroad industry. Other stakeholders were sincerely public-spirited, believing in the value of a public park, and were forebearers of the shift in moral ecology that would soon transition the old-west to new-west (see Chapter 2). But to see in sharpest relief the back and forth between utilitarian interests and the spiritual value of untrammeled nature, we need only look as far as the 1872 Yellowstone Act itself. The act has two clear and equal emphases: first, an anthropocentric purpose that the land be set apart "for the benefit and enjoyment of the people" and second, ensuring noneconomic spiritual value through protection wherein the government "shall provide for the preservation, from injury or spoliation, of all timber, mineral deposits, natural curiosities, or wonders within said park, and their retention in their natural condition."

MONEYLENDERS IN THE TEMPLE

Make no mistake about it though, America was still a nation whose relationship to nature was defined in terms of anthropocentric extraction, use, and control. The moral status of nature remained very clear: the value of natural resources rests in how they are *used*, through various extractive practices such as ranching, farming, mining, lumbering, and, increasingly, tourism. Thus, there was little environmental conflict because there was general consensus about what nature was good for. The emotional and aesthetic aspects of the establishment of YNP revealed small fissures in the predominance of this worldview, yet any sort of paradigm shift toward a spiritual or biocentric worldview would not come for several decades.

Early social conflict in YNP revolved around bureaucratic disagreements about who would manage its resources rather than higher-order moral disagreements that drive the debate today. Instead, early debates focused on how best to transition the park into the kind imagined "nature" that would provide tourists with the experience they came to expect. Yet because this was the first grand

Figure 1.4: A pile of American bison skulls waiting to be ground for fertilizer, mid-1870s.

experiment of its kind in world history, the federal government had to learn quickly, and on the fly. The floodgates rushed open. In the few years following the establishment of the park (1872), Yellowstone wildlife were being slaughtered by market hunters, poaching any and all animals at an industrial scale. The mass killing of bison during this period in American history is an important indicator of just how bad things had gotten. Reliable population estimates for North American bison ranged anywhere from 25 million to 75 million, until the late 1880s where this iconic gentle giant was hunted down to a shocking 23 individual bison, just narrowly escaping extinction by hiding in the Pelican Valley of Yellowstone Park. Figure 1.4 provides a visual representation of the magnitude of market hunting in the United States, and the threat that an unbridled utilitarian approach to nature posed to Yellowstone's resources.

Seeing Yellowstone's wildlife decimated, the public responded, most power-fully through new sportsmen organizations such as Forest and Stream. The public outcry about the destruction of Yellowstone wildlife led to the creation of new regulations and the strengthening of local and national sportsmen organizations. By 1883 pressure from these groups led the Secretary of the Interior to disallow hunting in Yellowstone. This was the first major conservation victory in the park's history. Two important lessons about the moralization of nature can be drawn from this management action. First, the campaign to end hunting in Yellowstone was the earliest display of political power by sportsmen groups in the region—stakeholders who still dominate the political scene today. This was not a purely altruistic act, however, but was a strategy to improve hunting in the region. These groups understood that Yellowstone would be more valuable if it served as a big-game reservoir where animals could safely repopulate and wander outside the boundaries of the park, where hunting was legal, thus ensuring a permanently healthy game population. Similar to the creation of Yellowstone, this major management decision to protect natural resources was at its root motivated by utilitarian interests, rather than a biocentric or spiritual logic. Second, the significance of disallowing hunting signaled the changing value of Yellowstone wildlife as it relates to tourism. Schullery (2004, p. 78) notes that the change in management (no hunting) "raised the importance and changed the role of wildlife in Yellowstone. Elk, bison, and other animals were no longer just walking lunchboxes or handy targets; they almost immediately assured a primary role in visitors' enjoyment of the park. Yellowstone pioneered the nonconsumptive use of large mammals among western recreationists."

Similar utilitarian values drove the burgeoning tourism industry. How could the area be managed wisely and efficiently, for the greatest number of people (and businesses) over the long term? A first order of business was to make the tourist destination safe, which meant ridding the area of threat number one in the American imagination: savage Indians. During the 1870s and 1880s, through numerous episodes, different Indian tribes were excluded from the area their ancestors had roamed for 11,000 years. Some tribes, such as the Nez Perce and the native-to-Yellowstone Sheepeater tribe, were forcibly and violently removed as they migrated through the park. Eventually all tribes were forbidden from entering through other measures, such as the construction of a fort at the park's entrance.

More and more money was made, and Yellowstone had its own "park grab" in the same way that other areas of the West experienced the gold rush and land grab. Unsurprisingly, the railroad was the central player in the park grab, and the completion of the Northern Pacific's line to the north entrance of the park boosted the number of tourists from 300 people in 1872 to 5,000 in 1883. By the turn of the century the Union Pacific Railroad and several other railroad companies began service to the park. More tourists meant a greater need for services and concessions, and Congress decided that private operators would handle tourism development through a system of government leases. Facing public pressure from angry tourists and eager businessmen, the Department of the Interior granted a major lease with monopolistic privileges to a group of men associated with the Northern Pacific Railroad. Known as the "Yellowstone National Park Improvement Company," these men began to develop their leases within the said contract, permitting them to mine coal, cut timber, build structures, control prices, and engage in myriad commercial developments, all of which were concentrated around the park's major natural attractions. Yellowstone was a public park, but it had quickly come under private control at the mercy of politically connected businessmen. It had become an amusement park of sorts, and by 1886 it was in great danger: poachers threatened wildlife to extinction, visitors and souvenir vendors chipped off parts of geyser cones to take home, vandals set forest fires, fragile thermal features became trashcans, delicate hot springs were rechanneled to heat buildings, coal and timber were mined, crops were planted and cattle were grazed, all the while "Congress, tired of the ceaseless problems, refused to allocate additional funding" (National Park Service, 2013).

The moral value of Yellowstone had undergone a radical transformation. Its 2 million acres had been reduced to a handful of "wonders" that tourists (who could afford it) enjoyed from the comfort of a stagecoach, saloon, or hotel. This was a far cry from the wild Yellowstone inhabited by indigenous peoples and Euro-American mountain men. If one of the primary goals of the 1872 Yellowstone Act was for the park to be a symbol of protest against rampant materialism and utilitarian use of western lands, it had failed. In many ways this is not surprising, given the fact that the park was, and still is, a bellwether for the nation's prevailing environmental values at different points in history. Thus during this slice of American history we might expect nothing else than YNP to change: from a wilderness threat to a tamed attraction, from something wildly uncontrollable to something orderly and understandable, from something dangerously remote to something comfortably approachable, and from something barren and useless to a rich commodity. Yet the social and physical construction of the park as a "natural" spectacle roused debates about its future, and the role of the government in promoting tourism and protecting its natural resources. Some argued that it should no longer be a public park, such as Kansas senator John Ingalls, who did not "understand what the necessity is for the government entering into the show business in Yellowstone... it should be surveyed and sold." Yet others sided with sentiments echoed by Missouri senator George Vest, that "the great curse of this age and the American people is its materialistic tendencies... [and] I shall vote to perpetuate this park for the American people."[5] Indeed, in the midst of the commodification of Yellowstone, deep down in the American imagination Yellowstone still represented a new moral paradigm *for* nature and *against* materialism, and if these values were to be fully realized, Congress would have to take a more hands-on approach to management.

In 1886 Congress took its first major step toward this end and assigned 50 soldiers from the U.S. Army to make "order out of chaos." For 22 years the Army offered as much protection as it could for the wildlife and geothermal features in

5 Quotes from documentary transcripts of Burns (2009).

the park. Eventually Congress would pass several laws that pushed the management of the area further into federal hands. An 1894 law "to protect birds and animals and punish crime in Yellowstone Park" gave teeth to wildlife protection and asserted the managerial power of the federal government over that of the states, by declaring that YNP "shall be under the sole and exclusive jurisdiction of the United States" (National Park Service, 2011). Along these same lines, the 1900 Lacey Act was the first comprehensive federal law establishing criminal penalties for taking, transporting, trading, or selling wildlife, fish, and plants.

Slowly but surely, the fissures in predominance of the utilitarian worldview became cracks, and more and more emphasis focused on preserving the biological, geological, aesthetic, and historical resources of Yellowstone. In response to these shifting winds of moralization, the federal government knew it needed a centralized management agency, as opposed to relying on a wide variety of agencies with conflicting philosophical approaches to management. On August 25, 1916, Congress passed the National Park Service Organic Act, establishing the National Park Service as an agency of the Department of the Interior, whose goal was to "conserve the scenery and the natural and historic objects and the wildlife therein and to provide for the enjoyment of the same... leaving them unimpaired for the enjoyment of future generations." Gifford Pinchot, the director of the U.S. Forest Service, opposed the bill, as did many of his colleagues. The establishment of the NPS did not by any means mark the end of Pinchot's brand of utilitarian resource management, but it did provide a new institutional platform through which the direction and purpose of the national parks could be renegotiated. This, combined with large-scale cultural, scientific, and socioeconomic changes in the United States, ushered in new ways of thinking about the moral status of nature, and new answers to the fundamental question: What is Yellowstone good for?

A Spiritual Moral Vision

With the conquest of the West, as in the conquest of Yellowstone, Americans lived out the romantic spirit of Progress. Led by the self-reliant mountain man, businessman, and railroad locomotive, progress was synonymous with growth and development. But the quasi-religious quest of limitless progress, and the unbridled rights of American individualism, did not provide the tools necessary to predict or grapple with its unforeseen consequences. In the wake of the conquest of Yellowstone, and in contrast to all the optimism of progress, some Americans wondered if we'd lost our way. Did nature have something more to offer? Is the Divine *in* nature, or standing far above a dead and disenchanted nature? What do these questions mean for how we should live our lives—for how we should manage protected areas like Yellowstone? These were fundamental moral concerns that simply could not be worked out in the current utilitarian resource framework. Americans needed an entirely new philosophical framework, one that re-imagined answers to ultimate questions about humanity's place and purpose in the universe.

If humanity's relationship to nature was motivated by human abilities to make use of nature, upon what moral ground could Americans stand to develop a new relationship to Yellowstone? Did there exist a purer moral realm beyond the reach of human interests and materialist dependence? Large-scale social change in American life helped set the stage for a new vision that would gain popularity in the 20th century. First, the myth about the West as a boundless frontier with an inexhaustible storehouse of riches began to erode. As with the park grab in the early days of Yellowstone, Americans began to see the limits and consequences of endless development, giving rise to new ideas about how to live in harmony with nature through conservation and preservation. Second, from the establishment of YNP (1872) to 1920, the number of Americans living in cities exploded from 10 million to 54 million. In the face of an industrial economy and deteriorating urban conditions, the appeal of nature as an escape from society began to grow. After World War II, Americans had more expendable income as well, allowing them to focus on quality of life rather than simple survival.[6] "Nature" as a physical and spiritual ideal offered respite from a city life that was increasingly crowded, impersonal, polluted, corrupt, and full of unsavory immigrants and self-interested industrialists. Nature stood outside this social environment. It was an alltogether separate and purer realm, a moral safe haven unaffected by the tricks and egotism of human power structures. In nature, especially "wild" nature like Yellowstone, Americans moralized nature through a new spiritual worldview aimed at curing the ills of urbanization and utilitarian materialism that plagued the nation. Here I will briefly describe this new moral relationship with nature, focusing particular attention on how the spiritual model sought to move beyond viewing nature as inert matter, but infused it with transcendental qualities, bringing it to life, and connecting it to emotional and religious sensibilities.

THEOLOGICAL ECOLOGY

The development of this spiritual approach to nature is heavily influenced by religious ideas rooted in 19th-century transcendentalist thought. These religious impulses, which were a stark contrast to a strictly materialist view of nature, made room for the inspiration of emotion, intuition, aesthetics, wildness, and divinity. Drawing from this general framework, I want to briefly consider two important religious concepts that influenced perceptions about Yellowstone's value and became important ideological foundations for moralization in later ecology and environmental movements.

The first is Henry David Thoreau's (1817–1862) concept of a divine community. He challenged the dominant utilitarian approach by arguing that nature is

6 Hays (1989); also see Inglehart (2008).

not a thing to be used but is a *community alive with spirit.* The historian Roderick Nash points out that the notion that nature is part of a created community stems from Thoreau's belief in an oversoul, or godlike moral force that held all things together. Thus, Thoreau could express that "the earth I tread on is not a dead, inert mass; it is a body, has a spirit, is organic and fluid to the influence of spirit" (Nash, 1989, p. 37). This togetherness entailed ethical demands that humans act in ways consonant with the moralizing belief that nature is a spiritual community. These ideas, notes Nash, "are remarkable for their total absence in previous American thought." Second is the idea that nature has God-given rights, and members of this divine community have intrinsic value separate from their utilitarian usefulness. The extension of rights to nature was part of a larger social and political movement whereby women, slaves, laborers, blacks, indigenous peoples, and other devalued groups were fighting for a place at the table of worth. While it would take until the 1960–1970s for nature to attain many of its legal rights (e.g., through the Endangered Species Act and the Wilderness Act), the roots of the rights of nature are found in this spiritual ethic—and this ethic reflected the natural rights philosophy and liberal values used in other movements.

In our quest to understand how Americans responded to the question "What is Yellowstone 'good' for?," the spiritual ethic responds resoundingly that it is good in itself. John Muir (1838–1914)—the founder of the Sierra Club, a preeminent pioneer of preservation, and patron saint of the environmental movement—famously asked a similar question in his writings on Yellowstone: "What are rattlesnakes good for?" Purposely choosing a species long devalued by American culture, Muir wonders how we might value such an ugly, vile, and deceptive creature. Muir's answer was simple; even rattlesnakes have intrinsic value and deserve the same rights as "Lord Man" because they are equal members of God's created community, of which humans were only one small part. Muir bemoans the low status of the rattlesnake, and makes his case for its value in Yellowstone: "Poor creatures, loved only by their Maker ... as if nothing that does not obviously make for the benefit of man had any right to exist; as if our ways were God's ways ... [rattlesnakes] are all, head and tail, good for themselves, and we need not begrudge them their share of life" (1898, p. 516). All living matter, even the most useless or ugly vermin, are "fellow mortals" who are "beautiful in the eyes of God" and fill the role "assigned them by the greater Creator of us all" (Muir quoted in Nash 1989, p. 39). This philosophical shift was rooted in a divine authority that bestowed intrinsic value and rights to *all* members of the sacred biotic community.

EMBODIED EXPERIENCE IN WILDERNESS

This new relationship with nature was not simply an abstract moralism or intangible spiritualism but was the product of direct experience with nature—Thoreau at Walden Pond, Muir in the Sierras. In the midst of their solitary journeys they encountered the land in visceral ways, seeking to discover a new place and purpose for humanity in the universe. They sought to connect the physical with the spiritual, the body with the mind. They drew on the romanticism of Ralph Waldo Emerson, tapping into the deep emotional pull nature had on many people—a pull first felt by Americans who glimpsed Moran's painting of the Grand Canyon of Yellowstone (Figure 1.1 above). This emotional expression of the human impulse toward nature went far beyond the calculating, efficient, controlling approach that measured nature's worth by its material resources. These deep emotional expressions flowed from physical interaction with the natural world. Thus the value of Yellowstone, and other wild areas, lay in its ability to offer a sharp break from society, providing the opportunity for individuals to immerse their bodies in a solitary environment with the hopes of finding this new aesthetic and spiritual enchantment.

Early pioneers of this new spiritual ecology wrote canonical texts based on their experiences in wilderness, establishing the connection between these new values and an individual's embodied experience in nature. These intellectual truths were most accessible in wild landscapes. For example, after a trip to Yellowstone, Muir wrote about his experiences, instructing readers about how they should comport their bodies and align their senses to best put this new spiritual approach to nature in practice:

> Look on, awe-stricken and silent, in devout, worshiping wonder … Walk away quietly in any direction and taste the freedom of the mountaineer. Camp out among the grass and gentians of glacier meadows, in craggy garden nooks full of Nature's darlings. Climb the mountains and get their good tidings. Nature's peace will flow into you as sunshine flows into trees. The winds will blow their own freshness into you, and the storms their energy, while cares will drop off like autumn leaves. (1898, pp. 515–516)

At the heart of this movement was a new understanding of wilderness. Indeed, the idea that wilderness was a doorway to the sublime and a refuge from society was a radical departure from prevailing ideas (Nash, 2001). Early American settlers influenced by the biblical view of wilderness saw it as a dark place of exile, the Devil's playground, and home of sinister beasts epitomized by the wolf. As described above, Yellowstone was first referred to as "Colter's Hell," and many of its geological features were given similar names that reflected American unease with wilderness, such as "Hell Roaring River," "Hell Broth Springs," and "The Devil's Caldron." This view eventually evolved as Americans learned how to tame this dangerous wilderness to harness its riches. Thus, wilderness in the American mind came to be synonymous with a storehouse of riches outside of society, where Americans went to collect needed resources.

For early advocates of the spiritual approach, the social world and the natural world were two separate domains. But the natural-material world became the doorway to the spiritual. Emerson believed that "the spiritual is not a realm apart from the natural but is instead revealed—and alone revealed—through the natural" (Dunlap, 2005, p. 70). The infusion of the spiritual into the physical—and into the embodied aspects of life—was the motivation for valuing wilderness, including parts of wilderness that were heretofore "useless" or damaging to utilitarian ways of life (e.g., top predators like the gray wolf). This meant that leaving nature in its original state gave it *more* value, because the less control humans exert over wilderness, the more natural this realm will remain, and the more humans will experience it as a site of spiritual renewal and hope. Fearing nature led to the human impulse to control it—and for Yellowstone that meant making it less wild and more approachable for tourists. Indeed, Muir encouraged Yellowstone's visitors to abandon their fear of wilderness, arguing that it is safer than any town park, and reminding them to cherish the opportunity to escape society:

> Fears vanish as soon as one is fairly free in wilderness... Fear nothing. No town park you have been accustomed to saunter in is so free from danger as the Yellowstone. It is a hard place to leave... You may be a little cold some nights, on mountain tops above the timber-line, but you will see the stars, and by and by you can sleep enough in your town bed, or at least in your grave. Keep awake while you may in mountain mansions so rare (1898, pp. 516–517).

Large tracts of wilderness, especially "mountain mansions so rare" as the ones in the Yellowstone that Muir describes, were especially valuable because they provided breathtaking views of aesthetic amazement not seen in other areas of the United States. And because this new spiritual model emphasized aesthetic experience as the primary source of knowledge, Yellowstone would become America's nature temple—the symbol and moral source of a nation's changing relationship with nature.

A Biocentric Moral Vision

The late 19th- and early 20th-century development of a spiritual approach to nature built an important philosophical framework in which to work out America's changing relationship to Yellowstone and the West. But spiritual values could only go so far toward protecting these now sacred areas. In a modern society in which all that matters are things that can be counted (e.g., market prices, arable land, cattle allotments, tourists), appeals to intrinsic rights or spiritual experiences would not transform prevailing institutions that relied on scientific, economic, and other technical metrics of value. What was needed was a more objective framework that could speak this language yet strive to fulfill the philosophical and spiritual goals of early environmentalist thought. Something more was needed in the process of moralizing nature—something of fact and reason, in addition to faith and emotion. Without it, how and who decides if a forest is "healthy"? How many bison make a sustainable population? How close to YNP can we drill before the underground geothermal features are affected? Without a scientific authority upon which to appeal, important questions about the how of preserving nature remained unanswered, and opponents could easily dismiss spiritual arguments as illogical, emotional, and antiscientific.

Ecology would provide the needed moral yardstick—a "scientific basis for ethics," as the famous University of Chicago ecologist Alfred Emerson (1946) once remarked. Even though ecology was the *scientific* study of the relationships between living organisms and their natural environments, early ecologists sought to work out *ethical* questions within a scientific framework. In this section I will introduce the biocentric worldview that developed in the early to mid-20th century, by briefly touching on the influence of two important figures: Charles Darwin and American ecologist/author Aldo Leopold. Their ideas were central in the continued moralization of nature, radically changing how humans viewed themselves, how they viewed their relationship to nature, and how they managed protected wilderness areas like Yellowstone. The growth of ecology during the 20th century, while initially motivated by moral concerns, would eventually become more and more specialized, focusing less on blending science and ethics and more on generating highly technical knowledge.

DEMOTING HUMANITY, PROMOTING NATURE

Darwin's *On the Origin of Species* (1859) and *The Descent of Man* (1871) dealt a crippling blow to age-old philosophies that placed humans at the center of the biosphere. The dualistic separation of humans and nature—aided by influential philosophers like René Descartes—guided humanity's view of itself and its dominionistic relationship to nature. Darwin's contribution lay in displacing humans from the center of the biosphere, throwing them back into nature, all the while abolishing the gap between human animals and nonhuman animals. His theory was an all-encompassing narrative in which humans were merely one species among many—all of which were connected to one source. Darwin concluded, "Man in his arrogance thinks himself a great work, worthy the interposition of a deity. More humble and, I believe, true to consider him created from animals" (quoted in Turner 1964, p. 162). Darwin's scientific conclusions provided hard evidence with which to challenge the anthropocentric foundations of a utilitarian extraction approach.

Early environmental ethicists such as Edward Evans took this science and ran with it. If humans were not a little lower than angels, as the predominant Christian narrative had taught, but were in reality a little higher than the ape, this meant that *homo sapiens* were no more deserving of rights and respect than the next species. Another early environmental ethicist, Howard Moore, who thought of his work as "simply the expansion of ethics to suit the biological revelations of Charles Darwin," took aim at human exceptionalism, arguing that humans are "not a fallen god, but a promoted reptile" (Nash, 1989, p. 53). These ideas were not far off from Thoreau or Muir, but the difference was that they were now made within the context of concrete empirical science. Muir's question in Yellowstone, "What are rattlesnakes good for?," now had a biological answer. Rattlesnakes were part of the grand chain of being, part of the narrative of life of which *homo sapiens* were equal members. All beings, from the snake to the human, were on an equal playing field, part of the same unfolding life process in which it was thought that all living things had an equal right to exist—or at least an equal right in the fierce struggle to exist.

RIGHTS AND THE BIOLOGICAL COMMUNITY

If the grand narrative of evolution dealt humanity a dose of humility, ecology would tell us how we should fit into this grand narrative, by connecting our daily lives to the web of life. Ecology could provide objective moral guidance by empirically showing the extent to which humans disturbed the web of life. The ecologist-historian-activist and patron saint of the environmental movement, Aldo Leopold (1887–1948), is well known for bringing science to bear on our moral duties to nature. The central concept in Leopold's work was the interdependence of all living things as part of a biotic community. This was as much a moral proposition as a scientific one. Leopold used the metaphor of an engine to describe how nature functioned, emphasizing the important purpose of every little cog and wheel, and cautioning that the removal of even one small part of the engine risks the functioning of the whole.

Leopold's ecological approach to nature assumed that value judgments about "good" and "bad" organisms are social constructions stemming from utilitarian and anthropocentric beliefs. For example, top predators like the wolf were considered "bad" animals because they killed livestock and because early American culture deemed them cruel and threatening. Yet Leopold argued that in making value judgments like these, we fail to see how the wolf functions as an important cog in the health of the biotic community. We must remember that the new goal should be permanence, or the preservation of as many "cogs and wheels" of the engine as possible. So, what good are wolves, then? Ecology could provide scientific answers about the ways wolves contribute to the functioning of a healthy ecosystem, such as their role in controlling important prey species' population dynamics. For example, since reintroducing wolves to Yellowstone in 1995 ecologists have been busy examining the cascade of effects this one species has on all other wildlife.

Leopold's work on the interdependence of all things had profound ethical implications that went far beyond the ostensibly amoral ecological science upon which it was founded. His famous land ethic states that "a thing is right when it tends to preserve the integrity, stability, and beauty of the biotic community. It is wrong when it tends otherwise" (1986, p. 262). The integrity, stability, and beauty of the biotic community obligated humans to extend rights to all nonhuman members of the community, because all members play an equal role in the flourishing of the whole. And to be equal members of the community, humans would have to restrain themselves, which would be difficult with booming industrial development and powerful new technologies. This ethical framework resembled the spiritual and philosophical appeals of Thoreau and Muir, yet instead of being rooted in spiritual experiences in wilderness, it was rooted in science about how ecosystems operate and how best we might preserve them. One cannot overstate the importance of Leopold's land ethic. While it was initially met with very little attention, it was the motivating force behind the environmental movement in the 1960s–1970s, and it is still the centerpiece of modern ecological science and environmental ethics.

TECHNICAL EXPERTISE

Writing in the 1970s and 1980s, the renowned Harvard biologist E. O. Wilson reflected on early ecology as a field interested in ethical questions. Yet with the subsequent increase of scientific knowledge in the field, Wilson argues that the field became more amoral in its research production. Ethics had gone underground, hidden beneath the specialized knowledge of the natural sciences. This was not necessarily a bad thing for Wilson, given that there was much to discover in the fields of ecology and biology. Yet Wilson was hopeful that after sufficient technical understanding, by the end of the 20th century the "questions [would] turn ethical again ... [because] the future of the conservation movement depends on such an advance in moral reasoning" (Nash, 1989, p. 82). As ecology became more of an abstract and quantitative science, and less of a blend of natural history and ethics (e.g., Leopold, Rachel Carson), those interested in moral concerns took shelter in the humanities. This specialization of knowledge altered the focus of conflict over the environment and put more power into the hands of highly educated institutions and experts.

The certainty of an objective approach made preservation a black and white issue now that the health of an ecosystem could be measured with numbers. But while the certainty of such an approach to nature was indeed a positive tool for social change, it also had a dark side, as it was used to justify the early expulsion of Indian groups in Yellowstone. Mark David Spence (2000) argues that "defining the value of wilderness in terms of animals and trees led advocates of preservation to view Indians as inherently incapable of appreciating the natural world." Indians in Yellowstone were described by early whites as "unscientific savages," unable to understand that "native hunting was an 'unmitigated evil' that threatened to undermine the entire purpose of the park," and thus Spence concludes that "Yellowstone provides the first example of removing a native population in order to 'preserve' nature" (2000, pp. 62–70). The biocentric logic was especially powerful because it had technical knowledge and the authority of science on its side, along with a deeply ingrained, yet increasingly veiled, moral vision about the intrinsic rights of nature and the value of intact ecosystems.

Social Change and the "Greater" Yellowstone Ecosystem

To bring this chapter full circle I now consider concrete ways in which this process of moralization led to social changes, ultimately altering how Yellowstone is currently viewed by the public, defended by activist groups, and managed by the government. Together, the new spiritual and biocentric moral visions directly challenged utilitarian logic and demanded radical revision of Americans' behavior. But it would take several decades for these new moral visions to be institutionalized in American culture and politics. The major reason for this is that the socioeconomic context in which these new ideas were born was not receptive to their idealistic message and ethical implications. But with changing socioeconomic conditions and an expanding educational system after World War II, these ideas about nature as a source of spiritual renewal and deserving of rights began to take hold. New institutions and practices followed. By the 1960s–1970s new legislation was in place, and a growing number of environmentalist groups successfully infused their moral vision into American culture. The institutionalization of these values, especially biocentric values, would redefine Yellowstone National Park into the "Greater Yellowstone Ecosystem," a redefinition that was as important as any event in the history of Yellowstone, for it defined new rules of the game and set the stage for intractable environmental conflict.

SWEEPING SOCIAL CHANGE

Most Americans in the late 19th century and early 20th century were not at a place to accept Thoreau, Muir, or Leopold's ideas with enthusiasm, given the socioeconomic effects of the Civil War, the Depression, and two world wars. But in the post–world war II decades Americans began to acquire more wealth and more education. Rising incomes meant that many Americans could favor preservationist goals, pursue amenities above and beyond necessities, and view leisure and recreation as an important component of a high standard of living. Nature became part of American consumption (e.g., vacations, recreation, local parks), rather than simply a source of production (e.g., mining, logging, ranching, farming). An expanding educational system meant that the educated elite were especially sympathetic to biocentric arguments, and a primary reason why education has long been the best predictor of environmental concern at the individual level. These broad changes explain the larger political opportunity structures within which moralization of nature led to the decline in the utilitarian approach, and the subsequent increase in American concern for a higher quality of life that favored environmental values. More Americans, in their own way, went on wilderness pilgrimages to experience spiritual renewal of the likes of

Thoreau and Muir, whether that was a family vacation to Yellowstone or a picnic in their local state park. These social changes led to the gradual entrance of spiritual and biocentric visions into the American consciousness, especially the middle class. Natural environments that were valuable only if developed were now most valuable if preserved in their natural condition.

In addition to beauty and recreation, social changes relating to public health and quality of life also opened the door for changing environmental attitudes. Rachel Carson's (1962) book *Silent Spring*, widely credited with launching the environmental movement, alerted the public to the deleterious effects of pesticides for human and environmental health. In addition to the increased scale of material alterations to the environment, polluting the environment became much more than an ethical issue; it had become a public health issue. The "web of life" in which everything was connected to everything else began to make sense to many Americans, if only because they now saw clear links between environmental pollution and diseases like cancer. These human health concerns, combined with growing interest in recreation and leisure, kick-started the environmental movement and led to the legal and political institutionalization of the spiritual and biocentric moral visions.

ENVIRONMENTAL LAW AND RATIONAL EXPERTS

The postwar boom in the interest and ability to seek out unspoiled nature meant that these areas were being destroyed at a staggering rate. Ironically, Americans were loving wilderness to death: wanting their own piece of paradise, they encroached, bit by bit, on beautiful areas like the GYE. Environmental organizations adapted to these threats and advocated for tighter federal control of wild lands. The Wilderness Act of 1964 was the first law to preserve areas "where the earth and its community of life are untrammeled by man, where man himself is a visitor who does not remain" (U.S. Congress, 1964). Legal scholar John Nagle (2005) notes that this was a law inspired by the spiritual values of wilderness, as much about preserving these religious sensibilities as it was about ecological and recreation interests. The Wilderness Act was an important legal mechanism, but for many, it did not go far enough.

During the mid-1960s the number of national and regional environmental organizations exploded; many of these groups were concerned with preserving wild lands (Brulle, 2008). Articles like Garrett Hardin's "The Tragedy of the Commons" (1968) made the case for tighter regulation of public areas. Paul Ehrlich's book *The Population Bomb* (1968) warned of long-term consequences of postwar population growth. Indeed there was a sense of apocalyptic urgency that produced more studies, new political groups, and tighter laws. Perhaps the most important new law was the National Environmental Policy Act (1969), which ensured that environmental factors be weighed equally with other factors in government decisions. NEPA institutionalized biocentric values into decision making by expanding the role of technical experts and standardizing the legal process, ensuring that the health of biotic communities would be central in policy decisions. For Yellowstone, this meant that management and policy decision making became highly bureaucratic and scientific.

The institutionalization of the biocentric vision through new environmental laws meant that the technical experts—scientists, economists, engineers, academics, lawyers, and the like—became central players in environmental controversy. How endangered are Yellowstone grizzly bears? This was a question now best answered by legal experts on the 1973 Endangered Species Act and by scientists with specialized skills to calculate the carrying capacity of grizzly bears in the Yellowstone ecosystem. The institutionalization of new bureaucratic processes such as NEPA, and the growing sophistication of environmental science, created a gulf between the small bands of professional experts and an uninformed and emotional public whose input into policy relied on spiritual and cultural experiences rather than technical specialization. That is not to say that the biocentric vision replaced spiritual concerns, but simply that in some cases spiritual concerns received their expression through technical science. Indeed, spiritual approaches to nature survived and thrived, for example, during the environmental movement, in the rediscovery of native spiritual practices, in commitments to "deep ecology," and today in many grassroots environmental movements.

FROM A PARK TO AN ENTIRE ECOSYSTEM

Throughout this chapter I have argued that since the beginning, the struggle to define Yellowstone was rooted in different visions about what nature is good for. The moralization of nature, and the resulting institutionalization of new environmental visions in the 1960s and 1970s—especially the growing importance of ecology and the passing of environmental laws—opened the door for watershed changes in how Yellowstone was defined and protected. First, scientific research in Yellowstone, especially during the 1980s, led to a new "hands-off" management approach allowing nature to find its own balance without human intervention. Second, and most important, developments in ecology led to the redrawing of the management bounds of Yellowstone to include land far beyond the park border, comprising a regional Greater Yellowstone Ecosystem.

With the boom in tourism and development, scientists and park leaders were grappling with what it meant for Yellowstone to be natural, and how best to promote "naturalness" through park management (e.g., the 1963 Leopold Report). In the past, park managers had exerted a heavy hand, interfering in the ecosystem through the extermination of wolves, raising and culling elk, feeding bears, and extinguishing wildfires. This was normal practice for much of the history of U.S. wildland management, yet this new approach advocated less intrusive management that let the ecosystem take its own direction rather than trying to impose stability through control. This was a difficult and controversial process. For example, park managers caused a public uproar, known as the "dump debate," when they prohibited feeding bears and closed garbage dumps where bears routinely foraged. Tourists were no longer allowed to feed bears from their car windows, a favorite pastime for many visitors. The public also enjoyed watching hundreds of bears forage through the trash every evening. The Park Service built seating for tourists to see the action, and park rangers on horseback often gave educational talks as the bears ate the trash. But in the new environmental context this was no longer seen as natural, and park managers began trucking trash out of the park. Bears struggled in the wake of the dump closings, many of them dying of starvation, until new generations of bears learned to forage more natural food sources.

At the same time, the concept of a "Greater Yellowstone Ecosystem" began to emerge based on Robert H. MacArthur and E. O. Wilson's (1967) work on island biogeography. The concept took hold in the 1970s and 1980s as a result of research on Yellowstone's grizzly bear population. Only two years after the Endangered Species Act was passed, the U.S. Fish and Wildlife Service listed the grizzly as a threatened species. This inspired scientific research to discover the causes of endangerment and to create mechanisms for preserving the grizzly. The brothers, and renowned researchers, John Craighead and Frank Craighead began the first research on grizzlies in Yellowstone, and the Interagency Grizzly Bear Study Team (IGBST) expanded their work in the 1980s. They found that Yellowstone grizzlies relied on an ecosystem that went far beyond the legal bounds of YNP. The important conclusion was that habitats outside the park were vital to the bears' survival, and yet these adjacent areas were the location of increasing road development, logging, mining, agriculture, energy extraction, and recreation.

For example, in the 1970s the construction of the Big Sky ski resort 19 miles from the YNP border, along with the suburbanization of adjoining wooded areas, split the Madison mountain range in two, impeding the northern half of the range for grizzly recovery. South of Yellowstone near Jackson Hole, WY, the U.S. Forest Service continued to grant leases for oil and gas companies to set up drilling operations in sensitive habitats. And, in all directions from Yellowstone, new cabins were built, and new recreational opportunities led to more development. The cumulative effect of these piecemeal infringements on the future existence of the grizzly bear (and all other wildlife) was a sign of a larger realization that the ecological and aesthetic quality of the park's resources depended upon expanding the bounds of protection to include connected landscapes far beyond the park's borders. Federal land managers, scientists, and conservation groups gradually reached a consensus that Yellowstone's management area (not the park's official borders) needed to expand from 4 million acres to about 20 million acres (Figure 1.5). By the mid-1980s the concept had taken hold, one indication being the 1985 U.S. Congressional hearings on the Greater Yellowstone Ecosystem.

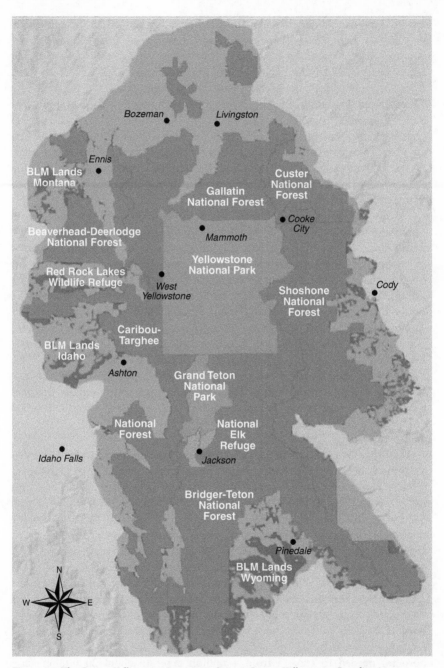

Figure 1.5: The Greater Yellowstone Ecosystem. Source: Greater Yellowstone Coordinating Committee.

The scientific and symbolic decision to expand Yellowstone beyond its legal borders had profound social implications. Not only had this decision included natural areas outside the bounds of the park but, perhaps more important, it also included all private land, towns, Indian reservations, ranches, farms, as well as another national park and seven national forests. This action came to have dramatic political and economic consequences, as we will recurrently discover throughout this book. Effective management of the park's resources now meant balancing the utilitarian, spiritual, and biocentric values of a dizzying array of local and regional stakeholders who resided within the growing bounds of the GYE. These changes are the culmination of a long history of shifting ideas about the value of nature, scientific theory, and public interest in natural areas. In many ways, the shift to a GYE represents the triumph of the spiritual and biocentric moral visions that ascribed new cultural meanings to the landscape.

Conclusion

In this chapter I have chronicled the complex moral history of Yellowstone, arguing that a process of "moralization" occurred that will come to have far-reaching consequences. Central in this moralization process were the historical entanglements between the utilitarian, spiritual, and biocentric visions of nature. The interaction between these different conceptions of what nature was "good for" had profound effects on how, through the years, Yellowstone was understood by the general public, and how it was managed by technical experts. Most important for our purposes moving forward, the moralization and sacralization of Yellowstone had important institutional effects—namely, the creation of new laws and the broadening of the park's ecological and political boundaries, constituting a "greater" Yellowstone ecosystem. With this in mind, the stage is set to consider in more detail the relationship between this process and waves of social change that would come to the GYE beginning in the 1970s. We continue this sociohistorical approach in the next chapter, examining the moral causes and consequences of social change, and its important role in eventual intractable conflict.

2. The New (Wild) West: Social Upheaval, Moral Devaluation, and the Rise of Conflict

On a chilly March evening in 1997, President Clinton's secretary of agriculture, the governor of Montana, and both of Montana's U.S. senators convened an important public hearing at a local high school, just steps from the famed Roosevelt Arch at the north entrance of Yellowstone National Park. As with most public meetings in the GYE, this night promised a rational discussion about policy and science pertaining to Yellowstone bison management. Delyla Wilson, from nearby Bozeman, had different plans. With her face painted a rainbow of colors, she rushed into the hearing carrying a five-gallon bucket of bloody and rotten bison innards, splattering them on the secretary, governor, and senators, whom she blamed for the mismanagement of Yellowstone's genetically pure bison herd. She quickly turned what was meant to be an evening of substantive dialogue over science and policy into a shocking episode of public humiliation.

Fast-forward 15 years to 2012 on the floor of the Wyoming House of Representatives, where Republican representative Allen Jaggi is pushing a bill that proposes a federal government takeover of New York City's Central Park, making it a wilderness area, and calling on Congress to reintroduce wolves and other endangered species into the middle of Manhattan. This six-page bill, sent to President Obama and U.S. Congress members, and its attempt to reintroduce wolves into Central Park, is a reaction to the federal government's immensely controversial reintroduction of wolves to Yellowstone almost 20 years earlier. While merely symbolic, this bill effectively expressed Wyoming's frustration with the federal government and non-Wyomingites meddling in their state.

These stories, not entirely out of the ordinary for hot-button issues in the GYE, are indicative of the tenor of environmental conflict in the area. Policy debates over wildlife, land use, and resource extraction in the GYE have a deep cultural side, one that is often overshadowed by the overwhelming technical and scientific framing of the debate. Indeed, the cultural underbelly of this conflict rears its head in surprising ways, through rotten bison entrails, cultural disdain for outsiders, distrust of science and the federal government, death threats on environmentalists, clashes at public protests, "ecoterrorist" bomb threats, trapping and poisoning of endangered species, and so on. This is the Wild West, indeed.

Yet, things have not always been this way. In fact, the main point of this chapter is that things couldn't have been this way, because the social and cultural conditions for conflict were not yet in place. We know from the previous chapter that there was early disagreement over Yellowstone, but on the whole, life in the GYE was not plagued with environmental disagreement because it resembled other rural American areas where the way of life was morally homogeneous, defined by farming, ranching, mining, and timber production. This utilitarian, yet deeply meaningful, old-west way of life characterized the GYE for much of its modern history. Since 1970, however, waves of demographic, economic, and cultural change have swept over the region and altered its way of life in radical ways. This dramatic change created the necessary social and political conditions for long-lasting conflict over natural resources.

I refer to this new social reality as the "new-west"—a flexible term used by researchers to describe a shift away from old-west extraction ways of life toward a new culture of in-migrants seeking noneconomic quality of life factors associated with aesthetic values and recreation opportunity (Jones et al. 2003; Krannich et al. 2011; Rasker et al. 2003; Shumway and Otterstrom 2001; relatedly, see Inglehart 1971, 2008). Thus, the term "new-west" signifies phenomena like population growth, environmental groups, tourists, second homes, chic art, outdoor recreation, and service industries. It replaces the image of a hardworking dusty rancher with "cappuccino cowboys" in designer cowboy boots, sparkly jeans, or a name-brand fleece (Rengert and Lang, 2001). It brings college-educated telecommuters, retirees, and outdoor enthusiasts into a world shaped by rustic settlers and cattle drives. Tight-knit sleepy mountain towns, made up of rugged farmers and ranchers struggling to make a living, were rapidly transformed into premier destinations for outdoor enthusiasts, environmentalists, and the mega-rich. Newcomers from far and wide—many from big cities—poured into the GYE. Some people simply came to live a "ski-bum" life, patching together service-sector jobs to pay rent. Others heard from afar about threats to the ecological health of the GYE, and came to protect the purity of the Yellowstone area. Others came to work for a federal government that since World War II was expanding its involvement in local GYE environmental affairs. Still others sought to build second homes in the area, buying up ranch or farmland for multi-million-dollar "ranchette" mansions with a view. But all came to play—to hike, ski, fish, raft, bike, rock climb, relax, watch wildlife—to live amid, and marvel at, some of the most pristine natural beauty America had to offer. And most important for our purposes, the new-west represents the establishment of a new moral order in the GYE.

My central argument in this chapter is that the causes and consequences of new-west change are part of a larger struggle to enact and sustain moral order, as competing groups erect new moral boundaries in the fight to transform their opponents' sacred stories and core intrinsic values from right to wrong, good to evil, and virtuous to virtueless. This is the broader social arrangement under which contemporary conflict now unfolds. Understanding more about these new social structures and institutions is fundamental to understanding the moral and spiritual conflict itself. For example, as these new-west immigrants spent more time in the region they began to notice the potentially harmful effects of traditional institutions and practices: local forests being cut, drilling permitted within a few miles of their vacation home, cattle grazing in the view of majestic mountain vistas, favorite fishing rivers threatened by mine waste, and their own tax dollars subsidizing government slaughter of sacred Yellowstone buffalo to protect livestock interests. The old-west way of life—its institutions, practices, policies, and moral commitments—became a target for many new-westerners. In the preceding chapter we examined the historical emergence of new value systems that directly challenged the moral foundations of American individualism and associated ideas about the old-west culture of resource extraction and production. These ideas remain central in this chapter, but I will narrow my focus considerably and turn my attention to how these ideas influenced—and were influenced by—socioeconomic changes in the GYE during the second half of the 20th century.

My argument draws in small part on Rory McVeigh's (2009) "power devaluation" model to understand processes by which socioeconomic change can trigger social conflict. In this model, changes in economic, political, and status-based "markets" alter relationships between groups in ways that can lead to devaluation in one group and award advantages in another. Incentives for conflict emerge when groups experience devaluation in one or more of these spheres of life. My analysis below of demographic, economic, and cultural change in the GYE focuses particular attention on feelings of "devaluation" among old-westerners, especially pertaining to losses in the local economic and status-based exchanges. As one environmentalist described it to me, "Old-westerners are caught up in massive change that they can't control." *Most important for our purposes, though, these dramatic social changes redefine what it means to be a "good" person, call into question entire generations of people and their life on the land, and claim—using new-west spiritual and scientific authority—that the old-west way of life is morally wrong.* I call this process "moral devaluation." It's not simply that long-time residents' way of life is outdated or no longer economically beneficial—but that, more profoundly, their relationship to the land is, and always has been, harmful and wrong. Once occupying an honorable status in the American mind, they are now the bad guys. These are challenges to what Stets and Carter (2012) term a "moral identity," or a theory of the self—meaning that old-westerners view these as attacks against their very personhood. New-westerners (along with support from Americans outside the GYE) institutionalized their new moral and spiritual vision of life on the land, favoring new laws to limit old-west activities and promoting "righteous" ways of interacting with nature. These challenges to the old-west identity and narratives, I found, actually *ramp up* the moral commitments of old-westerners, leading them to cling even tighter to that which is culturally meaningful to them.

In this analysis, the physical cannot be separated from the moral—this is a struggle not simply over beliefs, but over *physical* practices. How should land be physically used? How should land be physically enjoyed? The old-west moral vision of rugged individualism, private ownership, autonomy, and American progress was literally embodied in the physical practices of plowing one's land, grazing one's cattle, cutting lumber, or digging deep into the earth in search of minerals. These rigorous practices were once the pinnacle of what it meant to be a good, hard-working American, but they are now viewed by many in the area as ecologically evil and, in some cases, even illegal. Indeed, it is one thing to hear that your way of life is outdated or economically obsolete, but it is another to hear that it is morally wrong and spiritually bankrupt.

I will begin the chapter by describing what I mean by the concept "old-west." This will provide an important baseline from which to understand the emergence of the new-west beginning in 1970. Second, I will consider the social mechanisms that influenced the rise of the new-west, and then turn to a wealth of longitudinal data from the U.S. Census Bureau (1930–2010), Internal Revenue Service, Bureau of Economic Analysis (1970–2010), and other sources that describe specific demographic, economic, and cultural changes in the 20 counties of the GYE. I consider the big-picture moral implications of this socioeconomic transition on old-westerners themselves, focusing specifically on concepts I call *moral condemnation*, threats to *old-west sacred narratives*, and the perceived *moral hypocrisy* of the new-west lifestyle. Old-westerners and many environmentalists (many of whom are themselves new-west transplants) begin to question whether the gilded subdivisions, crowds of people, disappearing open space, pollution, and rampant commercialism is a morally superior alternative to the culture of traditional resource extraction.

From here I turn to examine how this process of new-west change actually resulted in protracted environmental conflict. Following research in the policy sciences, I designate environmental conflict in the GYE as "wicked," because the conflicts are seemingly unsolvable and reappear over and over again (Rittel and Webber, 1973). Wicked conflicts resist resolution because they are not solvable by scientific or technical means. Such conflicts are not, in the end, about true or false, but about right and wrong. I begin the final section by introducing the major stakeholders involved, describing the astoundingly wide array of individuals, groups, and institutions with varied interests in the GYE. I conclude with a comprehensive longitudinal analysis to make the case that conflict between these stakeholders is indeed intractable, and it emerged alongside new-west moral and cultural change. In contrast to the case studies that follow in Chapters 3, 4, and 5, I take a bird's-eye-view approach in the present chapter, to establish larger trends of conflict over time, with a host of institutional indicators (e.g., lawsuits, voting segregation, congressional attention, scientific disputes, public responses, interest group conflict, carrying capacity conflict). I conclude with a brief reflection on these findings, before turning my attention to the more fine-grained case studies in the chapters that follow.

The Old West, and Roots of the New

THE OLD WEST

In the typology of old-west and new-west, two categories are useful for understanding how the area has changed in recent years. I use these ideal types knowing that individuals in the GYE do not always act in accordance with these categories, nor do these categories map evenly upon all 20 counties in the GYE.[1] But despite the tendency of typologies to overgeneralize, these are nevertheless helpful categories for describing with accuracy the overall empirical reality that exists in the GYE. These categories also connect us to a rich literature on the new-west in the fields of sociology, economics, geography, and political science (Hansen et al., 2002; Johnson, 2004; Krannich et al., 2011; Power and Barrett, 2001; Riebsame and Robb, 1997; Robbins et al., 2009). I begin by briefly considering some of the enduring cultural qualities of old-west communities in order to provide a sense of what things were like before the influx of new-west change.

Like many other areas of the American West, new residents came to the GYE during the period when ideas about manifest destiny, rugged individual will, and inevitable progress were especially strong. For example, after the Civil War, American authors like Horace Greeley famously encouraged veterans and civil servants to take advantage of the opportunities provided by the Homestead Act, admonishing them that "Washington is not a place to live in. The rents are high, the food is bad, the dust is disgusting and the morals are deplorable. Go West, young man, go West and grow up with the country" (Spinrad, 1979, p. 155). Jackson Hole, Wyoming, is a great example of a GYE community whose roots are firmly connected to these old-west ideals. Yet ironically it is now one of the most well-known new-west communities in the United States. Not settled and developed until the late 19th century, its geographic isolation, altitude, and volatile climate discouraged agriculture, and thus homesteaders and other travelers sought out easier lands to develop. Nevertheless, Jackson Hole slowly

---

1 These counties are: Bear Lake, Bonneville, Caribou, Clark, Franklin, Fremont, Madison and Teton, ID; Carbon, Gallatin, Madison, Park, Stillwater and Sweet Grass, MT; Fremont, Hot Springs, Lincoln, Park, Sublette and Teton, WY.

grew, and by 1900 the small town numbered 638. The foundation of this town, like most in the GYE, was cattle ranching. More than 70 percent of the early residents were farmers or ranchers—and most others did work that directly or indirectly supported the industry. The National Park Service describes the lasting importance of the industry for towns like Jackson Hole:

> Cattle ranching became the economic mainstay of Jackson Hole. Virtually all homesteaders prior to 1900 started cattle ranches … cattle ranching is most important to the valley's history because it anchored early settlement in the valley, providing an economic base and the stability needed to establish viable communities. Ranching became and remained the economic mainstay through the World War II, when the tourist industry displaced it. The rancher and cowpuncher left a tradition that continues to be an important element of Jackson Hole's self-image. (1999, p. 10)

Old-west industries like ranching and farming cultivated relationships to land that went beyond simple economic dependence, to deeper affective bonds rooted in their physical practices with land and their interpersonal, community, and cultural experiences in particular physical spaces. One of the most basic types of "relationships to place" is the historical and familial connection to a particular parcel of land. These feelings develop over time as families live and work on specific lands that become part of their identity. Many of the early old-west ranches were small family operations, with only 57 percent owning more than 10 cattle, and a mere 3 percent of ranches owning more than 100 cattle (Daugherty, 1999). Thus, in contrast to large-scale corporate farming and ranching today, these were smaller family operations wherein the historical and familial bonds to local land were strengthened through the generations (illustrated in Figure 2.1). The fact that many families legally owned these physical spaces intensified their feelings of attachment. Not only were these lands part of a family's cultural identity, but through private land ownership they became part of their legal family identity as well. To own and control land was perhaps the distinctive trait of 19th-century America, and ranching is an important part of the dominionistic legacy of the old-west. Thus, concerns about private property control as they relate to physical spaces are an important part of antifederalistic individualism beneath the old-west worldview. Increasing governmental and environmental regulation, therefore, would come to represent a fundamental challenge to libertarian values of individualism, dominionism, and private property rights—and, by extension, a fundamental challenge to one's familial identity.

Old-westerners' deep attachment to physical places also lends itself to a certain spiritual connection to the land, providing a sense of purpose and belonging in the world vis-à-vis the land. This spiritual connection flows from the practical rituals acquired over the years from storehouses of generational expertise; it is rooted in learning through hard work and reliance on tradition. As in many rural communities in the United States, old-westerners view the acquisition of

Figure 2.1: *Top left*: GYE rancher cutting hay for a long winter. Source: Grand Teton National Park Natural History Association. *Top right*: GYE rancher with his children. Source: Jackson Hole Historical Society and Museum. *Bottom*: Sign at the top of the mountain pass between Teton County, ID, and Jackson, WY. Source: Photo by author.

this practical knowledge as a distinctive quality and process setting them apart from urbanites and others who they believe have lost the practical skills required to establish an authentic connection to the land—a connection defined by care, control, and productivity. Thus, this is not a spirituality made up primarily of abstract beliefs or ideologies but is the product of years of physical ritual (e.g., plowing, feeding, watering, harvesting, teaching) that over time make a place come alive with a kind of spirit and meaningful presence. This shared experience binds together old-west families and communities.

ROOTS OF THE NEW-WEST

As new spiritual and biocentric value preferences became more institutionalized during the 1960 and 1970s, many Americans sought to align these interests with the type of lifestyle offered by rural landscapes and areas rich in natural amenities. Since the 1970s, population gains in rural areas across the United States exceeded metropolitan population gains, for the first time since the early 1800s (Daniels, 1999; Johnson, 1998). This larger trend was most pronounced in the American West, where in-migrants came to occupy large areas of pasture, rangeland, and forest. Motivated by new environmental values and amenities, the rural population of the American West grew faster than other areas of the United States. The GYE, in particular, was one of the fastest growing rural areas in the nation. What was it about the GYE that gave rise to unique demographic, economic, and cultural change? To answer this, I focus on how emerging spiritual and biocentric value preferences interacted with three factors: the romanticization of the old-west, the abundance of natural amenities, and new opportunities for post-cowboy employment.

Tourism may have exploded in the GYE from the 1970s onward, but it has a long and storied history in the area, beginning with the popularity of dude ranches in the 1920s in Wyoming and Montana. Wealthy elites, usually from cities in the East, paid to experience a created version of the cowboy life. Many wanted to get their hands dirty experiencing the more authentic and physical work of ranching, while others preferred to enjoy a more relaxing version of rugged western life in stunning luxury. Dude ranches signify the romanticism of the American West that emerged in the late 19th century. Americans began to feel nostalgia for the bygone days of the frontier—a way of life that supposedly no longer was possible in more modern days. They lamented the death of the unfettered and free explorer, miner, trapper—the American cowboy writ large—who embodied the American spirit in their conquest of the Wild West.

These feelings of nostalgia, and the general cultural appeal of the frontier and the Wild West, were an important foundation of new-west tourism. The imagined West became an important commodity and defining part of American popular culture. Best-selling western novels by the likes of A. B. Guthrie (*The Big Sky*, 1947) and Louis L'Amour (nearly 100 novels) burned into the modern American imagination the mythical, adventurous, dangerous, action-filled, mountain mythology of the old-west. In 1988 The *New York Times* called L'Amour, who at the time had 200 million copies in circulation, "one of the world's most popular writers" (Barron, 1988). Movies like *High Noon* (1952), *Cheyenne Autumn* (1964), and *Butch Cassidy and the Sundance Kid* (1969) provided another way to experience the sights, sounds, and feelings of the cowboy life. From 1945 to the mid-1960s Hollywood pumped out 75 western movies a year, one quarter of all films released (Hine and Faragher, 2000). But Americans also wanted firsthand experiences of the old-west, and when tourists came to the GYE, they carried with them these myths that shaped their expectations of what they would see and do. Demand from out-of-state tourism began to climb. By 1963 Wyoming benefited from out-of-state travelers to the tune of $100 million— three times as much as had been spent only 15 years earlier. Montana received about $72 million annually during the same time period, and by 1988 was up to $1 billion (Smith, 2008).

The increase in tourism does not itself explain why so many Americans would chose to call the GYE their permanent (or second) home rather than just another vacation destination. Prior research suggests that natural amenities have a lot to do with making the jump from vacationer to resident. These studies find associations between settlement patterns and proximity to natural amenities—especially natural amenity areas within shouting distance of mid-sized rural communities (Deno, 1998; Frentz et al., 2004; Rasker and Hansen, 2000; Rudzitis and Johansen, 1991). Tourists came to see the grandeur of YNP, but they also spent time in the communities near the park, like Bozeman, Jackson, Cody, West Yellowstone, and Big Sky, where they could enjoy natural recreation amenities (e.g., ski, hike, raft) in addition to cultural amenities (e.g., art, shopping, theater, old-west historical tours). Because the majority of rural amenity population growth is near ski areas, national parks, and universities, in-migrants are looking to get out of large metropolitan areas without completely severing ties with the big-city amenities (Booth, 2006). The blend of natural and cultural amenities provided the best of both worlds, thus was ideal for Americans seeking a high quality of life in a rural western environment. The unique ecological value, combined with the fact that the area was still relatively undeveloped and "characterized by unrestricive land use policies" (Gude et al., 2006, p. 131), made the GYE a prime candidate for population growth and development.

Research on migration shows that many of the transplants who came to the GYE did so for noneconomic reasons (Winkler et al., 2007, p. 479). These were retirees or financially well-off individuals who, unlike most immigrants to new areas, came for the amenities. Research shows that people who move to areas like the GYE first decide that they wish to live near natural amenities, and then they look for jobs—thus the process is "migration first, then jobs" rather than "jobs first, then migration" (Knapp and Gravest, 2006; Rasker et al., 2012; Snepenger and Johnson, 1995). As the GYE became more populated, new sectors emerged and job opportunities followed, allowing others to move into the area as well. The 1980s and 1990s were especially successful eras for the rural West— job growth in this region outpaced the nation by almost 60 percent (Beyers, 1999), and the West saw more new businesses, higher per capita job growth, and greater income gains than any other region (Robbins et al., 2009; Travis, 2007). As we will see in the data below, most of these gains were in an exploding services sector that propped up the new natural amenities–based economy. But the new-west also brought growth in the self-employment sector, which was made possible by new technologies. With new access to media technologies, the chasm between rural and urban access to goods and services was shrinking, and with web access, "footloose" individuals could live in rural high-amenity areas yet still manage their investments, engage in global commerce, attain education, and consume popular media. Also called "modem cowboys" by some observers, these new quality-of-life migrants relied on these technologies to thrive in this "post-cowboy" economy—an economy that now looked very different from the homogeneous agricultural economy that had sustained generations of old-westerners.

The Rise of the New-West

In what follows I present a wide range of longitudinal indicators of dramatic demographic, economic, and cultural change in the GYE. The focus here is to simply get all of this evidence on the table, and then in the next section to consider its implications. In these data, my units of analysis are the 20 counties that comprise the GYE. It it an ideal unit of analysis, given that most social, political, and economic decision making in the GYE happens at the county level. While I am interested in the aggregate of these 20 counties, I also show how characteristics of the new-west are not evenly distributed across all 20 counties. For example, Sublette County, WY, is heavily reliant on natural gas development yet is also experiencing changes characteristic of the new-west. Thus, to provide more nuance, I isolate a sample of four GYE counties most exhibiting new-west characteristics (Madison, ID; Gallatin, MT; Teton, ID; Teton, WY) and a sample of four GYE counties that are perhaps more old-west than they are new-west (Bear Lake, ID; Caribou, ID; Hot Springs, WY; Sweet Grass, MT). These are indicated as "New-West GYE" and "Old-West GYE" on the figures that follow. New-west counties contain cultural hubs like Bozeman, MT, and Jackson, WY, and therefore exert the most social and political power in the region. This is not to suggest that there are only four new-west counties in the GYE, but is merely meant to be a helpful heuristic tool for comparison. Last, when relevant, I provide a sense of the external validity of these findings by comparing the GYE to the United States as a whole and to the three states in which the GYE is contained (Wyoming, Montana, Idaho).

DEMOGRAPHIC CHANGE: NEW FACES IN OLD PLACES

Figure 2.2 displays population growth from U.S. Census data spanning 1930 to 2010. Note a couple of important points about this chart. First, percentage

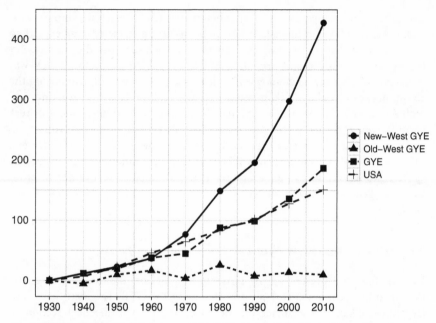

Figure 2.2: Percentage population change, 1930–2010. Source: United States Census Bureau.

increases in population for the GYE, new-west sample, old-west sample, and USA are similar from 1930 to 1970. But from 1970 onward, the sample of new-west counties explodes upward, whereas the sample of old-west counties remains constant. New-west counties grew at an extraordinary rate compared to the rest of the country, and the slope is sharpest from 2000 to 2010. Those with knowledge about the American West know that it experienced population growth in the 1970s—even in some rural areas—and thus these data may not be entirely surprising. However, the majority of population growth in the American West was in metropolitan areas or rural areas near larger cities, and thus the fact that rural GYE counties grew as they did is remarkable, especially given that they grew for noneconomic reasons relating to natural amenities. As further evidence of the uniqueness of this population change, consider that compared to all 3,080 counties in the United States, Teton County, ID, ranked 12th in percentage population growth from 2000 to 2010 (U.S. Census Bureau, 2010). Similarly, Sublette County, WY, saw a percentage increase of 73 percent from 2000 to 2010, ranking it 10th among all 3,080 U.S. counties. Indeed, these figures show that population dynamics changed rapidly in the GYE over the course of 40 years, as more and more transplants poured into the area from 1970 onward.

But who were these people, and where did they come from? Using additional U.S. census data I constructed Figure 2.3 to chart the percentage of GYE residents

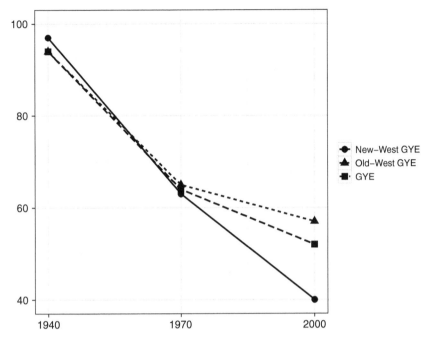

Figure 2.3: Decline in native-born GYE residents. Percent born in state, 1940–2000. Source: United States Census Bureau.

born in the state in which they currently reside. For example, are ski bums living in Jackson Hole actually from Wyoming? Are environmentalists in Bozeman actually from Montana? Are farmers in Ashton really from Idaho? The hypothesis here is that as old-western communities developed, most residents were tied to their family ranch or farm, and thus a higher percentage of old-westerners in the GYE were native to the GYE. Figure 2.3 displays these data using three available cross sections from 1940, 1970, and 2000 U.S. Census data. In 1940, in all counties in the GYE about 95 percent of residents were born their state of residence. These measures begin to drop precipitously, but there are no differences between the GYE, new-west, and old-west counties from 1940 to 1970. Yet from 1970 onward differences emerge, and by 2010 only 40 percent of residents in the sample of new-west counties are native-born, whereas nearly 60 percent of the old-west sample are native-born.

For more nuance about migration patterns, consider Figures 2.4 and 2.5. Using 2010 IRS tax data, they map trends of county in-migration and out-migration for two very different GYE counties. The top map in Figure 2.4 displays migration data from a typical GYE old-west county (Hot Springs County, WY), and the bottom in Figure 2.5 from a typical GYE new-west county (Gallatin County, MT).

Figure 2.4: Migration patterns in a typical old-west county (Hot Springs County, WY). Source: Internal Revenue Service Tax Statistics and Bruner (2011).

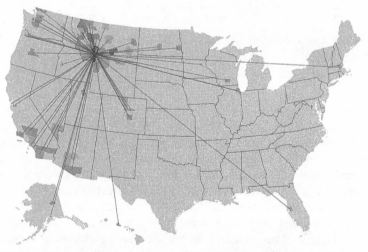

Figure 2.5: Migration patterns in a typical new-west county (Gallatin County, MT). Source: Internal Revenue Service Tax Statistics and Bruner (2011).

From these maps it is clear that Gallatin County has more migrants coming and going from areas outside the GYE. In this sample, Hot Springs County does not send or receive people from outside the state of Wyoming. These data look similar for many other counties in the GYE that exhibit new-west characteristics. The big picture to be culled from these migration data is that the population boom since

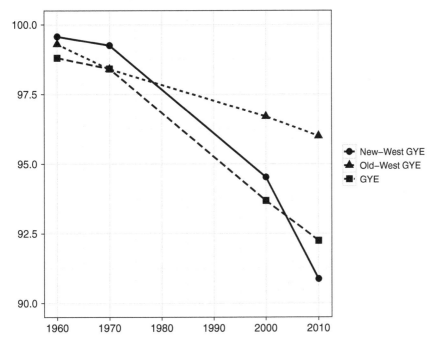

Figure 2.6: Percentage white (non-Hispanic) in GYE counties, 1960–2010. Source: United States Census Bureau.

the 1970s is made up of more transplants who are "outsiders" in the sense that they are not native to the GYE.

These are "outsiders" in another sense of the word. Since the forcible removal of indigenous populations, the GYE has been almost exclusively inhabited by whites, with the exception of Indian reservations such as the Wind River. The racial makeup of the GYE, however, has changed in recent decades. Figure 2.6 charts the percentage white (non-Hispanic) population in the region from 1960–2010. Prior to 1970 some counties in the GYE were 100 percent white. After 1970 this began to change rapidly, except in the sample of old-west counties. Many new-west communities saw increases in their Hispanic population, largely the result of a growing services and construction economy. In places like Jackson Hole (Teton County, WY), Hispanics make up 24 percent of the county's population aged 17 and younger (U.S. Census Bureau, 2010). There is considerable local discussion in the GYE about changing racial/ethic dynamics, especially given the fact that the Hispanic populations struggle to find affordable housing in the same communities that rely on them to provide the low-wage services required to sustain new-west privilege. Furthermore, many Hispanics working long hours in service industries or new construction may have different values, beliefs, and

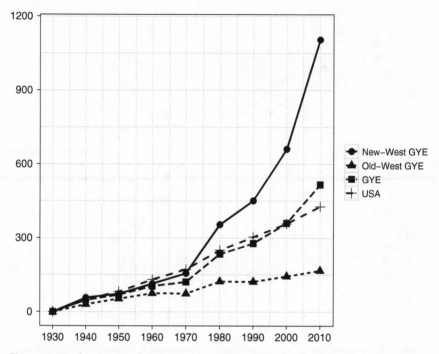

Figure 2.7: New housing growth (percentage increase) in GYE and nationally, 1930–2010. Source: United States Census Bureau.

attitudes about GYE land, given that many do not have the time or finances to enjoy the natural amenity lifestyle.

When new-westerners arrive, where do they live? Figure 2.7 uses housing data to chart the percentage increase from 1930 in housing units in the GYE. At first glance this graph looks very similar to the population data in Figure 2.2. This is due to the fact that there was no housing infrastructure in place to accommodate the massive influx of new residents, and thus most transplants either built new homes or moved into recently built units. Also similar to Figure 2.2, the percentage increase in housing units remains relatively similar between 1930 and 1970. But after 1970 major differences begin to emerge, and the increase in housing units in new-west GYE counties rapidly escalates from 1970 to 2010.

As a national comparison, consider that Teton County, ID, ranked second among all 3,080 U.S. counties in new home growth from 2000 to 2010. Many of these new housing units in Teton County are nestled up against the remarkable Teton mountain range. Just across the Teton mountain pass in Jackson, WY, public real estate data from 2012–2013 show that average home prices in this town hover just above $3,000,000. As a comparison, average home prices in

Figure 2.8: Luxury guest ranch in Three Forks (Gallatin County, MT). Source: Photo by Chris Pfadt, Grey Cliffs Ranch.

adjacent old-west GYE counties range between $100,000 and $250,000. Academic research on residential development in the GYE shows that in addition to new units in towns like Jackson and Bozeman (Figure 2.8), many of these new units are in the most scenic—and ecologically sensitive—parts of the rural GYE. Residential development in these sensitive rural areas increased 350 percent from 1970 to 1999 (Gude et al., 2006).

Given the paucity of private land in the GYE (32 percent), ranch- and farm-land are a primary source for residential development. Some ranches and farms are turned into multihome developments, others into single-family mansions on several acres, and others are converted into modern-day dude ranches. As shown previously, many new residents are nonnative "outsiders," thus it is not surprising that a large portion of ranch sales are to out-of-state buyers. Travis et al. note that "most large ranch buyers these days are from out of state ... in Sublette County, 29 of 81 buyers, or 45 percent, had out of state mailing addresses. The largest number of buyers in Carbon County—18 of 43, or 42 percent—were also from out of state. Again, because many out-of-state buyers secure local mailing addresses, these numbers are probably underestimates" (2002, p. 12). Not all ranches turn into residential developments, but most residential developments were at one time ranches or farms. Many ranchers choose not to sell, however, and instead hold on to the land or make easement agreements with organizations

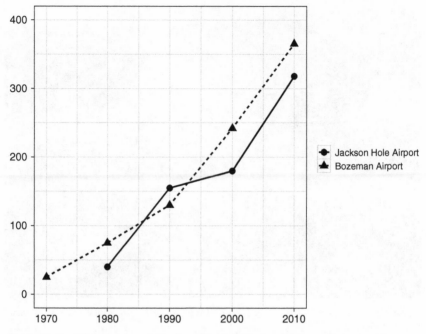

Figure 2.9: Growth in new-west air travel to GYE. Number of enplanements (in thousands), 1970–2010. Source: Bozeman Yellowstone International Airport and Jackson Hole Airport.

like the Nature Conservancy. Nevertheless, the rise of new housing units is closely linked with out-of-state residents and developers purchasing old-west land for the purpose of supplying the housing demands of a growing population.

The quintessential family road-trip vacation to Yellowstone is an iconic pilgrimage that many Americans make, but for new-westerners who relocate as permanent or seasonal residents, access in and out of the GYE by plane is essential. Living close to an airport is associated with an increase in rural residential development in the GYE (Gude et al., 2006). Because the area is so far from a large metropolitan area, access to flights in and out of the region became a vital mechanism for new-west growth. It was also becoming an important need for the burgeoning "footloose" class in high-tech industries. Data from the Bozeman Yellowstone Airport and the Jackson Hole Airport show that access to air travel grew rapidly alongside new-west trends explored above (Figure 2.9). Access to airports, shown here, is an effect of population growth, but it is, perhaps more important, a cause of new-west growth as well. Thus, airports are a key ingredient influencing the choice to make the GYE a permanent home, because new-westerners know they can enjoy all the natural and cultural amenities, while also having quick access to the outside world.

ECONOMIC CHANGE: DEATH OF THE COWBOY

The influx of new people, new values, and new national laws in the 1970s made it difficult for old-west industries to thrive. Traditional work practices such as ranching and farming were, for many new residents, at odds with spiritual and biocentric ideals that emphasized natural amenity preservation. Figure 2.10 displays longitudinal data from the Bureau of Economic Analysis (1970–2010) measuring the total percentage of income from ranching (includes farming) and mining industries in the GYE. Other industries (not displayed) that make up the rest of total income are nonlabor, government, services, finance, real estate, manufacturing, and construction. As the chart clearly demonstrates, both ranching and mining industries, while important culturally to the old-west image, did not make up the majority of income, as they did did in 1900, and as these data show, declined rapidly since 1970. Mining rose rapidly from 1970 to 1980—as boom and bust industries often do—but then steadily declined in the decades that followed. Ranching, which accounted for nearly 12 percent of all income in 1970, declined rapidly in the decades that followed until in 2010 it accounted for less 1 percent of all income. The ascendancy of the environmental movement led to new restrictions that hampered these already suffering industries. A 1979 federal GAO report signaled that things would not be getting any easier for industries like mining: "At one time, 90 percent of all Federal lands were available for mineral exploration and development. However, beginning with the passage of the Wilderness Act of 1964 ... successively more and more public land throughout the United States has been declared off-limits to mining."

In a detailed project report released in 2002 entitled "Ranchland Dynamics in the Greater Yellowstone Ecosystem," the Center of the American West at the University of Colorado-Boulder examined in detail the causes and consequences of ranchland change in the GYE (Travis et al. (2002); also see Gosnell et al. (2006, 2007)). It provides an important on-the-ground description of trends pictured in Figure 2.10 and is worth quoting in detail to explain how the ranching and agriculture industry has changed:

> GYE ranchland is in an unprecedented state of flux ... Large sections of GYE ranch lands are already, or soon will be, in the hands of relatively new owners and many of these newer owners place a higher value on amenities and invest-ment than on livestock production. As one realtor put it to us, new buyers are experienced at asset management, and bring these skills to bear on their ranch properties. Scenery, wildlife, and recreation often constitute more important assets in today's ranch market than livestock production capacity ... there have always been amenity and investment components to ranch ownership (including, of course, dude ranches in the region dating to early settlement), the current non-agricultural market for ranches is unprecedented: Some 40 percent of all buyers in the last decade can be classified as buying for amenities,

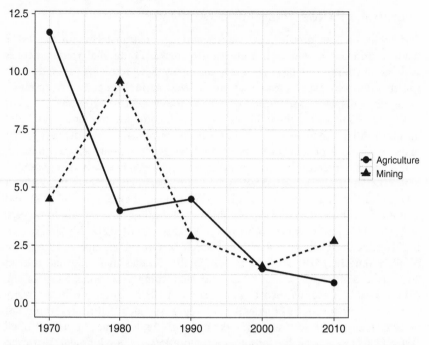

Figure 2.10: Decline of mining and agriculture (ranching, farming) in the GYE. Percentage of total income by industry for mining and agriculture. Source: Bureau of Economic Analysis (2012). Note: In 1997 the BEA implemented a new classification scheme, switching from the long-standing Standard Industrial Classification Scheme (SIC) to the North American Industry Classification Scheme (NAICS). Data include both schemes, and thus data from 2000 and 2010 are based on the NAICS. I followed Yuskavage (2007) for converting industry data in the 20 counties of the GYE across this time period.

investment or conservation. In some places, like the Star Valley in northern Lincoln County, new owners have removed cattle entirely, dedicating 400-plus acre blocks of land to home sites. (Travis et al., 2002, pp. 2–3)

The transition of private land in the GYE from traditional ranchers to a varied group of landowners, including absentee owners focused on amenity or conservation values instead of livestock production, means that a new set of values is inscribed into the GYE landscape. These new values are seen above in the aggregate decline of these old-west industries, but perhaps equally revealing of this change is growth in new industries. Figure 2.11 presents additional data from the Bureau of Economic Analysis and charts personal income in the GYE by industry, comparing ranching and mining with new-west industries typical of the new-west, including services, nonlabor, government, and construction. Unsurprisingly, ranching and mining flatline from 1970 to 2010. The three fastest

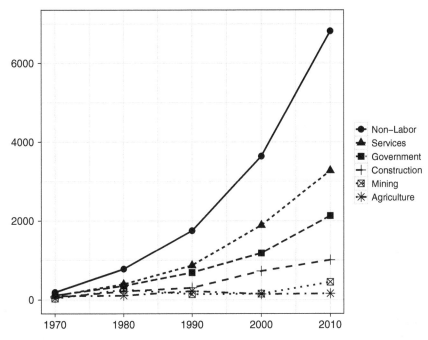

Figure 2.11: Changing sources of personal income in the GYE by industry, from 1970–2010 (in millions of dollars). Source: Bureau of Economic Analysis.
Note: See note in Figure 2.10 for information about combining SIC and NAICS codes. The Services indicator combines the following NAICS categories: Information; Professional, scientific, and technical services; Administrative and waste management services; Educational services; Health care and social assistance; Arts, entertainment, and recreation; Accommodation and food services; Other services, except public administration. See Yuskavage (2007) for more information.

growing sources of income over this time period are nonlabor, services, and government. Nonlabor income (i.e., dividends from investments, rent, transfer payments such as retirement and Medicare) grew fastest, shedding light on a new-west economy that in many ways is in direct contrast with the labor-intensive practices of the old-west. That the category "nonlabor" supplanted ranching and mining is itself ironic given the labor-intensive image of the hardworking rancher. The services industry also grew rapidly following 1970 with the emergence of tourism, recreation, hospitality, and other services at the foundation of a natural and cultural amenity economy.

This growth occurred differently for different areas of the GYE. Classic old-west towns like Cody, WY, became tourist destinations, but they looked and felt very different from GYE ski resort destinations. Nevertheless, recreation in all shapes and sizes grew across the GYE: camping, four-wheeling, horseback riding, snowmobiling, bird-watching, hunting, rock climbing, fishing, snowshoeing, and resort skiing. For example, recreation visits to the park during winter, mostly by snowmobiles, more than doubled in the 10 years between 1982 and 1992, growing from 47,294 to 105,536 (Yochim, 2009). The type of recreation growth across the GYE was largely determined by an area's proximity to natural amenities—for example, a gateway community like West Yellowstone, MT, became a hub for snowmobiling into the park, an area like Fremont County, ID, became a hub for fishing because of its pristine alpine lakes and streams, places like Jackson Hole, WY, and Big Sky, MT, built massive ski areas on local mountains accommodating skiers as well as the rich and famous, and outfitter-led hunting expeditions became popular in many areas, especially near the migration corridors on the Yellowstone Park boundary. As I will demonstrate in later chapters, some of the most heated environmental conflicts are rooted in old- and new-west differences about what constitutes morally appropriate recreation (e.g., motorized vs. nonmotorized).

There is some hope, however, for old-westerners in this post-cowboy economic milieu. While traditional ways of making a living have declined, the overall health of the regional economy has improved. Decades of economic expansion in other industries have provided more economic opportunities than before, for those old-westerners willing to adapt to winds of change. For example, Hunter and colleagues (2005) compared long-time residents in high-growth, high-amenity areas like the GYE with nongrowth, nonamenity areas, and they found that long-time residents in high-growth, high-amenity areas actually have higher annual incomes. Another book-length study about economics in the Mountain West concludes that "during the period in which natural resource industries were contracting sharply, the region showed impressive economic vitality" (Power and Barrett, 2001, p. 157). Thus, there is more economic opportunity for those old-west residents willing to adapt—a task that is easier said than done, given their attachment to traditional utilitarian beliefs, practices, and narratives.

As discussed, one of the main culprits of old-west economic decline is the institutionalization of environmental policy that favored tighter restrictions and protection. But again, research has shown, somewhat counterintuitively, that environmental protection actually increases economic performance in high-amenity rural areas like the GYE, even for long-time old-west residents (Holmes and Hecox, 2004; Lorah and Southwick, 2003; Rudzitis and Johansen, 1991). Net of a host of other factors, the more public land in a nonmetropolitan western county, the higher the per capita income for the county (Rasker et al., 2012). For GYE areas like Gallatin County, MT, $2,655 of annual per capita income (7 percent of total per capita income) is explained by the presence of the county's protected public lands. Similarly, a county in the GYE exhibiting old-western characteristics like Hot Springs County, WY, sees an increase of $633 of annual per capita income for its protected public lands. Thus, even in counties like Hot Springs, long-time residents who may no longer find economic value in ranching, mining, or logging benefit economically from environmental protection of public lands.

But presenting these figures to old-westerners who have lost a ranch, or who are struggling to change occupations, is of little help. What is most salient for them is their sector of the economy, and the cultural decline and moral devaluation that has resulted from its decline. Thus, even with the upsurge in the regional economy with the new-west, old-westerners continue to support antienvironmental and antigovernmental efforts, even when these may actually harm their future economic prospects. But despite economic changes, "the historical orientation toward agriculture and natural resource extraction strongly shapes and influences local values and attitudes, resulting in what Power (1991) refers to as a rearview mirror' version of the local economy" (Reading et al., 1994, p. 361).

CULTURAL CHANGE: "GO WEST YOUNG, EDUCATED, CULTURED (WO)MAN"

Here I want to dig a bit deeper into the characteristics of new-westerners as they relate to cultural change. We know from the population and migration data above that these were "outsiders" in the sense that they are out-of-state transplants. We also know that many of these new residents work in the services and nonlabor industries associated with recreation and "footloose" occupations. But here I want to consider more specific characteristics of new-west residents as they relate to long-time old-westerners—focusing on age, education, gendered employment, and cultural interests.

Despite the fact that many retirees sought out the new-west lifestyle in the GYE, data from the 2010 U.S. Census show that new-west counties in the GYE are still much younger than old-west counties. For example, the average age in new-west GYE counties is 31.3, whereas in old-west GYE counties it is 43.35. Moreover, new-west counties are getting younger (from 35.1 in 2000 to 31.3 in 2010), whereas old-west counties are getting older (from 39.05 in 2000 to 43.35 in 2010). One reason old-west communities are aging is because ranching has proven more difficult, meaning the family ranch is no longer a viable option for young people. This is also part of a larger national trend, where rural communities that rely on agriculture are aging (Wuthnow (2010) explores these dynamics in the rural Midwest). Data from the USDA show that in many GYE counties the average age of ranchowners has indeed increased over the years. The fastest growing age demographic of ranchers in the GYE are those who are 65 and older. In 1969 the percentage of agricultural proprietors in the GYE hovered between 10 and 13 percent, but by 1997 the percentage 65 and older climbed between 25 and 30 percent (USDA, 1968, 1997). The decline of multigenerational ranches in the GYE means that young people born into a ranch family are either forced to diversify ranch operations to include recreational opportunities

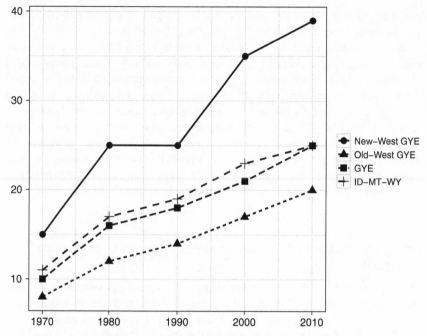

Figure 2.12: Increasing levels of education in the GYE, by percentage with college education (four years or more). Source: United States Census Bureau.
Note: 2010 data are drawn from the Census Bureau's American Community Survey.

or to fold the ranch altogether and move out of the area in search of other economic opportunities. This shift away from the multigenerational ranch was also influential for young women. The emergence of the new-west economy meant different opportunities for these old-west young women whose horizon of opportunity was typically limited to supportive roles—in the home and around the ranch—characteristic of gendered extraction industries.

In addition to becoming younger, the GYE also became more educated. Figure 2.12 displays data reporting the percentage of residents in a county with a college education, 1970–2010. On this chart I include an aggregate measure for Idaho, Montana, and Wyoming to give a sense of education levels in the states containing the GYE. These data demonstrate that since 1970 the percentage of residents with a four-year degree increased fastest in new-west counties. Old-west counties grew slowest over this time period, but they began with lower levels in 1970. By 2010 nearly twice as many people in new-west counties had college degrees than in old-west communities. These figures further paint the cultural portrait of the new-west, because educational attainment is particularly important for predicting a wide variety of attitudes and behaviors relating to environmental activism. Furthermore, the authority of different types of education is central to conflict in the GYE insofar as university education (e.g., biology, ecology) is often pitted against a more practical old-western knowledge that is passed down through the generations and can be learned only through physical experience on the land. In the next section I will explore in more detail the moral and cultural implications of these demographic differences.

A younger and more educated demographic tells us quite a bit about how GYE culture has changed over the years. Another avenue by which to explore cultural change is the 2012 EASI Culture Index, an average of cultural activities in each GYE county. This index measures culture using economic census data that aggregates various aspects of "culture," such as the number of employees working in museums, historical sites, and performing arts centers. The average score on the culture index for the United States is 100. Thus, according to this scale, "a higher value [than 100] indicates more than average cultural activities near the geography" (EASI, 2012). Many of the old-west counties in the GYE (e.g., Caribou County, ID) register in the 50's, whereas typical new-west counties (Teton County, WY, and Gallatin County, MT) are much higher than the U.S. average with scores in the 180's and 190's. The GYE as a whole scores a 120. These data provide another angle to understand cultural change in the region, suggesting that the new-west offers a type of cultural sophistication and opportunity that is very different from traditional old-west counterparts.

The Moral Effects of New-West Change

It is useful to now consider the big picture implications of this transition for old-westerners, with a particular focus on their relation to ongoing environmental conflict in the area. The central point here is that the new-west raises issues that reach much deeper than any sort of surface-level interpretation of population growth or economic change. The rise of the new-west challenged the entire old-west culture. It did more than devalue old-westerners' economic or political purchasing power—it devalued them as a moral people. Many old-westerners reacted by *ramping up* their commitments to their old-west ways of life and finding other ways to preserve their old-west traditions. Throughout my research I identified three moral problems old-westerners had with the rise of the new-west: first, *moral condemnation*, by which I mean the old-west moral vision of what constituted a "good person" and a "good life" is now morally wrong; second, challenges to the beliefs, symbols, and rituals of *old-west sacred narratives*; third, the perceived *moral hypocrisy* of the new-west lifestyle. I end by considering how all of this change actually intensifies old-westerners' moral commitments, despite the challenges that the old-west culture faces moving forward.

MORAL CONDEMNATION

What does it mean to be a "good person"? What does "good" behavior toward the natural environment look like? I discussed at length in Chapter 1, and earlier in this chapter, the inextricable link between the old-west vision of a good person and physical interaction with the land, especially the hard work of ranching, farming, mining, and logging. Old-westerners do not think about or analyze their relationship to the land; it is who they are, it is part of their daily routine. Thus, these practices cultivate what Stets and Carter (2012) call a "moral identity," or theory of the self. I found that this old-west identity is also strong among long-time residents who may never have worked the land, but nonetheless "pick up" this moral identity as members of the old-western culture that has guided the behavior of communities of settlers in the GYE since the late 1800s. This moral identity created cultural expectations defining what it meant to be a "good person" vis-à-vis the land: practical knowledge, discipline, dominionism, hard work, physical transformation of land, and resource production. Constructed from both reality and mythic nostalgia, this moral identity attempted to simplify life to its most basic and real elements, where what it means to be a good person was straightforward, and right and wrong were clearly defined.

With the shift to protect natural amenities through environmental regulation (e.g., Endangered Species Act of 1973), accompanied by a decline in the number of people working in extraction industries, the old-western moral identity became harder and harder to verify, and old-westerners increasingly experienced negative emotions. Long-timers take it especially hard—or as one author describes it,

> The older cowboys are a bitter breed. Their community is dissolving as more ranchers fail to make a living and as more sons and daughters turn the family ranch into a subdivision. Their sense of place in society is threatened. They have always felt proud of what they did and who they were. They have, in fact, even felt righteous. Now, suddenly, they are the bad guys. (Russell, 1993, p. 12).

The widespread authority of the old-west moral vision continued to wane. Although once aligned with widely shared American ideals, growing public concern and further environmental regulation directly condemned extractive practices, and by extension condemned old-westerners' view of themselves. The beliefs and practices of the old-westerner—long held to be the pinnacle of what it meant to be a good person—was not only morally wrong in the eyes of many, but was now legally wrong. Furthermore, the effects of these changes—and the negative emotions that came along with them—were felt most acutely by old-westerners who were part of several generations of families who helped build this moral identity through the cultivation of western lands. It is the feeling that you are wrong, your parents (and their parents) were wrong, and all the time and energy you spent raising cattle, harvesting timber, or extracting minerals were not only harmful to the lands you love but are deemed by science, public opinion, and the law to be unethical.

CHALLENGE TO OLD-WEST SACRED NARRATIVES

I use the concept of "sacred narratives" here as an organizing term to describe the deeply important and life-guiding beliefs, symbols, and rituals of old-westerners. These sacred qualities are the basis for social integration into old-western culture and structure its moral boundaries. They originate from western experiences and the nation's historical and mythic *imagining* of the western experience. They are not fixed doctrine or dogma, they are not stored in a church or city hall, but they manifest themselves as flexible and fluid elements of a cultural tool kit that old-westerners have historically used to make sense of their lives. Here I identify three important old-west sacred narratives—manifest destiny, rugged individualism, antifederalism—and briefly comment on how the new-west represents a challenge to these sacred beliefs, symbols, and rituals.

Shared memories of manifest destiny and westward expansion were a continual source of inspiration for Americans who dreamed beyond their horizon. Manifest destiny has its roots in early 19th-century ideas that Americans had a divine obligation to spread what Thomas Jefferson referred to as an "empire of liberty" (White, 1993). It was indeed an empire in another sense of the word, given the ruthless military force that would be needed to conquer the continent. Manifest destiny was more an intentional strategy for proponents of westward expansion than it was some sort of sui generis ideal in the American consciousness. To convince the public, manifest destiny became a powerful blend of American exceptionalism, romantic nationalism, and material promise. Its main tenet is that Providence (i.e., God) favored liberty and self-government. Even as early as 1775, Princeton's leader, John Witherspoon, preached manifest destiny and westward expansion, exclaiming: "True religion, and in her train, dominion, riches, literature, and art have taken their course in a slow and gradual manner from East to West ... from thence forebode the future glory of America" (Hine and Faragher, 2000, p. 3). The West, with its undeveloped landscapes and uncivilized indigenous populations, was, as the narrative went, a frontier awaiting the spread of liberty and self-government. And with this spread would come further glory to America. Eventually the nation fulfilled this Divine responsibility, forcibly through violent military action, and through incentivizing policies like the Homestead Act of 1862, which allowed 600,000 families to freely own parcels of land in the West. Indeed, the "great experiment of liberty" and progress toward "self-government" in the West was under way, providing future generations the opportunity to live out the purest of American ideals in the purest of landscapes.

The rugged landscapes which westerners came to inhabit required the sort of rugged individualism that the God of manifest destiny favored. They were rugged in the true sense of of the word. Thus, ideas about rugged individualism are an important element of old-west beliefs, symbols, and rituals. We glimpsed in the last chapter the prototypical rugged individualist as the self-sustaining mountain man conquering the West in the name of progress. In the 20th century ideas about the Wild West took hold in books and movies, and the masculine western outlaw who blazes his own trail became a popular manifestation of rugged individualism. Similarly, we might include the rancher and farmer, who, against all odds and risking everything, yield just enough to survive. These narratives provide Americans powerful moral lessons about the "great experiment of liberty," self-reliance, and hard work. But what have we learned about the new-west that might challenge these defining moral commitments?

During my fieldwork I spent time with dozens of long-time residents whose parents and grandparents had engaged in the type of work symbolic of rugged individualist cowboys. Because of new-west changes they had lost the sort of autonomy that is at the heart of individualism, finding themselves in service industries that are neither "rugged" nor "individualistic." For example, a former rancher from Sublette County, WY, converted his ranch to a tourist destination for horseback rides. He spends his time taking reservations, organizing consent forms, and slowly leading groups of tourists, in single-file lines, through the trail loops around his property (Figure 2.13 depicts a similar scene from Fremont County, ID). This is a far cry from the Wild West cattle drives that his family once led. Another old-westerner, from Teton County, ID, sold his farm and now takes tickets at the local ski slope—perhaps the only ticket taker at the elite resort in an authentic belt buckle and cowboy hat. Many other old-westerners I interviewed cook, do laundry, do maintenance, or work as custodians at luxury guest ranches and hotels, serving elite tourists from big cities around the United States. Even residents whose families have no connection to traditional extraction industries still cling to rugged individualism typical of cowboy mythology. These new-west occupations are in many ways viewed as the antithesis of rugged individualism, especially for old-westerners working in hospitality and service industries. They have lost autonomous control as they are more or less relegated (or perceived to be relegated) to the role of servant, and thus the work does not carry the weight of satisfaction relative to their old-west symbols and moral archetypes.

Related to rugged individualism are commitments to self-government and antifederalism. For proponents of manifest destiny, the West as a wild and open place—far from Washington and the bureaucracies of the East—was especially amenable to the spread of self-government. Intense feelings of self-governance and skepticism of the federal government in GYE states like Wyoming, Idaho, and Montana have given rise to a strong moral commitment to antifederalism. After World War II antifederalism in the GYE grew stronger with social transformations that swept over the area, along with the unprecedented intrusion of the government into local communities. The American West was the "arena in which an expanded role for the federal government first took hold" (Limerick,

Figure 2.13: Former ranchland being used for tours on horseback. Fremont County, ID.
Source: Photo by author.

2011). Ironically, the involvement was somewhat a double-edged sword for westerners because in the 15 years following the war, the expansion of the federal government brought sustained economic growth in the West. Many in the West still welcome the assistance of the government through subsidies and tax breaks. But there are deep-seated antigovernmental and antienvironmental values, which for many old-westerners are two sides of the same coin. The deep-seated cultural ideals about self-government *shaped the meaning of public lands*, thus the expansion of the United States Forest Service, Bureau of Land Management, National Park Service, and other governmental agencies—many of which were perceived to be "in bed" with environmental groups—meant that environmental controversies were "not just interested in the conventional sense of an economic stake, but values... at a deeper level of human response... and that fear occasionally expressed itself in a burst of paranoia that tended to attribute change to conspiracy" (Cawley, 1996, p. 69). New-west values tend to favor the expansion of federal government in the GYE, thus stirring up passionate responses from old-westerners whose cultural ideals about self-government, private property rights, and radical liberty have been trampled by Uncle Sam's oppressive bureaucracy.

MORAL HYPOCRISY?

Are the environmental values that characterize the new-west really that publicly minded? Is the moral high ground upon which many proponents of the new-west stand really that sturdy? Is the science to which environmentalists in the GYE appeal actually objective and pure? Does the new-west economy, driven by tourism and growth, really promote quality of life or protect the health of YNP and surrounding lands? These questions are frequently asked by old-westerners in response to feeling morally devalued and condemned by new-west changes. Old-westerners voice widespread skepticism about the purity of prevailing moral commitments in the GYE, and many feel that for new-westerners, environmental values are a wolf in sheep's clothing. Accusations of moral hypocrisy are especially strong toward elite residents who are some of the most ardent supporters of environmental restriction while at the same time complicit in the most ecological harm characteristic of new-west change.

Research on the ecological effects of the new-west shows that these perceptions about moral hypocrisy are warranted. A primary characteristic of the new-west is rural residential growth, and housing growth in the GYE is occurring at a rate faster than population growth. Recall that Teton County, ID, ranked second among all 3,080 U.S. counties in new home growth from 2000 to 2010. In 2005 GYE conservation biologists, wildlife experts, and other researchers convened a three-day conference to discuss new-west problems, and they concluded that the development of private lands in the GYE is the biggest threat to its ecological health. One year later a seminal study was published documenting the social and ecological effects of rural residential growth in the GYE, concluding that

> In comparison with urban development, the ecological effects of rural residential development are likely to be larger, because low-density development consumes more land, resulting in more extensive habitat conversion and fragmentation. Also, rural residential development tends to be distributed in areas with high biodiversity due to biophysical and factors and natural amenities ... [and] may alter ecological processes on adjacent and even distant public lands. The socio-economic consequences of rural residential development are related to environmental degradation, cultural changes, and costs of community services. Rural on-site septic systems for sewage disposal often overflow, leading to water quality problems. Rural residents commuting long distances to work and shopping burn more gasoline, increasing air pollution. Employment opportunities and traditional ways of life are rapidly changing as farms and ranches are subdivided and converted to home sites ... In the GYE, most new growth is low-density, dispersed development that is more costly to provide service to to than compact development. (Gude et al., 2006, p. 133)

Many old-westerners wonder, then, how their way of life is cast as the villain, when the new-west brought more housing developments, more tourists, more pollution, and more commercialism. Of course the answer depends on who is included as "new-westerner" in these claims of moral hypocrisy. Few professional environmentalists live in multi-million-dollar ranchettes, and some elites do not think twice about environmental harm, so long as they get to enjoy the area's natural amenities. Research also suggests that there is wide variation between different types of new-west residents (Smith and Krannich, 2000), but the perception of moral hypocrisy remains nonetheless. The perception persists because many of the most powerful and visible elites in the GYE vocally favor environmental regulation, and do so through generous financial support of local environmental groups. Many old-westerners question the motives behind their involvement, suspecting that it is not about a moral commitment to environmental values, but a strategy to maximize their own interests. This process is analogous to work in economics on "positional goods," meaning the value of goods like real estate or social status depends on how much one has in relation to everyone else. Thus, these residents have a vested interest in stopping further growth and change, and they are more likely to support environmental policies that preserve scarcity and increase their social status.

Perhaps new-westerners of this kind are simply another in the long line of groups to occupy the GYE, exploiting its people and resources for their own short-term benefits in the name of a moral and spiritual good. The earliest indigenous peoples who were labeled by whites as "unscientific savages" were the tragic victims of such hypocrisy, which was used to justify their removal from Yellowstone on behalf of a moral obligation to protect its wonders. In reality, of course the relationship between old-west and new-west does not compare to the violence perpetrated against indigenous GYE peoples, but the perceptions are similar in that old-westerners feel that they are the victims of a new "quality-of-life" conquest cloaked in moral virtue and objective science.

THE SURVIVAL OF THE OLD-WEST?

The data and discussion above might seem to imply that the old-west way of life will inevitably decline until it fades into distant memory for most Americans and GYE residents. But old-west beliefs, symbols, and rituals are not fading—they are alive and well in new ways. Understanding how the old-west continues to thrive in the face of economic decline and moral condemnation is essential to understanding environmental conflict in the region.

First, and perhaps most important, the moral identity of the old-west lives on through recreational practices that are deeply symbolic, and even sacred. Because of the new-west shift toward diverse land use and enjoyment of natural amenities, the type of recreational practices an individual (or community) engages in has more cultural influence in shaping one's moral identity than do work practices. In a sense, how one recreates and enjoys the land says as much about a person today as farming or ranching did 50 years ago. Of course, the lines can blur—new-westerners hunt wolves and old-westerners go skiing—but on the whole, recreational practices are a sharp dividing line between old-westerners and new-westerners. For old-westerners, the moral commitments to individualism and antifederalism are vital to protecting their culturally meaningful recreational practices, many of which are stigmatized as consumptive or dominionistic, such as motorized recreation and hunting. Thus, what constitutes morally appropriate recreation is at the heart of the conflict, and moral debates about what the land is good for again remain central, as they did in the establishment of the park and with the decline of extraction industries in the 20th century. Thus, when environmentalists and the federal government target old-western forms of recreation they are targeting age-old old-west beliefs, symbols, and rituals that are alive and well in the GYE.

Second, the new-west itself perpetuates the survival of the old-west. The new-west reappropriates dominant old-west symbols for tourists eager to live out the tales of the Wild West they had read about and watched in popular media. So while "real-life" American cowboys are becoming a thing of the past, the beliefs, symbols, and rituals of the cowboy live on. They live on in cultural artifacts as simple as license plates (Figure 2.14), or in the daily reenactments of town square shootouts (Figure 2.15), and in the myriad other tourist sights and sounds that offer neatly packaged cultural experiences of old-west life. But the new-west also preserves old-west ideals in its environmental values and in the pursuit of untamed wilderness. Wilderness represented freedom. In protecting wilderness, the new-west seeks a new frontier in the form of protected lands, but, equally powerful, seeks a frontier that represented the innate search for wildness and a yearning for a purer realm of unhinged individual experience somehow lost in American modern times.

The fact that the old-west survives despite the decline of its traditional extraction industries means that it continues to exert a powerful influence over environmental issues in the region. Despite the sovereignty of biocentric and spiritual environmental values in the new-west, the persistence of old-west ideals and practices looms large in battles over environmental right and wrong. These battles have erupted into full-fledge environmental policy conflicts between sets of stakeholders who are forced to navigate a cultural and moral context that is much more complicated than it was only 40 years earlier. With a better understanding of this context, I now turn to the conflict itself as it developed in the GYE throughout the late 20th and early 21st century.

Environmental Conflict

Thus far I have built the case that the rise of the new-west had profound consequences that went well beyond surface-level indicators of economic growth

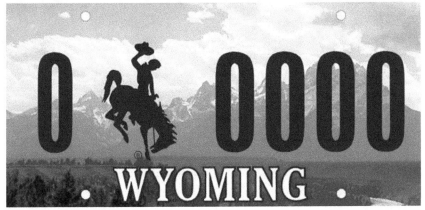

Figure 2.14: *Top*: Wyoming license plate circa 1983, iconic logo in front of agricultural fence. *Bottom*: Most recent Wyoming license plate with iconic cowboy logo in front of natural amenities of the Teton Mountain range.

and demographic change. These new-west social structures and institutions are part of a larger cultural struggle to enact and sustain a new moral order. Here I will provide evidence to argue that this process, which as I showed above occurred from 1970 to the present, resulted in a dramatic increase in environmental conflict over the same time period.

I define "conflict" to be a social process by which two or more individuals or groups struggle for control over meanings, power, and resources. Instances of social conflict involve actions that are oriented to secure an individual's or group's interests, over and against interests of competing individuals or groups. Social conflict requires resources to pursue these different goals—resources that

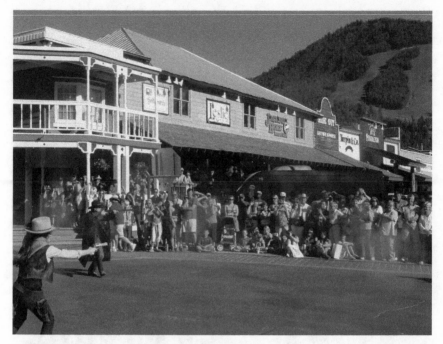

Figure 2.15: Reenactment of old-west town square shootout in Teton County, WY. Tourists, shops, and ski slopes in the background. Source: Photo by author.

I define to include cultural, symbolic, moral, and spiritual meanings, in addition to technical (e.g., ecological know-how, legal resources) or material resources. Sociologists like Lewis Coser, and more recently Steven Tepper, remind us that "symbolic and economic conflicts are cut from the same cloth" (Tepper, 2011, p. 4). A renewed focus on the symbolic dimensions of conflict in the GYE will not only improve our understanding about the influence of moral and spiritual mechanisms in environmental contexts, but it will improve our understanding about how these mechanisms award prestige, status, and economic gain. Thus, I do not restrict social conflict to the pursuit of economic interests but take a broader approach to interests to include norms, meanings, beliefs, and cultural values, such as a group's way of life (Thompson et al., 1990) or beliefs and feelings about the sacredness of nature.

Within the GYE, then, social conflict occurs at multiple levels, depending on the environmental problem. Conflict is as subtle as the disapproving look in the grocery store from an old-western cowboy toward an environmentalist. It is the daily struggle for rhetorical advantage in the editorial section of the *Jackson Hole News and Guide* or the *Bozeman Daily Chronicle*. It is a professional documentary alleging backroom deals struck between pro-wolf advocates and

U.S. Fish and Wildlife bureaucrats. It is a tea-party protest in downtown Jackson Hole, or on the steps of the Montana state capitol, against federal control of natural resources. It a protest asserting the sanctity of the wolf. It is an activist handcuffing herself to the bottom of a government agent's pickup truck ready to haul buffalo to slaughter. It is a ubiquitous bumper sticker reading "Wolves: Government-Sponsored Terrorists." It is the thousands of New Yorkers writing letters entreating the U.S. Forest Service to shut down natural gas drilling in the GYE. It is a Wyoming judge and a Washington D.C. judge engaging in judicial warfare against one another over snowmobiling in the park. It is moral outrage over the government's slaughter of 6,600 genetically pure buffalo since 1995. It is the millions of public letters sent to the federal government petitioning one Yellowstone policy or another.

One thing to notice about this cluster of examples is that environmental conflict and social conflict are seemingly synonymous in the GYE. The interaction between old-west residents and new transplants or environmentalists is in large part structured by economic, cultural, recreational, and political differences concerning humanity's relationship with the natural environment. What one "does" with the environment in a practical sense shapes many of the social markers that separate different groups. Do you work the land as a rancher, or do you work at a desk in town? Do you ride a snowmobile, or cross-country ski? Do you wear a cowboy hat, or a Patagonia brand hat? Do you drive a truck, or a Subaru? Does your vehicle have a gun rack, or a bike rack? Spending time in the region, one quickly learns just how salient are different environmental tastes, practices, and beliefs to the identity of the region and its people. In one sense, the natural environment structures the entire social system in the GYE. Thus, environmental conflict becomes difficult to separate from social conflict, and vice versa. As one might suspect, then, concrete environmental problems become social problems, with clearly drawn lines between different social groups and different environmental solutions. It is in such a context that resolvable problems become "wicked problems."

WICKED CONFLICT

Research in the policy sciences defines "wicked problems" as those that are seemingly unsolvable and tend to appear over and over again. In their seminal article, where they coin the term "wicked problems," Rittel and Webber (1973) argue that barriers built into certain policy problems make them unsolvable by scientific or technical means. They are unsolvable by scientific means because, as in the case of the GYE, they are not about true or false, but about moral right and wrong. Or, in other words, they become cultural problems in which different groups struggle to construct their own versions of right and wrong. The term "wicked" refers not to a problem that is ethically deplorable, but as a way to describe a policy problem that is malignant, vicious, or tricky, as opposed to problems which are set up in a way that the sciences can adjudicate to provide policy solutions with little pushback from divergent stakeholders.

The last four decades have produced a core set of recurrent and "wicked" environmental problems. One example is conflict over wildlife management, with unending controversies over wolves, bison, and grizzly bears. Equally contentious, and cycling in and out of the courts for decades at a time, is motorized recreation (e.g., snowmobiling) in Yellowstone and Grand Teton national parks. Oil and natural gas extraction also continue to be at the forefront of conversations about natural resource management in the GYE. These intractable policy issues result in long-drawn-out lawsuits, millions of dollars in research and lobbying, lengthy administrative rule, and intense pleading from interest groups for support from the local, regional, and national public. When decisions are made, or concessions won, they are often short lived, reversed at the judicial level, or put on hold in hopes that more scientific knowledge about a problem will make decision making easier. This circular and hostile process tends to repeat itself over and over again.

Greater Yellowstone Ecosystem Stakeholder Arena

A variety of stakeholders are involved in this ongoing, and "wicked," struggle over environmental issues in the GYE. I group stakeholders into five larger categories: *interest groups, citizens, bureaucratic agencies, elected officials,* and *technical experts.* From a practical policy standpoint, this diverse cast of characters, and their different cultural epistemologies and visions of what nature is "good" for, makes it nearly impossible for them to strike long-term agreements. In this section I briefly describe each of these categories of stakeholders, clarifying their social location in the GYE arena, highlighting their unique interests, and describing their epistemology (how they form knowledge about environmental issues).

INTEREST GROUPS—ENVIRONMENTALIST AND WISE USE

As of 2012 there were an astounding 242 nonprofit interest groups working on issues in the GYE. Building on the *Greater Yellowstone Conservation Directory,* I created a database of every group working in the region. I then collected every mission statement and complete budget data, as well as other background information such as address and founding date. These data were collected from GuideStar, individual group websites, and through direct contact with individual groups. I cluster my description below of these groups into two categories: *environmental* and *wise use.* The extraordinary number of groups operating in this small rural area indicates the importance of the GYE as a national treasure to be protected, and as a lightning rod for debate over the meaning of Yellowstone for different groups.

All environmental interest organizations in the GYE share the general goal of large-scale ecosystem preservation of the region's public and private lands. There is consensus among these organizations that to protect GYE flora and fauna, human development and extraction industries must be curbed by implementing tighter restrictions on land use and expanding the reach of untouched wilderness areas. Beyond this general goal, there is great diversity among environmental groups. Some of these groups are more community-minded (e.g., Teton Valley Trails and Pathways, Idaho Smart Growth) and others focus on education (e.g., Montana Outdoor Science School, Teton Science Schools).

While environmental nonprofits have been active in the area since the late 19th century, "the size and scope of the nonprofit community has exploded over the past 25 years" (Cherney, 2011, p. 16). Today there are 183 environmental groups in the region, commanding a combined annual budget of $150 million, numbering over 500 employees, and administered by over 700 board members. Indeed, these groups are a considerable force for environmental conflict and change, rivaling the power of the area's bureaucratic agencies.

Throughout the course of my research I identified three breeds of GYE environmental groups: *local-professional, local-grassroots,* and *national-professional.* Local-professional groups have broad support from mainstream locals and wealthy transplants, and they focus on science-based solutions for policy, as informed by biological, ecological, legal, and policy research. A prototypical example is the Greater Yellowstone Coalition. This large organization has considerable support both within and outside the GYE, with almost 28,000 supporters worldwide, and financial support from businesses spanning San Francisco to Portland. In 2012, its total assets reached nearly $8 million. It has four offices throughout the GYE, including a new state-of-the-art headquarters in Bozeman. In my interviews with various employees it was clear that they are very well educated in the environmental sciences, law, and policy. The coalition's mission statement makes explicit that "science should guide the management of the region's public and private lands" GYC (2013). Many employees and volunteers are career environmentalists, regularly moving between different nonprofits within the environmental sector. These groups, and their employees and volunteers, have high levels of social capital and are fluent in the professional skills needed to raise funds, navigate political relationships, interpret biology and ecology, and engage in strategic litigation.

I refer to the second breed of environmental groups as *local-grassroots,* typified by the Buffalo Field Campaign (BFC)—a group that is the subject of Chapter 3. These groups are far less prevalent, yet they exert considerable influence over policy and are no strangers to public conflict. Their social location is different from local-professional groups, in that they are less cosmopolitan, less institutionalized, and made up of younger and more idealistic activists.

Their budgets are considerably smaller. Many supporters of groups like these are influenced by national grassroots movements such as Earth First! The BFC has a former volunteer who assists with the occasional lawsuit, but its day-to-day tactics rely less on technical and scientific expertise and more on direct action in the field (e.g., sit-ins) and generating public support by drumming up media attention (e.g., videotaping buffalo being harassed by the Department of Livestock). I found that GYE locals often refer to these groups pejoratively (and at other times lovingly) as "hippies" or "tree-huggers." Unlike local-professional groups, local-grassroots groups root their epistemology not solely in the natural sciences, but in the deep cultural significance of nature and wildlife. For these sorts of groups, and the people who support them, the environment has important cultural and spiritual value, and is thus deserving of vigorous protection.

The last breed of environmental group is national-professional. In this category I include groups such as the Sierra Club, Defenders of Wildlife, and the Nature Conservancy. These groups are very similar to local-professional groups with their highly educated technical and science-based approach to conservation. Their budgets are also very big, enabling them to fund fleets of lawyers, scientists, and policy experts. For example, in 2010 the The Nature Conservancy had nearly $1 billion in revenue, with nearly $6 billion in total assets. National-professional groups have a strong influence in the GYE because they are able to mobilize their national constituency in a hurry. In 2011 Defenders of Wildlife mobilized 14,564 individuals, over the course of 45 days, to send letters to the federal government opposing the delisting of wolves from endangered species protection in Wyoming. Almost all of these signatures came from outside the GYE, some even outside the United States. One leader of a local-professional group complained to me that despite the fact that these national-professional groups do a tremendous amount of good in the region, they are at times disconnected from the concerns of everyday life in the GYE, given that the majority of their staffs are in Washington or elsewhere (although most of these national-professional groups do keep offices and staff in the GYE). This can make it difficult for local-professional groups despite their hard work building trusting relationships with different stakeholders in the region, especially private landowners.

At loggerheads with many of the ideals and practices of these environmental groups are wise-use groups, such as hunting and motorized recreation interests, which seek to resist or loosen restrictions on recreating in national forests and national parks. For example, local groups like Lobo Watch, Friends of the Northern Yellowstone Elk Herd, and Save Western Wildlife advocate elk conservation through aggressive opposition to wolves, because of the threat wolves pose to the viability of hunting. Motorized-use groups are also very influential. Based in nearby Pocatello, ID, the Blue Ribbon Coalition is a powerful national organization spanning all 50 states. Constantly clashing with many of the environmental groups previously mentioned over motorized pollution and the right to access public lands, the Blue Ribbon Coalition slogan clearly states its

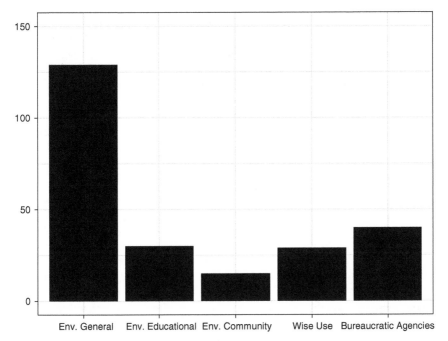

Figure 2.16: The distribution of interest groups and bureaucratic agencies working in the GYE.

goal: "Preserving our natural resources FOR the pubic instead of FROM the public" (caps in original).

Under the umbrella of wise use are many extractive industry groups, which, as described above with the shift to the new-west, view that their livelihood is threatened by increasing federal regulation. Groups such as these include the Multiple Use Coalition, the People for the West, the Montana Stockgrowers Association, the Wyoming Heritage Society, the Montana Logging Association, the National Wool Growers Association, and the American Farm Bureau Association, to name a few. Because of their economic pull and their historic heritage as part of the old-west, these groups wield an incredible amount of influence on Capitol Hill. And, as we have seen with other economic vs. environmental issues in the United States, their power and persuasiveness are often contingent on the health of the economy.

CONTENT ANALYSIS OF INTEREST GROUP DATA

With this brief introduction to interest groups, it will be helpful to get a feel for the number and location of these groups who are doing battle. For the purposes of Figure 2.16, I split environmental groups focusing on education concerns and community concerns (based on their mission statements) into separate categories. Bureaucratic agencies are not interest groups, but they are included in this graph as a comparison, and are discussed below. Based on a content analysis of every group, this graph demonstrates that there are several times more environmental groups operating in the GYE than there are wise-use groups (or bureaucratic agencies). The majority of interest groups are within the GYE, and the average euclidian distance from YNP (calculated using latitude and longitude) is 180 miles (the median distance is 288 miles).

LOCAL, NATIONAL, AND GLOBAL PUBLIC

Many American citizens get involved in the conflict through the aforementioned groups, but it is also useful to examine how local, national, and international citizens are involved in the conflict. Members of the public include long-time GYE residents, recent transplants, recreationists, tourists, and those who know about Yellowstone but have never been to the area. These groups of people outside the GYE can also shape the political process. For example, one of the most common ways that citizens have become involved is through writing public letters when a policy change is being considered by state and federal agencies. I say much more below about how these letters are an important indicator of the tenor and intractability of the conflict. I spoke with Al Nash, the public spokesperson for YNP, about the locational diversity of the letters received by the National Park Service. During our conversation at a 2012 public hearing in Jackson Hole over the controversial new snowmobile plan for the park, he remarked to me that the "Park Service weighs all comments the same, while acknowledging that these issues may affect local communities more. But, it is an international resource, and we steward it in such a way. There is just so much emotional attachment to this place from all locations."

Similarly, at another public hearing in Bozeman in 2012 I spoke about the diversity of public interest with David Jacob, a lawyer who manages public comments for the National Park Service and incorporates them into policy making. With regard to citizens from outside the GYE, David said, "One thing that is interesting but doesn't get talked about is our doctrine 'enjoyment from afar.' The National Park Service believes that there is a benefit for a person in Florida to simply know' that Yellowstone Park exists. They may never come to the park, but they benefit from the knowledge that it is being protected." Both of these quotes, from two very influential Nationl Park Service staff members, demonstrate that when it comes to debate over Yellowstone's resources, consideration is not limited to the GYE, nor is it limited to national environmental groups—citizens everywhere have a voice at the table. This has frustrated many long-time locals who loathe the power of "outsiders" to influence policy for which local GYE communities bear the brunt of the consequences (e.g., New Yorkers supporting, but not dealing with the consequences of, the reintroduction of wolves).

BUREAUCRATIC AGENCIES

The GYE contains two national parks, six national forests, three national wildlife refuges, 5 million acres of private land, and two Indian nations—all within 20 counties spread across three different states. As one might imagine, this dizzying spatial and physical array of natural resources creates a thorny institutional framework within which 28 different local, state, and federal bureaucratic agencies attempt to manage the region (National Park Service, U.S. Forest Service, Animal and Plant Health Inspection Service, Montana Department of Livestock, U.S. Fish and Wildlife, U.S. Geological Survey, U.S. Department of Agriculture, Bureau of Land Management, etc.). Prior to the emergence of "ecosystem management" in recent decades, these agencies could more easily work independently from one another because the boundaries of jurisdiction were clearly drawn. For example, the Forest Service could work with extractive or environmental interest groups independently, without worrying about stepping on the toes of the National Park Service. But with the GYE now managed as one *whole* ecosystem, these 28 different agencies are charged with supervising a single entity, creating a powderkeg of different perspectives. These struggles happen across different political hierarchies and authorities, institutional cultures, institutional incentives, and political alignments.

The grand experiment of managing an entire ecosystem proved to be more difficult than many thought, and to address these problems the U.S. House of Representatives Committee on Interior and Insular Affairs held an oversight hearing on Greater Yellowstone in 1985. The goal of this subcommittee was to sort out the diverse interests in the region in order to develop some sort of solution to the bureaucratic mess. Susan Clark aptly summarizes the Congressional Research Service's 1987 report on the 1985 congressional hearings:

> [The committee] concluded that there was general agreement on the area's importance, but that the diversity of perspectives was manifest in the varied land management policies of the federal agencies, which showed a "thin mantle of inter-agency cooperation." The report confirmed the obvious—that thousands of separate decisions produced overall management of the area. The wide range of management agencies, organizations, and interests, combined with a lack of consensus about policy, created a complex context. Conflict was everywhere evident in the management debate then as it is now. (2008, p. 34)

There have been major efforts to foster mutual cooperation and coordination, most notably by the Greater Yellowstone Coordinating Committee (GYCC), made up of leaders from the National Park Service and the Forest Service. The committee did not really take hold until 1990 when it released a statement of intent and "Vision for the Future" document describing its ecosystem management policies, including its intention to coordinate activities between YNP and the six neighboring national forests. Most notably, the document explicitly promoted a shift to "ecosystem values" and "ecosystem integrity... across administrative boundaries." Yet there was consensus that the committee had no real administrative teeth for making this happen. Most environmental groups "dismissed the document as business as usual and did not actively support the agency effort" (Pritchard, 1999). Extractive industry groups, however, took the document much more seriously because of the explicit nature in which the GYCC advocated "ecosystem values" over and against the utilitarian value of natural resources. Extraction groups vociferously opposed this shift, making their presence known in dramatic fashion, at public meetings about the GYCC:

> Wearing yellow ribbons around their arms, people from outside and inside the GYE disembarked from buses to throng one of the public hearing sites in Bozeman. A representative of Montana Senator Conrad Burns began the session by effectively lambasting the agencies and the document [GYCC "Vision for the Future"] to the cheers of the folks with yellow armbands. Testimony was emotional—one woman castigated the Vision, then waved a small flag and recited the Pledge of Allegiance. A few quiet "environmentalists" and scholars stood up to defend the document as a reasonable exercise in cooperation, or to praise the naturalness of the GYE. Clearly, the politics were so highly charged that ideas about ecosystems or coordination of the simplest plans got lost in the dust. (Pritchard, 1999, p. 294)

Even though the local public overwhelmingly rejected the 1990 Vision document, the GYCC has made notable progress over the last 20 years, bringing bureaucratic agencies within the GYE into conversation and collaboration with one another. To the GYCC's credit, this first attempt in history at large-scale ecosystem management gained international notoriety, with a captive audience that was curious to see how this grand experiment might unfold. Indeed, it is still very much a long-term work in progress, and at present, the continued fragmentation of the methods, interests, and goals of the 28 different bureaucratic agencies remains a central cause for conflict in the region.

ELECTED OFFICIALS

Various local, regional, and national elected officials are also heavily involved in environmental conflict in the region, including members of presidential administrations, governors, judges, congresspersons, state legislators, county officials, and town officials. The influence of these officials tends to fall along party lines. Republican party officials are more supportive of economic development through traditional extractive commodities. They also, unsurprisingly, tend to favor less regulation on recreation on public lands, as evident in George W. Bush's administration's role in increasing the number of snowmobiles in Yellowstone from zero (the Clinton administration's plan) to 950 per day. Democratic officials tend to support more regulations on extractive industries and motorized recreation. For example, in 1996 President Clinton famously approved a $65 million government buyout of Crown Butte Mines Inc., to stop the company from mining gold 2.5 miles from Yellowstone's northern border.

Indeed, Republican and Democratic presidential administrations, governors, judges, and other elected officials working in the GYE have relied on contrasting philosophies about natural resource management, but to reduce political conflict in the region to sheer partisanship is overly simplistic. For example, the late Republican U.S. senator Craig Thomas, a rancher from Wyoming who had one of the most conservative voting records during his 18 years in Congress, is now deeply admired by environmentalists for protecting the Wyoming Range area from oil and gas drilling. Similarly, environmentalists constantly express frustration with Democrats, including their U.S. senators and the Obama administration, for caving to extraction industry interests, ignoring the effects of global warming, or dragging their feet on other hot-button issues in the GYE. So, while there is a general trend in the region along party lines, history has shown that issues of conflict depend more on the individual politicians or judges who are in power at a given time.

TECHNICAL EXPERTS

Yellowstone is the ideal laboratory for biologists, ecologists, and a host of other natural scientists. Perhaps no other natural region in the world commands as much scientific attention as the GYE. It is the world's largest intact temperate ecosystem. With the reintroduction of wolves in 1995, it now holds all of the original species known to inhabit the region. It also contains over half of the world's geothermal features, fueled by the largest supervolcano on the continent. Yet, even ostensibly objective scientific research about these vast resources finds its way into the environmental fray.

Historically, the role of technical experts, and the value of scientific information, has always been at the center of GYE conflict. In 1965 microbiologist Thomas Brock identified a new organism living in the 160-degree waters in the Lower Geyser Basin of Yellowstone. From this organism biochemist Kary Mullis was able to develop a gene-replicating procedure that enabled the creation of DNA fingerprinting, and this molecule is now referred to as the "Swiss army knife of molecular biology." This discovery won Mullis the 1993 Nobel Prize in Chemistry. The discovery of this organism also led to "an explosion in 'bioprospecting' in Yellowstone by high-tech companies interested in developing, patenting, and marketing other useful new organisms" (Schullery, 2004, p. 3).

This led to conflict about whether bio-prospecting in Yellowstone aligns with the values of the park, if it is appropriate for companies to benefit from a public resource in this way, and how it should be regulated.

All of the hot-button issues, such as this one, command a massive amount of scientific research, and many of the scientists working in the area are embedded in one or more stakeholder groups discussed above. Scientific findings can point toward important solutions to conflict, yet in many cases the questions they answer provide more fodder for debate and can obscure the deeper conflict over values that goes unnoticed. What appear to be questions over science are politicized and become deeply intertwined with social aspects of the conflict: Are wolves healthy for the ecosystem? What is the effect of snowmobiles' sound on wildlife stress levels? Will mining operations near the park contaminate its geothermal features? What is the impact of rural home development on wildlife migration corridors? These sorts of questions are both cultural *and* scientific, yet the majority of resources are poured into understanding the scientific aspects of these environmental problems (e.g., decibel level of a snowmobile). But because many of the scientists are (at least perceived to be) affiliated with partisan stakeholders, or with "liberal" academia, scientific findings of those involved in the conflict engender a deep distrust. This same sentiment appears over and over again at public meetings, in written letters, in qualitative interviews, and in informal conversations. The irony is that even though there is a deep distrust of scientific evidence between stakeholders, there is nevertheless an overwhelming obsession with obtaining "hard" scientific evidence in the hopes that it will settle "wicked" environmental disputes, when in the end the abundance of hard scientific evidence becomes just another basis for discord.

The Rise of Conflict, 1870–2012

Environmental conflict in the GYE can be measured in a variety of ways. I have touched on some of the ways that the structure of the stakeholder arena breeds conflict. Throughout this chapter I also shared stories and anecdotes—from the rise of the new-west, to the arrangement of hundreds of interest groups—that describe the type and tenor of the conflict. Here I provide a slightly different angle, focusing on the emergence of the conflict over time. To do this, I constructed various across-time indicators of conflict from a wealth of legal, scientific, political, and socioeconomic data. These different data sources provide a bird's eye view of the conflict from several different angles, and when taken together depict the rise in environmental conflict in the region. The *timing* of this rise in conflict is especially interesting, because it correlates with my earlier arguments about the rise of the new-west—especially the restructuring of the moral and cultural landscape of the GYE after 1970.

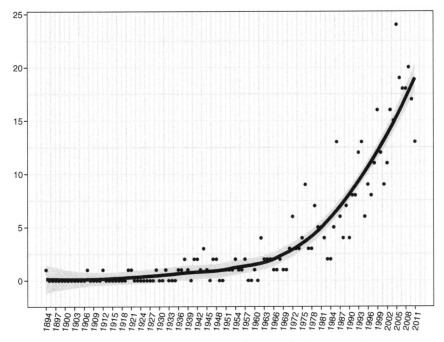

Figure 2.17: Annual number of lawsuits concerning Yellowstone filed from 1894–2011.

LEGAL CONFLICT

Figure 2.17 displays the number of lawsuits filed in U.S. federal and state courts from 1894 to 2011. As these data show, very few lawsuits were filed prior to the 1960s. Then, from 1970 to 1980 the number of lawsuits grew from less than 1 per year to an average of 4.2 per year, and by 2000–2010 it had quadrupled to 16.2 per year.

The first lawsuit filed in 1894, thirty-two years before the establishment of the National Park Service, concerned the construction of wagon roads in "what is known as the Yellowstone National Park." At this time in history there was still uncertainty about the meaning of the park and how the government would legally protect its resources. Of course, the socioeconomic changes that would bring about rapid growth in environmental conflict would not come to fruition for another 80 years. Many lawsuits remain in the state and federal courts for decades at a time, cycling through appeals, vacated by one court and then upheld by another. For example, litigation pertaining to winter-use recreation in Yellowstone has been tied up in the courts since 1998, with dizzying back-and-forth decisions on the same issue. Tortuous litigation like this costs millions of dollars for the interest groups and government agencies involved and fails to resolve environmental problems for the long term. One environmental group leader commented to me about the ubiquity of legal conflict in the region, suggesting that "for many people involved in the conflict it is more about the fight than about the health of the ecosystem. It's the satisfaction of fighting for the environment, through constant litigation, or otherwise. It's about the life purpose it gives them."

The growth of environmental organizations is also a major reason for the explosion of legal conflict in the region. Many environmental organizations have teams of well-trained lawyers who are vigilant of all happenings in the region, rarely hesitating to initiate litigation. Entire environmental organizations exist solely for this reason, such as the national group EarthJustice, which provides legal representation at no cost for more than 1,000 clients, "because the earth needs a good lawyer." EarthJustice is heavily involved in litigation issues in the GYE, and it has an office in Bozeman. Its 2011 total revenue eclipsed $34.5 million. Smaller operations, such as the local Cottonwood Environmental Law Center, similarly initiate lawsuits on behalf of local groups that lack the resources or technical knowledge to litigate on their own.

INTEREST GROUPS AND COUNTERMOVEMENTS

The number of interest groups in the GYE is also correlated, in a variety of ways, to the historic rise of "wicked" conflict. With more stakeholders in the region pursuing disparate values and goals for the ecosystem, more conflict has ensued, as Figure 2.17 demonstrated with the dramatic increase in legal conflict. Figure 2.18 displays the number of new interest groups founded from 1870 to 2012.

As these data show, there is a dramatic increase from 1970 to 2012. This is especially true during the decade between 1990 and 2000, when 71 new interest groups were founded, creating 30 percent more interest groups in the GYE in just 10 years. During the 1970s, many of the hot-button issues were beginning to take shape: whispers about the return of the wolf; concerted efforts to stop timber, mining, and oil development; the explosion of motorized recreation in Yellowstone. As these issues took hold, interest groups formed— many of them environmentalist (as Figure 2.16 showed)—as a way to combat the already entrenched interests of extractive industries. These environmental groups began to see success in the late 1980s and early 1990s, and with such success, counterenvironmental groups began to form. For example, with the federal reintroduction of wolves in 1995—a major victory—several anti-wolf groups emerged to save elk populations they used for hunting and to challenge the symbol of the wolf, which represented increasing federal intrusion into their way of life. Similarly, and around the same time period (1990s), concerns were raised about the polluting effects of motorized recreation, resulting in tighter restrictions on recreating in Yellowstone and surrounding public lands. These

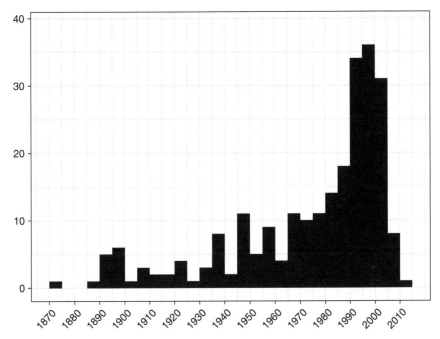

Figure 2.18: Annual number of GYE environmental interest groups founded from 1870–2010. Source: Northern Rockies Conservation Cooperative (2012), GuideStar, Internal Revenue Service, and direct communication with groups.

restrictions created a countermovement whereby new motorized recreation groups were formed to fight intrusions on individual liberties regarding recreation—something that was unheard of (and not needed) just 20 years earlier.

GROWING POLITICAL POLARIZATION

Another lens through which to examine conflict in the GYE is through formal political indicators. Here I focus on two important aspects of political conflict: congressional hearings and voting segregation between "cultural hubs" and rural GYE residents. First, congressional hearings are an important method by which committees collect and analyze information at the beginning stages of the legislative process. Second, research on congressional hearings has shown that they can be a "gold mine of factual information about all the public problems of the nation" (Galloway, 1959, p. 26). The Senate Library notes that "hearings are among the most important publications originating in Congress" (U.S. Congress Senate Library, 1979). Past public problems warranting attention from Congress range from the famous 1966–1967 Ku Klux Klan hearing to the 1996 hearing on high gasoline prices.

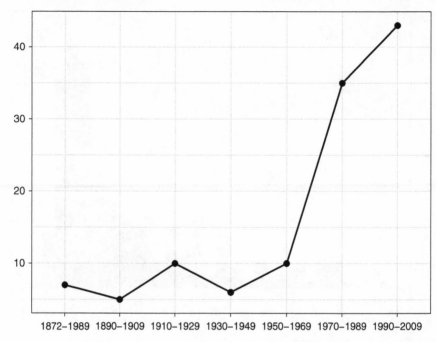

Figure 2.19: United States congressional committee hearings concerning Yellowstone, 1872–2009.

Variation in the number of hearings about the Yellowstone area tells us how the nation—and in particular Congress—views the GYE conflict as a public problem. Figure 2.19 displays data tracking the number of congressional hearings that included Yellowstone National Park. The data come from full-text searches of every congressional hearing from 1872 to 2012, and thus include all committee prints, transcribed testimonies, exhibits, histories, and all other information relevant to the hearing. As the graph shows, the attention to Yellowstone as a public problem was relatively stable from the founding of the park in 1872 until about 1970, when congressional attention grew rapidly thereafter. This trajectory parallels data above on lawsuits and the growth of environmental groups, as well as my larger argument about the implications of the post-1970 rise of the new-west. The rise in congressional attention to the GYE is related to increases in litigation and environmental interest groups, but these data also indicate the emergence of the GYE conflict as a public problem deserving of valuable congressional time and energy.

The second source of political conflict that is relevant to larger environmental conflict in the region has to do with voting segregation between urban and rural GYE residents. Here I refer to "urban" loosely to mean the cultural hubs of Jackson Hole and Bozeman. Figure 2.20 compares presidential voting patterns

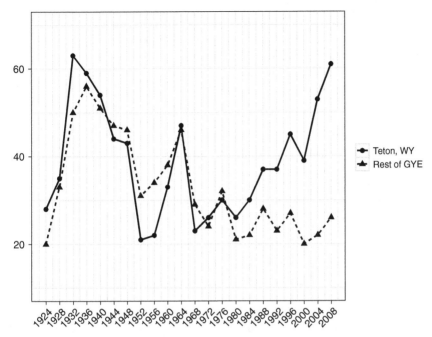

Figure 2.20: Voting segregation in the GYE. Percent voting Democrat in presidential elections 1924–2008. Teton County, WY, is separated to reveal typical new-west differences.

for Teton County, WY (home to Jackson Hole), versus an aggregate measure of all other GYE counties. The graph charts percentage voting Democrat in presidential elections dating back to 1924. The data demonstrate that up until the 1970s Teton County and other GYE counties were virtually identical in the percentage voting for presidential candidates. After the 1976 election, however, voting patterns shifted dramatically, with Teton County overwhelming favoring Democratic candidates. This trend grew even more rapidly from 2000 to 2008.

These political trends suggest that GYE environmental conflict is spatially structured. There is a growing divide in the region between cultural hubs (Jackson Hole and Bozeman) and more rural areas of the ecosystem. These cultural hubs control the flow of environmental information through the media (e.g., *Jackson Hole News and Guide, Bozeman Daily Chronicle*, local news stations). During the decades that followed 1970, these areas became home to the majority of environmental interest groups, educated elites, and wealthy benefactors; they are still the gateways for tourism and economic development. Similar to national politics, where those from "Main Street" feel overshadowed, ignored, and controlled by elites in New York and Washington, environmental conflict in the GYE is influenced by similar cultural differences.

PUBLIC CONFLICT OVER SCIENCE

In 1969 Congress passed the National Environmental Policy Act (NEPA). This was one of the first laws to establish a broad legal framework for protecting the environment. The purpose of NEPA is to ensure that all branches of government dutifully consider the environment prior to taking any action that could "significantly" affect the quality of the environment (U.S. Congress, 1969). If an action might significantly affect the environment, NEPA requires a complex set of procedures that include preparing environmental impact statements (EISs) and the solicitation of public comments on a draft of the EIS. EISs have been completed on all sorts of "actions" that might affect the GYE environment, ranging from oil and gas development to installing cell phone towers, and from protection of wildlife habitat to the construction of bridges and roads. Each EIS is extremely detailed, spans hundreds of pages, can take years to complete, and relies heavily on current scientific knowledge to describe the positive and negative environmental effects of a proposed action. Each EIS also proposes a list of alternative actions that might be better (or worse) than the proposed action. For example, the 2012 EIS for snowmobiling in Yellowstone is nearly 300 pages long and draws on a massive amount of scientific research to propose four alternative actions. After the draft EIS is released, the agency is required to invite the public to read the document and solicit the public's input through local public hearings and invitation for public comment (written letters).

Figure 2.21 displays data on the number of EISs completed for the GYE. These data come from Northwestern University's database of environmental impact statements. This database includes all EISs issued by federal agencies since 1969, when NEPA was signed into law. The graph compares the number of EISs within the GYE (506 total) to EISs outside the GYE in Idaho, Wyoming, and Montana (1,503 total). These three western states serve as an appropriate comparison group because EISs are common in non-GYE areas of these states, whereas comparison to a state outside of the region, would skew the data in favor of the GYE. I standardize the data to permit comparison by displaying the percentage of total EISs.

The percentage of total EISs completed in the GYE began to increase in the late 1980s and then grew sharply in the 2000s. This is in contrast to non-GYE areas in Idaho, Wyoming, and Montana, where the percentage of total EISs stabilized from 1990 to 2012. The dramatic rise in GYE EISs from 1990 to 2010 indicates that government agencies were either engaging in more actions that significantly affected the environment, or, as I have argued, the social and moral context developed in earlier decades in such a way that it created a hypersensitivity to environmental actions, and thus resulted in more EISs. As people flocked to the GYE, including wealthy transplants and environmental groups with expertise in ecology and law, federal agencies received more pressure to scientifically evaluate their management actions.

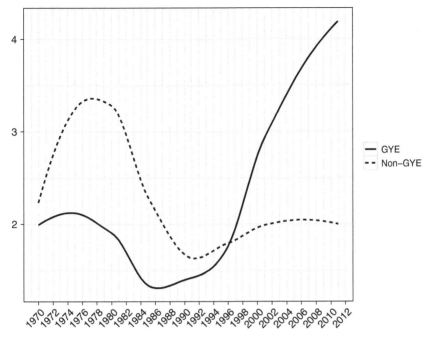

Figure 2.21: Annual number of environmental impact statements conducted, GYE and non-GYE, 1969–2012. Source: Collected by author at Northwestern University's Transportation Library. Individual EISs organized and geocoded by author. Data include both draft and final EIS reports.

Public debates during the EIS process are especially contentious in the GYE because nearly every action the government takes is perceived by at least one group to be significant enough to warrant an EIS. While NEPA intended EISs to assuage conflict by providing scientific evidence that should objectively adjudicate between opposing groups, the reality is that EISs often become just another politicized aspect of the ongoing cultural conflict. At a 2012 town hall meeting in Jackson Hole, one resident expressed his frustration to me about the intractability of the process and the obsession with science instead of common sense, remarking that "it is pretty obvious why our government is in trillions of dollars in debt. I was on the county commission for a year and we spent money on these things [EISs] and they very rarely are any better than what common sense would have you do."

The second major step in the NEPA process is to solicit public comment about the draft EIS. This includes holding public meetings to discuss the EIS and providing a 30 to 45 day comment period for the public to write letters providing feedback and making arguments for or against the planned action. The agency will take these comments into serious consideration before making a policy decision.

In an interview with me, a high-ranking National Park Service NEPA/Environmental Impact project manager explained that a small EIS project will get less than 100 public comments, whereas a more controversial or "regular" EIS project will receive between 200 and 300 comments. The number of comments, he said, "generally represents how important and controversial an issue is to the public." To give a sense of the magnitude of the conflict in the GYE, the 1993 draft EIS about the effects of introducing wolves into Yellowstone received 160,284 comments from July to November. More recently, the 2002 draft EIS for snowmobiling in Yellowstone received 307,592 comments (about 625,000 comments have been received on this issue since 1999). EISs in the GYE are among the most controversial in the nation, as is evidenced by the hundreds of thousands of citizens inside and outside the GYE engaging in debates that are about much more than an EIS's scientific veracity but, more important, are about the implications of an EIS for their moral and spiritual vision of how nature should be "managed."

CARRYING CAPACITY CONFLICT

In 1798 Thomas Robert Malthus argued that unchecked population growth would quickly lead to human and environmental catastrophe. Known as "Malthusianism," this theory became controversial because of its ethical implications concerning population control, but its general idea about the carrying capacity of ecosystems remains at the heart of many of the environmental problems in the GYE. Many areas of the country can better handle population growth because they have the room to grow and policies that allow for growth. In the GYE, however, most of the land is public, and thus conflicts often arise over restrictions on the development of private lands.

Here I focus on two different aspects of conflict about carrying capacity: growth in tourism in Yellowstone Park and growth in new home development. First, many new visitors to Yellowstone are surprised by the lack of roadways in the park. The current two-lane road system was built during the 19th and early 20th centuries, with routine maintenance taking place over the years, but no plans to widen or expand the timeworn road system. Most other built-environment features of the park have also been preserved with the same compulsion, and there has been no significant expansion of the park since the 1960s. Even new campgrounds or visitor center improvements are met with great controversy.

The one thing that *has* changed in the park, however, is the number of people driving these roads, staying in the lodges, walking the geyser boardwalks, and generally enjoying the park's resources. Figure 2.22 displays the number of visitors to Yellowstone and Grand Teton National Park from 1904 to 2010. It is clear that from the 1950s onward, the number of visitors Yellowstone has increased dramatically, while the accommodations and infrastructure they encounter has largely remained constant. So while the trajectory of visitors

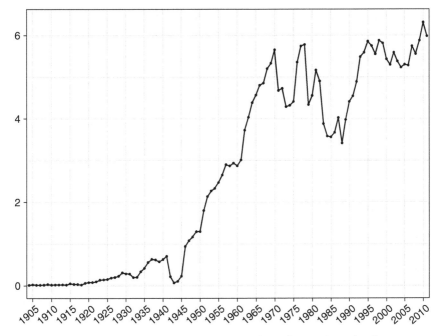

Figure 2.22: Annual number of visitors to Yellowstone and Grand Teton National Park, 1904–2010. Source: National Park Service.

continues to climb, the trajectory of policy is moving in the opposite direction, toward tighter preservation. These irreconcilable trends have led to protracted conflicts over even the most minor issues: employee housing, upgrading board-walks, modernizing campgrounds, improving bridges, concessions contracts, the ethics of cell phone towers, and so on.

The growth in local land development throughout the GYE is the second major source of carrying capacity conflict. Nearly all of this development involves building new homes. As noted earlier in this chapter, some counties in the GYE ranked in the top five of all 3,080 U.S. counties between 2000 and 2010, for population growth and new housing units. This has become a source of conflict for the many people who worry that the wholeness of the ecosystem is being frag-mented by all of these new homes. In their study of rural home growth in the GYE from 1880 to 1999, Gude et al. (2006) found that "rural development [has] been exceptionally rapid in the private lands surrounding Yellowstone." Many of these new homes are retirement condos or seasonal cabins. This dramatic increase exerts a great deal of pressure on protected areas, can block wildlife migration routes, and in general has made ecosystem management more contentious as environmental groups try to slow the growth through tighter zoning restrictions.

I asked a prominent member of the Montana Stockgrowers Association about these changes, and he responded sharply that environmentalists better "be careful what they wish for with the decline of ranching," because in his words it comes down to two choices, "cows or condos." Thus, ranching advocates argue that with the new-west push to eliminate ranching in the GYE, ranchers are left with no choice but to sell their land to real estate developers, which in the end, they argue, is more detrimental to the ecosystem than continued grazing of cattle would be. Some environmentalists view this as a false dichotomy, yet the debate over cows or condos frames the conflict, with no end in sight as more and more in-migrants build homes on their own slice of paradise.

Conclusion

This chapter demonstrated that widespread social change has swept over the region in the last 40 years. With this, a new "Wild West" was born—but now with higher stakes and more stakeholders. I showed that the *moral* causes and consequences of this social change are particularly important. Many long-time residents began to feel that the community life they had inherited and cherished had now become unrecognizable. These feelings are part of a larger process of moral "devaluation" that occurred, by which I mean that transformations in economic, political, and status-based relationships challenged time-honored ideas about what it means to be a "good" person, how one *ought* to make a living on the land, and the virtue of an old-west way of life. These *moral* foundations were rethought, revalued, and ultimately redefined through new laws, institutions, and economic policies. These sweeping changes created the necessary moral and political conditions for long-lasting conflicts over the area's natural resources. The second part of this chapter demonstrated that "wicked" conflict emerged after 1970, and continues to persist to present day. Using a variety of new data, I find that there is considerable legal conflict, interest group conflict, political polarization, congressional committee attention, public conflict over science, and carrying capacity conflict—much of it correlating with, and following the general pattern of, findings in the first section of this chapter. This bird's-eye view of moral and environmental conflict sets the stage for a finer-grained analysis in the case studies that follow. It is to these in-depth studies of contemporary conflict that I now turn my attention.

3. Buffalo Crusaders:
The Sacred Struggle for America's Last Wild and Pure Herd

At 4:45 a.m. I quietly rolled out of my sleeping bag for another morning of buffalo reconnaissance, stepping gently along the cold dusty cabin floor, careful not to wake the other activists. I quickly gathered my patrol gear—headlamp, maps, snow boots, binoculars, bear spray, and countless layers of wool. Rubbing my sleepy eyes, I made my way out of the cabin toward the beat-up Subaru station wagon that was, like me, slower to move in these subzero temperatures, and struggling to heat up before a long morning of work. I met three other activists outside—Jayla, Dave, and Pike—and together we packed up the car with cross-country skis and snowshoes. Dave double-checked the batteries in the video camera and two-way radios, and we made our way through the darkness down the dirt road away from camp, toward the border of Yellowstone National Park, to patrol and protect America's last remaining wild bison herd.[1]

Jayla, a young white woman from California, with a half-shaved head and long crinkly dreadlocks to match her wooly sweater, rubs her hands together struggling to get warm in the back of the station wagon with Dave, a white, middle-class, and self-proclaimed "wanderer of sorts" from Maryland who came West to "find meaning" by helping to "stop the slaughter of this sacred animal." I sit in the passenger seat alongside Pike, a long-time volunteer from the Midwest, and the leader of our morning reconnaissance. As part of the Buffalo Field Campaign (BFC), we embark on this dark morning—like BFC activists have every morning and night for 16 years from November to June—motivated by the official mission to be the "only group working in the field, every day, to stop the slaughter and harassment of Yellowstone's wild buffalo."

After a short 10-minute drive around Hebgen Lake toward the YNP border, we agree to split into two groups, with Jayla and Dave skiing along the Madison

---

1 I use "bison" and "buffalo" interchangeably. "*Bison bison*" is the proper Latin name for the animal, and "buffalo" is the popular, and culturally meaningful synonym.

River and nearby Horse Butte to get a count of buffalo outside of YNP, and, at Pike's suggestion, he and I take the video camera to various lookout points in search of footage of potential Montana Department of Livestock (DOL) mistreatment of buffalo. We watch closely for government agents on horseback and four-wheelers, and keep an eye to the sky for helicopters these agencies use to aggressively haze buffalo back into the park. We check different capture facilities around the area to make sure they are not making preparations for buffalo containment and slaughter. After a couple of hours of patrol, Pike and I decide to snowshoe across the border into YNP to record the number of buffalo on their way out of the park toward Highway 191. We record 76 buffalo over the course of three hours, and as we slowly snowshoe past each furry giant, Pike talks reverently and reassuringly to them, telling one large bull that "its OK buddy, we are here to protect you, you big sacred boy" and a nearby female that "we love you, you have nothing to worry about, you precious thing." We eventually trudge our way through the deep snow and make our way toward the car to meet Jayla and Dave before heading back to camp to give our report and prepare the next patrol group to head out for the evening shift.

An important historical hallmark of Yellowstone is that it is "the only place in the world where a wild bison herd has survived continuously since prehistoric times" (Yellowstone Park Foundation, 2013). The government's recent management (hazing and slaughter) of America's only genetically pure and fenceless free-roaming bison herd has become one of the most contentious, intractable, and long-lasting political disputes in the GYE. And, as we would expect in the GYE, this issue hinges on scientific disagreement—in this case, the biology and ecology surrounding the disease brucellosis (*Brucella abortus*), and the extent to which the disease threatens Montana's livestock industry. These scientific, economic, and legal debates play out in the local, federal, and tribal courts, in state legislatures, and in the agencies charged to manage public lands and wildlife. Scientific disagreements about the disease brucellosis have polarized the political debate and have slowed any sort of major movement on the issue for the last decade.

But the BFC—the most heavily invested and effective social movement organization working on the issue—has in recent years found considerable success by shifting the focus of the debate *away from* science and technorationality, toward the deeper cultural, moral, and ultimately *religious* dimensions of bison management. My argument in this chapter is that the BFC has found success in the midst of this dense scientific and economic stalemate over disease and risks to livestock production because it has largely eschewed technical debates in favor of an aggressive form of moral protest rooted in, and legitimated by, Indian spirituality. *The BFC has successfully infused the conflict with moral and spiritual feeling that had otherwise been viewed as incommensurable with rational management policy.* It has erected rigid and uncompromising moral boundaries around these animals, a good example of what Durkheim describes as "the extreme strictness of the prohibitions that separate the sacred from the profane" (2001, p. 237). Unlike the wolf issue, where moral and spiritual commitments tend to remain beneath the surface and are not linked to a particular religious framework, the BFC has, in radical and public ways, brought to the fore deeper moral and spiritual questions, *ultimately making this a public religious conflict as much as a scientific one. I contend that by making this a matter of expressive moral and spiritual obligation, the BFC is able to sidestep scientific rabbit holes of intractability, and at the same time raise to the surface what the debate is really about.* It is able to focus the debate on its own moral logic, organized around the moral value of genetic purity, on the "wildness" of free-roaming buffalo, on the animal's direct link to native spirituality, on ethical lessons humans must learn from buffalo, and on the future of the GYE, as the BFC sees it, moving away from old-west extraction toward a return to indigenous spiritual values of nature.

Because it has been successful at bringing the bison issue to the fore of GYE and national wildlife politics, I chose to focus my case study of this GYE conflict on the BFC in particular. How has its moral and religious culture influenced the policy conflict? How does it understand its own moral culture, and its religious roots? How does it bring this culture to bear on the policy conflict? Why is it successful? To do this, I participated in the BFC full time, living in its camp, and participating in activism and communal life during its busiest time of year, when mistreatment of the buffalo is most likely (Spring).[2] In addition to participant observation and in-depth interviews, I collected thousands of BFC written documents and conducted computational content analysis on full texts of every newsletter and press release and selected video transcriptions. To supplement these BFC-specific data, and to examine the influence of the BFC in the policy arena, I drew heavily on broader textual data from the conflict not related to the BFC, including thousands of written public comments from everyday citizens, organizations, and political institutions, as well as legal documents, transcriptions of field hearings in Montana, and United States congressional hearings about the issue.

In addition to my substantive argument that the BFC has been successful because it has brought moral-spiritual concepts to the surface in what is otherwise a techno-rational intractable conflict, my research on this group also aims to expand sociological knowledge about the relationship between moral culture and human behavior. My interest in this question is motivated by a paradox that I quickly discovered during my fieldwork: the BFC is a moral protest movement with a clear institutional logic motivated by very public and expressive commitments to indigenous religion, yet I found that BFC activists— who sacrifice so much to be involved—were largely unaware of, and unable to

2 I participated early in Spring 2012.

coherently articulate their personal moral and spiritual motivations. Why is there a mismatch between the moral logic of the BFC and the motivations of individual activists? This is especially curious, given the costs these activists incur, risking health, living in poverty, getting arrested, and so on. What does it mean, then, that BFC activists act in ways that appear to be motivated by deeply held moral and spiritual beliefs that are consistent with the BFC's institutional logic, yet they are unable to recognize the moral and spiritual dimensions of their own actions or to articulate them when asked? Does this mean that they are not actually motivated by moral and religious commitments? This paradox creates a unique opportunity engage in ongoing discussions in sociology of culture and sociology of religion about the role of culture in action, and why individuals who are immersed in strong moral cultures still struggle to give consistent reasons for their behavior (Mills, 1940; Swidler, 1986, 2001; Vaisey, 2009).

My argument is that BFC volunteers are indeed motivated by deeper moral and spiritual commitments to the buffalo, but that their post hoc explanations of their activism and self-sacrifice are often incoherent because they are filtered through larger countervailing cultural narratives and habits of talk that lead them to "mute" strong moral and religious claims. This moral and religious "muting," as I call it, is the product of these volunteers' background (middle-class, white, younger, liberal, and secular) and immersion in particular cultural narratives fostering suspicion of organized religion and universal moral claims. I focus particular attention on how changes in American religion during the late 20th century affected the perception of organized religion. I also touch briefly on how habits of talk about right and wrong are influenced by individualism and moral relativism in American life. These findings provide clues about how some stronger elements of culture can organize and pattern others. Namely, while I show that BFC activists are indeed motivated by clear commitments to right and wrong about the buffalo, their embeddedness within larger, stronger cultural narratives structures how they construct explanations for their behavior.

Overview of the Issue

Experts estimate that over 30 million bison once freely roamed the United States. But in a matter of decades this number was reduced to a startling 23 single animals. During the 19th century, buffalo became the target of mass hunting efforts, but, more important, the U.S. government itself ordered their slaughter as a military strategy to rapidly and effectively destroy the cultural lifeblood and material sustenance of Native Americans, making it nearly impossible for tribes to survive on the plains. In 1873 the U.S. secretary of the interior, Columbus Delano, laid out this plan clearly, explaining that "the civilization of the Indian is impossible while the buffalo remains upon the plains. I would not seriously regret the total disappearance of the buffalo from our western prairies, in its effect upon the Indians, regarding it as a means of hastening their sense of dependence upon the products of the soil and their own labors" (U.S. Department of the Interior, 1873). Narrowly escaping extinction, the 23 surviving wild buffalo found sanctuary in a remote area of Yellowstone. Over the course of the 20th century this small population of 23 was restored to about 3,000–4,500 bison that make up the "Yellowstone herd" today (Plumb and Sucec, 2006). Bringing bison back from the brink of extinction is widely considered one of America's most successful conservation achievements.

Most important to this cultural, moral, and political issue is the fact that the Yellowstone herd is the only "pure" population, meaning it is *genetically unique* from all other buffalo in the United States because it is the only continuously wild herd with the genetic makeup linking it to the original ancestral populations that once freely roamed the United States. Unlike all other bison, the Yellowstone herd has not been cross-bred with cattle (called "beefalo" by some environmentalists to denote genetic impurity), and continues to be America's only free roaming and unfenced population. Because of the genetic and historical uniqueness of the Yellowstone herd, the battle over the buffalo is as emotionally charged as any issue in the GYE. It plays out along familiar socioeconomic lines, between old-west coalitions and new-west coalitions, who have sharp disagreements about the historical importance, usefulness, purpose, threat, and future of this animal.

Directly at the center of the controversy is a seemingly unresolvable scientific dispute over a disease called brucellosis (*Brucella abortus*), which can cause infected livestock and wildlife to abort their fetuses. The Yellowstone bison population contracted brucellosis in 1917, likely from local cows (Meagher and Meyer, 1994). The disease poses an economic threat to ranchers, who must slaughter affected cattle herds, but, more important, a single case of brucellosis can threaten the reputation of an entire state's livestock industry. Fortunately, all cattle herds in the United States are "brucellosis-free," but in the GYE bison and elk still carry the disease. The state of Montana became brucellosis-free in 1985, and as a result, in 1989 state agencies implemented heavy-handed management techniques to ensure that cattle and bison remain spatially separated.

But free-roaming bison care little about risks to industry, and every year—as they have for thousands of years—move out of the deep snow and limited winter vegetation in YNP to embark on their instinctual migration across park boundaries into lower-elevation public and private lands along the park's western and northern borders. As these unfettered beasts move across the human-made borders of YNP into human civilization, onto public and private property, they raise concerns about the spread of brucellosis to cattle. To address this threat, various interim management plans were implemented in the 1980s–1990s. Yet it was not until 2000, after 67,500 public comments from American citizens, that the Interagency Bison Management Plan (IBMP) was implemented for the State of Montana and YNP. These plans involve state agency capturing, slaughtering, or aggressively hazing buffalo back into the park, chasing them for miles at a time with horses, four-wheelers, and helicopters. For example, in 1997, during a particularly hard winter, 1,084 bison were slaughtered in government facilities on the border of the park, wiping out 43 percent of the Yellowstone bison population. Similarly, in 2007–2008 over 1,600 buffalo were slaughtered or shot, most without being tested for brucellosis. In 2008 the Government Accountability Office (GAO) audited the 2000 IBMP and concluded that these agencies were not fulfilling adaptive management practices as defined by law. There have been efforts to revise the plan, yet the issue remains intractable because managers have found it nearly impossible both to allow this migratory animal to freely roam, and at the same time to reduce industry fears about brucellosis transmission to cattle.

To date, however, there has *never* been a documented transmission of brucellosis from bison to cattle (White et al., 2011). Unending debate ensues about the reasons why there has never been a documented transmission. On one side, mainstream environmental groups cite hordes of scientific evidence about disease resistance, the probability rates of transmission, and in-depth biological and ecological evidence about bison behavior (e.g., bison thoroughly clean their birth sites, thus removing opportunity for cattle to come in contact with a placenta or other fetal fluids carrying the disease). On the other side, the ranching industry, state agencies supportive of traditional extractive practices, and sympathizers in the National Park Service argue that there has never been a documented transmission of brucellosis only because of their preemptive and heavy-handed action to maintain separation between cattle and bison.

These disagreements have led to a long-lasting political conflict over the future of this iconic animal on public and private land surrounding YNP. Legislators representing old-west livestock areas of Montana have introduced bills intended to severely restrict the free-roaming Yellowstone herd. Commenting on the issue in 2013, Republican Montana senator John Brenden rhetorically asked, "Why do you want to spread this creeping cancer, these wooly tanks, around the state of Montana? Trying to bring back the buffalo in big herds across Montana is like bringing back dinosaurs. And who wants dinosaurs in Montana? I certainly don't" (Robbins, 2013). These sentiments express underlying disdain for the buffalo rooted in threats to old-west ways of life, competition for subsidized grass on public land, threats to private property rights, and the larger struggle for an idealized version of the West. Groups like the BFC understand this and are quick to publicly point out that "it's not about the disease brucellosis," but an insensitivity to the sacred qualities of this animal. Instead, argues BFC, "the livestock industry continues to wage its 150 year 'war on the west'... and the disease [brucellosis] is merely a convenient excuse to kill bison" (Buffalo Field Campaign, 1998).

Figure 3.1: Buffalo Field Campaign headquarters.

The Buffalo Field Campaign

GROUP OVERVIEW

After the slaughter of nearly 1,100 Yellowstone buffalo in 1996–1997, Mike Mease and Lakota activist Rosalie Little Thunder created a nongovernmental environmental organization that came to be called the Buffalo Field Campaign. Motivated by the "genocidal assault on native cultures" and the death of thousands of "sacred Yellowstone buffalo," they began running daily patrols, recording video of agency actions in the field, organizing grassroots advocacy, and staging civil disobedience. Mease, a middle-aged, rugged caucasian man with shoulder-length hair, explained to me that before starting the BFC, he had cofounded an environmental group focused on "using video as an advocacy tool," and was "flown around the world to sneak into places and get footage that no one else was getting." From this experience, he says, he developed the BFC and focused the organization on the use of morally shocking media to raise awareness and change policy. BFC headquarters are located in a small log cabin near the north shore of Hebgen Lake (Figures 3.1, 3.2, 3.3, 3.4), in the foothills of the towering Madison mountain range, where bunks (or floor space in teepees or yurts) and warm meals are provided to volunteers interested in participating in the movement. The BFC has managed to be very effective despite very few resources. Its total annual revenue ranged from about $84,644 in 1998 to $239,304 in 2012. About 90 percent of its budget comes from individual contributions. Campaign cofounder Mike Mease and executive director Daniel Brister are currently the only full-time paid employees, receiving relatively meager incomes of roughly $10,000 and $20,000, respectively. This is in sharp contrast to larger environmental groups in Bozeman

Figure 3.2: Buffalo Field Campaign headquarters (cont.).

or Jackson Hole, whose budgets are in the millions and whose executive director salaries can easily top $100,000.

Since 1997, more than 5,000 volunteers have come to participate from every U.S. state and dozens of countries. During my stay, there were usually between 12 and 16 volunteers, all from outside the GYE: from Boston, Minnesota, Connecticut, Maryland, Georgia, California, Switzerland, and Germany. For Mease, sometimes the biggest challenge for the group is "figuring out how to live together in community in this tiny little cabin ... but we must learn to live in community like the buffalo teach us. It's not always easy, but we struggle to make it work." Despite the heavy influence from Native American values, executive director Daniel Brister notes that many volunteers are young, white, and tend to come from middle-class backgrounds (2013, p. 49). Some volunteers go by "forest names"—like Chipmunk, Grumble, Peaches, Frog, Willow, Felony, and Smoosh—which, according to Brister, are used in lieu of their birth names "because they could not be traced back to social security numbers or arrest warrants by law-enforcement officers paid to monitor or identify activists" (2013, p. 24).

Some days in the field volunteers find themselves in the heat of the battle: capturing action-packed video, protesting, getting arrested, or engaging in direct-action interventions to stop bison slaughter (Figure 3.5).

Figure 3.3: Main room of BFC headquarters. Source: Photo by author.

Figure 3.4: Bunk and floor sleeping space for volunteers. Source: Photo by author.

Figure 3.5: *Left*: Volunteer on reconnaissance, keeping watch for buffalo and government agents. *Right*: Activist engaged by government agent as he films inside hazing trailer. Source: Buffalo Field Campaign.

Other days, however, volunteers find themselves conducting less exciting work, whether involving long, quiet days on snowshoes or cross-country skis patrolling for hours without much to film, setting up traffic signs on the highway as bison make their way out of the park, or simply dwelling for hours in the wilderness alongside the buffalo (Figure 3.6). Because the BFC practices a form of intentional communal living, volunteers spend just as much time keeping the camp and community in working order: cooking meals, splitting wood, cleaning, organizing winter gear, editing video, writing newsletters, legal fact-finding, making phone calls, going into town for supplies, and various other tasks. Every night the group gathers for a mandatory organizational meeting to discuss the day's work, make announcements, raise intragroup concerns, orient new volunteers, assign tasks for the next day, or share a poem, song, or other expressive form of art to honor the buffalo.

INDIGENOUS RELIGION AND THE BFC

I was unsure about what to expect when I arrived on my first day at the BFC. What would it be like to practice such close-knit communal living, to not know other volunteers, to engage in direct-action protest? I had just spent a week and a half observing old-westerners, so I needed to quickly shift my frame of reference. Stepping into the cabin for the first time I was greeted by two young women sitting on the couch meditating into their mugs filled with steamy coffee. One was the daughter of a musician from Boise, ID, and the other came west from Georgia to "help out the cause for a few weeks." As we engaged in some friendly small talk, I glanced around the cozy rustic cabin, and was at once drawn to an old laminated sign perched at eye level above the meal table. I walked over and

Figure 3.6: *Top left:* Keeping warm out in the field. *Top right:* On skis watching a buffalo herd near Horse Butte. *Bottom left:* Filming armed government agents in the field. *Bottom right:* Snowy patrol on bicycle inside Yellowstone Park. Sources: BFC and photos taken by author.

read it (bold type in original):

> This space is intended to be a **sacred space** for honoring the Buffalo Nation, this dwelling, and all of the various beings who pass through this camp. An altar is traditionally a place set aside for reflecting on the sacred and transforming negativity, through the placement of special objects and the burning of incense and sacred plants.
> **It is not a place for thoughtlessness and junk.**
> Please refrain from degrading this space in our home that has been reserved for honoring the Buffalo—the reason we are all here.

Looking up, one of the young women noticed me and said, "That's sort of the code we live by, ya know?" During my time with the BFC, and in my subsequent research on the buffalo conflict, her words stuck with me. I became interested in the spiritual content of this mission statement. It emphasized that this cabin was a "sacred space." It was not just a "dwelling" but, more important an "altar" to be employed by activists for "reflecting on the sacred"—not to be "degraded," but to be used only to "honor the buffalo." Next to this laminated sign was a second one of similar length, size, and of related content. It was a prayer letter from an elder Santee Indian, encouraging members of the BFC to remain steadfast in their work despite the bloodshed and slaughter of his people's relative, the buffalo.

Even though most BFC leaders and volunteers are nonnative, they have appropriated indigenous Indian religious beliefs, which they use as baseline motivation for the movement's commitment to the buffalo. My goal, then, became to dig beneath the BFC's religious motivations—as well as a researcher might—through in-depth reflection on what participants believe, what they do, what they say and don't say, what they write, what they film, and how it affects the larger GYE policy conflict over the buffalo.

According to Mease, the BFC is motivated by "a common theme amongst all the tribes I had worked with that believes these animals to be super sacred... and I felt it was part of my job to reconnect this cultural gap." The BFC's vision of the human–buffalo relationship is especially influenced by Lakota creation narratives. Lakota people believe that humans and the buffalo originated together inside of the earth. Were it not for the buffalo, humans would not have been able to emerge from under the ground to the surface world. The Lakota creation legend, as told by Lakota elder Rosalie Little Thunder, tells of the buffalo caring for people as they struggled to survive on the surface of the earth. She explained that the buffalo made an agreement with humans, "The buffalo said, I will give you food, I will give you clothing so you can be warm, I will give you my flesh to eat and to survive, and when I am in need, you must help me, too." The Lakota creation narrative, and the sacred agreement between the buffalo and people, is similar in other tribal creation narratives, such as the Crow, Santee, and Pawnee, and is the basis for first nations'—and the BFC's—sacred relationship between humans and the buffalo.

Not only are buffalo considered *literal* relatives, but they are partners on an inseparable journey that began thousands of years ago. The ties that bind buffalo and humans are deeper than a simple historical linkage, but more powerfully an unbreakable bond that was almost tragically fractured during the 19th-century slaughter of bison. Because the Yellowstone herd of about 3,000–4,500 is the last remaining genetically pure and free-roaming herd, it is viewed as a tenuous link to their ancestors and to the creation narratives that give their communal lives meaning. Chasing Hawk of the Cheyenne River Sioux tribe describes the GYE "policy" issue in stark religious terms, eschewing the technorational specifics of science, law, or politics, "We are the buffalo people, the Lakota People. When they kill [the Yellowstone] buffalo, they are killing our brothers and sisters, grandpas and grandmas. The State of Montana did not see this. In fact, our religious significance is nothing to them." (Brister, 2013, p. 44). At a spiritual gathering in Rapid City, SD, in 1997 Chief Arvol Looking Horse—the 19th-generation keeper of the Sacred White Buffalo Calf Pipe, an indigenous representative to the United Nations, and collaborator with the Dalai Lama and Desmond Tutu—pleaded for policy change. In the wake of another massacre of Yellowstone buffalo, he urged policy makers to consider the spiritual crimes being committed against buffalo and indigenous peoples:

> I, Chief Arvol Looking Horse of the Lakota, Dakota and Nakota Nations would like to address the serious issue of our relative the Buffalo Nation. With the teaching of our way of life from the time of being, the First People were the Buffalo People, our ancestors which came from the sacred Black Hills the heart of everything that is. Our ceremonies consist of Seven Sacred Rites and with these rites we walk with the buffalo nation as our relatives. Through their blood line exist our spiritual values. It is our responsibility to protect them. As 19th Generation Keeper of the Sacred White Buffalo Calf Pipe, I pray for health and well being of many nations. I humbly ask all nations to respect our way of life because in our prophecies if there is no buffalo then life as we know it will cease to exist. Hecetu yelo! (Looking Horse, 1997)

The BFC's own organizational charter, the "Buffalo Bill of Rights," draws direct inspiration from these Indian narratives about the spiritual importance of buffalo. The first and most important of the BFC's "Buffalo Bill of Rights" reads, "1. To be honored with respect to their cultural and spiritual significance to the Indigenous people of this continent."

Thus, as I discovered within minutes of being in the BFC cabin that first day, indigenous religious beliefs and practices are, and always have been, a central part of the BFC's institutional makeup. These cultural values push the work forward and make it meaningful. In its engagement with the policy issue, the BFC has successfully secured a place at the table for deeper moral and spiritual concerns that have long been seen as incommensurable with rational management and policy. Even though BFC leaders and most volunteers are nonnative, and in many cases not conventionally religious, the BFC actively infuses these beliefs into what is generally understood to be a singularly technical conflict over science, law, and politics. They do this all the while recognizing that this is a useful tactic to be successful, because, as Mease explained to me, "Science has become a store-bought thing anymore, that whoever invests in the science project get the results they want... *so we don't use science to shut these guys down or show their irrelevance*" (emphasis added). Thus, during his road shows across the United States, and in his meetings with government agencies, tribes, or the general public, Mease finds it more useful to emphasize the point "that these buffalo have meaning and souls and hearts, and I mean I always try to bring up that aspect of them because that's the one aspect that is never brought up, and those meanings matter." With this in mind, the remainder of this chapter will consider in greater depth the inner logic of the BFC's moral protest, to understand how the moral culture of the BFC operates, and to consider its successful effect on the larger policy conflict. I focus on three particular aspects: purity, wildness, and ethics.

The Moral Logic of a Movement: Purity, Wildness, Virtue

In this section, I consider how the BFC's unique moral logic influences the bison policy conflict. My goal is to unpack the particularities of the BFC's inner cultural logic, and demonstrate its effect on policy decision making, by focusing on three key aspects. I organize these factors around larger contextualizing narratives, because, as I argued in the introductory chapter, such narratives often frame our beliefs and behaviors about what is right and wrong—they tell us who we are, what we should do, and why it all matters. After laying out this moral logic, I present results from a computational content analysis of BFC materials, comparing the BFC's use of moral, spiritual, and technorational logic with that of other stakeholders involved in the conflict.

PRESERVING GENETIC PURITY

The first aspect of the BFC's moral logic is a profound concern for preserving genetic purity, the narrative about which goes something like this:

> Once upon a time tens of millions of native bison roamed the lands that we now call North America. All but 23 bison were brutally slaughtered at the hands the U.S. government. This sacred remnant of 23 Yellowstone bison was bred to save what is now the last native and genetically pure bison population. We now have 500,000 buffalo in the United States, but nearly all of these are "beefalo," as they have been polluted and cross-bred with America's new sacred animal, the cow. All bison are not created equal. The continued control, hazing, torture, and slaughter by the government and livestock industry of this pure remnant is an act defiling the sanctity of an animal that is still on the brink of extinction. The cattle industry, and those who collaborate with them, are complicit in the longstanding conquest against the buffalo. The moral boundaries are clear, and there is no room for compromise. We must remain steadfast and vigilant to do whatever it takes to protect the few remaining genetically pure and sacred bison whose link to the past is irreplaceable.

The emphasis here is on the survival of a genetically pure remnant, and the fact that government agencies and livestock interests are flagrantly transgressing what the BFC views as a very serious moral boundary that, when violated, cannot be restored. One problem is that much of the American public is unaware that relatively few genetically pure bison are left in the United States. Many people unfamiliar with the issue see buffalo in other areas of the United States, whether Oklahoma, South Dakota, or elsewhere, and assume all buffalo are the same. A central goal of the BFC is to publicize the fact that even though they are physically indistinguishable to the eye from buffalo in Yellowstone, they are "beefalo," not as valuable because they are not genetically unique. But the issue is not just their genetics. Mease explained to me that it goes much deeper, and that even though with the naked eye "you can't physically tell the difference, their nature and their beings are very different."

The BFC is very clear in its "no-compromise" policy about preserving genetic purity. On one long afternoon of patrol, I discussed this issue with a head volunteer, as we snowshoed atop a long, picturesque ridge on the border of Yellowstone. As we sloshed through the snow and talked about this concept of purity, he continually emphasized that the BFC draws a hard line about about the importance of Yellowstone buffalo compared to America's population of beefalos. He remarked that "it makes us appear as though we are uncooperative, or that we are always negative... but fuck man, there used to be 30 million of these sacred creatures until we wiped them out, and now there is controversy about protecting a couple of thousand?" Mease, further told me that their uncompromising belief in the value of genetic purity has indeed led to strife with fellow environmental groups. He explained to me, with frustration in his voice, "What bothers me about [other environmental groups] is their ability to compromise and buy into this idiocy... but once again there has to be one group that doesn't compromise. There has to be one group that stands up and says 'no, this isn't right!' And whatever, we're gonna turn some people off, we're gonna turn some people on, but that's how it has to be." He continues, "So many of those larger groups are just professionals that compromise, but when you come down to the last 3,000 buffalo, there is no more room for compromise. There is no more selling out, you know. As I like to say it, there's 40 million cattle in the United States, and there's [about] 3,000 buffalo... then it's like come on, we can't make enough room for us to have wild buffalo again in this country? We don't want to? That's the scariest thing, we don't want to."

For first nations people, the concern with genetic purity is tied to a long, dark history of repeated conquests by Euro-Americans destroying their culture. Chief Jimmy St. Goddard of the Blackfeet Nation understands the management actions against the Yellowstone bison herd as one event in a long history of pollution and cultural destruction, emphatically stating that "it's basically desecrating everything we're about. We call it historical post-traumatic distress disorder that happens to us Indians, when this continues to destroy our culture... all of these tribes are affected and we need to band together to stop this killing of the Yellowstone herd... [but] one group of euro-americans who think with their hearts, and believes in these sacred mammals, is the Buffalo Field Campaign... Most of them are whites... [but] they are truly good people who want to protect these sacred animals."

The BFC's public claim that preserving genetic purity is a sacred obligation that ought to be included in the "rational" and "technocratic" decision-making process has been politically effective in recent years. Mease explained to me that despite government manipulation, "The sacred element... [has] been received better as of late... the doors are opening and those more sacred and more spiritual aspects are coming in." This has largely happened through the recognition of treaty rights by public officials in charge of bison management through the Interagency Bison Management Plan. With the help of the BFC, Montana's tribes have capitalized on this momentum and have, for the first time, secured a seat at the decision-making table. At a January 2013 Montana-Wyoming Tribal Leaders Council Board meeting they unanimously approved a resolution demanding Montana stop hazing Yellowstone bison. One tribal spokesman remarked on the motivations behind this resolution, declaring: "It's time that people start understanding how sacred the bison are." In their resolution, they urge the governor of Montana, the Montana Legislature, the U.S. Department of the Interior, Yellowstone National Park, the U.S. Department of Agriculture, and the U.S. Forest Service to protect the "genetically distinct" buffalo that live in Yellowstone and to recognize that the "revered buffalo" is a "sacred species" and "inseparable from the identities, traditions, cultures, beliefs, and religious practices of American Indians and an indigenous way of life." At the center of this vision and strategy is the idea of purity.

WILDNESS

In addition to their genetic purity, what makes Yellowstone bison especially sacred is that they are the only herd in the world that has remained continuously wild since prehistoric times. Thus, like purity, this related concept of wildness is an incredibly important, and inviolable, marker of veneration. I discovered the following narrative that organized this concept, which goes something like this:

> Buffalo were created to be wild; to be unfettered by artificial constraints. They were created to roam free. This is how it was, and how it should be. But as we see throughout human history, wildness threatens human lust for control, and thus in the last 150 years humans have successfully tamed nearly all wild buffalo through fencing, feeding, killing, breeding, and other "management" and domestication techniques. In this conquest they destroy what is sacred. Now they are taming and controlling the world's last remaining wild buffalo, and armed with sophisticated science, private land rights, and economic logic, they wage a war on wildness itself. We must oppose any management policies that suppress the intrinsic rights of the buffalo to roam free, and work to create new policies that favor the expression of wildness lived out by the Yellowstone herd.

The BFC's moral vision of wildness is part of a larger stream of environmental thinking that I describe in Chapters 1 and 2, which developed out of religious impulses in 19th century transcendentalist thought. Under the umbrella of what I call the "spiritual moral vision," it views wildness and wilderness not as something to fear, something to control, or something to benefit from economically—as it was for much of American history—but as something uncontrollable, a source of noneconomic benefits, uncontaminated by the ills of human influence, of pure moral conscience, and a place where humanity might reconnect with the mysterious and the divine. It is in wildness that human and nonhuman animals could fully flourish.

I routinely discussed these concepts with BFC volunteers. On one car ride back from evening patrol, I talked with a few BFC volunteers about the concept of "wildness," asking what it means and how it relates to the work of the BFC in the policy arena. Our lead volunteer, Elena, reflected on her year and a half with the BFC, describing to me that "when the government attempts to control buffalo through hazing they are removing their wildness. And this wildness is the fount of their sacredness. It's, you know, what makes these animals special, and it's why we try so hard to protect them." I pressed a bit, asking how an ideal like "wildness" could ever be attained. She responded confidently, "Oh, yea thats a good question, but its pretty easy for us. Wildness for the buffalo means that they are *completely* free to roam outside of the park, to the lands that they have roamed since the beginning. When they can do this they will be unconditionally wild. Thats how I see it." Leaf, a volunteer from northern California, chimed in from the back seat, clarifying Elena's description, remarking that "its more like different degrees of wildness. The more the better. These buffalo are wild, yes they don't have fences. But they are kept out of certain areas, off of certain land at certain times, and so we won't stop until they are left alone completely."

Since the establishment of YNP, there has been unending disagreement over ideals of pure "wildness"—what it means, whether it's possible, how we might go about promoting it, and so on. These longstanding debates, and the contrasting philosophical approaches to the question, underlie most natural resource conflicts in Yellowstone and other protected areas. The disputed wildness of buffalo was a jumping-off point for some BFC activists to lament about other issues relating to wildness in modernity. For example, during one afternoon patrol Alexa, David, and I cross-country skied along a snowmobile path, and as snowmobiles went by we began talking about the ethics and symbolism of machines in Yellowstone Park. Alexa complained that "Yellowstone is just a tourist money maker. That's all it is." I gently probed, asking her what would satisfy a requirement for pure wildness, and she said, "We need a wild space where no humans are allowed, ever." This sort of black-and-white idealism is of the same sort that undergirds the BFC's approach to the buffalo. It is an ideal that has the potential of being reached if buffalo are "left alone completely," and thus the BFC marches on toward that goal, with its unique form of uncompromising idealism.

While Alexa's hope for completely removing humans from the area might be a huge task, smaller roadblocks stand in the way of achieving the ideal of pure wildness for the Yellowstone herd. One is, quite literally, the 8.5-mile stretch of highway that runs north–south from West Yellowstone, MT, along Yellowstone's western border. This road is both a symbolic and a physical boundary, which makes it difficult for Yellowstone buffalo to safely follow their ancient migration routes outside the park. In recent years the BFC has spent a

Figure 3.7: *Left*: Photo of Highway 191. Volunteer at bottom right is recording video. *Right*: Photo of buffalo hit by semi truck on highway 191. Sources: Photos by author and BFC.

lot of time patrolling the highway, keeping watch over buffalo that come near the road, and erecting large orange traffic signs to alert drivers, or slowing traffic with their Subaru wagons. During one patrol, we drove this 8.5-mile stretch up and back for several hours, patrolling what was more than merely a physical asphalt boundary. For the BFC the highway is a symbolic moral boundary of modern human intrusion. The left photo in Figure 3.7, from this day's patrol, shows a common sight where buffalo pass over this highway filled with semi trucks and transfixed tourists—who for the BFC embody everything that is *not* wild. Watching these sacred animals navigate this dangerous environment (the photo on the right shows a Yellowstone buffalo struck by a semi truck) often infuriated BFC volunteers, and was a clear example of how the wildness of the buffalo was being compromised, especially if tourists or semi truck drivers tried to disrupt or hurry the natural pace of the buffalo by honking or revving their engines.

The BFC has found success in aligning traditional environmental ideals about wildness with its particular policy issue. I focus on specific policy outcomes below, but in terms of attracting a motivated volunteer base, the issue of preserving wildness rings true for many who are sympathetic to the broader spiritual moral vision I presented in previous chapters. For many who travel to the American West from other areas of the country, volunteering for the BFC allows them to live out the ideal they desire to protect. One volunteer, Amani, explains her reasoning along these lines: "I volunteered because bison symbolized freedom and abundance. Now I know they are more than symbols, they are truly wise, majestic creatures who add wonder and beauty to our environment." Like the desire to preserve their genetic and spiritual purity, the struggle to free the wild Yellowstone herd from the last remaining shackles of human control and interference is an uncompromising ideal, which I will show has altered management policies in recent years.

BUFFALO VIRTUES, OR BECOMING A BUFFALO

BFC participants believe that buffalo model virtues that humans should adopt if we want to live better lives together. I discovered a guiding narrative that goes something like the following:

> We humans have lost our way in our increasing pursuit of power, wealth, scientific mastery, and control. Our families and communities have been fractured. As a result, we no longer care for one another, and despite our "progress," we remain detached from nature and one another. Fortunately, the Yellowstone buffalo herd offers us an ethical paradigm based on community, unity, caring for the least among us, gender equality, servant leadership, patience, environmental sustainability, and peacefulness in the midst of injustice. Despite our continued mistreatment of the Yellowstone herd, they peacefully lead by example. We would do well to follow in the path of the buffalo, and reorient ourselves and our communities around the set of life-giving virtues they personify. We must align our policies not with human thirsts for power, wealth, or technocratic control, but fight peacefully to realize a way of life as it is lived in caring community, as exemplified by the Yellowstone herd.

The BFC is clear that the buffalo are much more than bundles of organic matter with mechanical-like propensities: buffalo are dynamic beings that feel emotion, have personalities, and behave with conscious conviction. BFC volunteers recognize human forms and personalities in these animals, and most often this anthropomorphism is related to the things buffalo seek to teach humans about how we should live. Moral lessons we can learn from the buffalo are aimed at the root of who human beings are and how we ought to coexist together. I encountered these sentiments everywhere during my time with the BFC and in my subsequent interviews and archival analyses. As one BFC leader put it, "The buffalo have stuff to teach us. They have ways to show us humanity: don't shit in your own bed; think about next year; take care of everyone instead of just the rich." He continued, "They have neat ways of showing people how things could work in society, but yet we don't follow their ways." The abusive treatment of the buffalo is a manifestation of the fractured nature of human community, says Mease, and "is the epitome of the problems we're facing in the bigger world, that hey, in certain circles none of us matter, and never will." An op-ed written by a volunteer and published by the BFC, "Lessons Learned from Wild Bison," makes a case for 14 specific moral lessons taught by the buffalo, including, "You are your brother's keeper, Let the women lead, Persevere in the face of difficulty, Do a job thoroughly, Protect the children, Foster creativity, Express feelings and emotions, and Care for your home, the earth."

But certain moral lessons are particularly important for the BFC's moral logic. In the midst of political polarization and political corruption in the United States, the buffalo provide a right model of human governance. According to Mease,

Figure 3.8: A bull bison visits buffalo remains just outside YNP. BFC decribes this as the mourning process for his relatives. Photo by BFC.

because the buffalo are "a very family- and herd-oriented animal," their leader is "not a dictator like our leaders tend to be in this world, but their job is to make sure the entire herd survives." This picture of selfless leadership is of particular importance to Mease's leadership style, and for many of the volunteers, who tend to espouse a peculiar mix of liberal, libertarian, and quasi-anarchist views about American politics. Mease reflects on the failures of the Obama administration, bemoaning, "You know, we all voted for Obama for this massive change and I think all of us who had faith in him got a lot of our eyes opened that, hey, he's still owned by the same money that Bush was owned by, you know, and that all these guys are corrupt assholes by the time they become high up in politics because you can't advance up in politics without being owned." But there is no political ownership in the buffalo herd, and there are no corrupt or dictatorial "assholes." For Mease, we must look no further than the communal-focused leadership in the buffalo herd for a model of good human politics.

Another key lesson humans need to learn from the buffalo is the intense concern for every member of the community, especially when members are lost. This is seen most powerfully in the BFC's description of buffalo mourning rituals. When buffalo are killed during a haze, hunt, or slaughter, buffalo have what the BFC calls a "Wake of the Buffalo," or a "Mourning Ceremony" (Figure 3.8).

Thus, after 44 wild bison were killed in February 2013, the BFC released a statement explaining in stirring detail how the herd conducted its communal mourning ritual:

> Two days later we watched as more than a hundred buffalo approached these killing fields. They found the remains of their relatives strewn across the land like fleshy boulders left behind by glaciers. We watched in sorrowful awe as the buffalo approached the gut piles. Their tails shot up in the air as they ran from remain to remain, discovering what was left. Enormous bulls bellowed like roaring dragons, mouths agape, bodies arched, and pawing the ground. The buffalo placed their faces close to the flesh left behind, nuzzling their muzzles into the earth where the buffalo had fallen. They sniffed at fetuses still sheltered in their mother's flesh whose lives were ended before they were born. The buffalo circled and scattered, ran to each other and away again. Sparring, bumping, running, pawing and crying out in their deep emotion of their discovery. Watching, we could only think of it as a wake, a mighty wailing of the buffalo. Back and forth they ran, frantic, between the gut piles that had been their friends, their family. Like chieftains in their own right, fathers of their clans, the mature bulls lingered the longest, as the mothers and grandmothers led the young ones on in an ancient procession, their deliberate footsteps slower in their sorrow.

In this statement, the BFC challenges those who rationalize buffalo killing or explain away the process of animal mourning, arguing that "the depth of relationship the buffalo share is timeless, intense, and far beyond most people's willingness or ability to accept or understand. Indeed, it is easier, more convenient, to ignore or pretend that it doesn't mean anything." In this rational "blindness" we deny ourselves "the honest power of love, the gift of respect, and the aid of wisdom." The buffalo serve as a model of the sacred power of communal bonds and "[the buffalo] are patiently waiting on the brink for us [humans] to catch up." Beneath these beliefs about, and descriptions of, buffalo mourning ceremonies is the narrative that in modernity we have lost deep interpersonal connections, and with them, the deep sense of care and respect characteristic of intimate communities. The buffalo mourning ceremony is one example of the buffalo guiding us toward more communal ways of life. As one BFC leader put it, "It's time we get back to community and taking care of one another. These are all things the buffalo are trying to teach us if we'd just open our ears and listen."

This is all, in a sense, a process of "becoming" a buffalo. Our wildlife policies should follow suit, argues the BFC. Some take this more literally than others. In a sort of reversal of anthropomorphism, and in an attempt to literally live out the example set by the buffalo, I found that BFC participants would often personify buffalo forms and personalities. Late one morning I had finished digging a small trench and came inside to warm up over a cup of coffee; upon entering the cabin,

Figure 3.9: Protest at Montana Fish, Wildlife and Parks headquarters. Photo by Buffalo Field Campaign.

I stumbled on two volunteers crouched down, playfully sparring like buffalo. With their index fingers as horns, they kicked dust off of the cabin floor, bumping into one another, bellowing buffalo sounds while circling the main room of the cabin. As I made my way around them, careful not to get caught in the battle, I sarcastically remarked, "Sorry to break up the fight, ladies, I'll be quick." One of the women looked up, laughed, and responded, "Just doing our best impression, its actually kind of fun to be a buffalo, you should try it." Outside the confines of camp, BFC activists often dress up as buffalo at protests (Figure 3.9) and at direct-action demonstrations in the field (Figure 3.10). The act of becoming a buffalo is part of their expressive form of moral protest. Indeed, the women sparring like buffalo in the cabin is merely a playful act, but it is part of their commitment to expressive tactics of moral protest that in this case blurs the lines between human and buffalo.

BFC activists also believe that the buffalo are aware of the GYE policy conflict, know that they are at the center of it, and understand that the BFC is on their side. For example, on one afternoon of patrol, four of us sat in a car on the shoulder of the highway, watching 25 buffalo meander out of the park onto the road, as they commonly do. Coming up to the road they formed a single-file line and stopped in the middle of the road for 15–20 minutes, completely blocking traffic. Pleased at the sight, one volunteer remarked from the back seat, "The buffalo are forming a barricade in the road to protest the highway!" Another volunteer yelled out the window, "Take your time sweet baby ... you're right, these people can wait!" Here again the BFC attributed purpose and symbolic meaning to the behavior of the animals. The buffalo had, in their view, joined the movement and staged a protest in the road that day.

Figure 3.10: Protest in the field, disrupting government hazing operations. Photo by Buffalo Field Campaign.

Also common is the sense that the Yellowstone buffalo recognize BFC activists and are aware that they are helping them. Mease told me a long story of a buffalo who had killed a dog and was being searched for to be killed by the DOL and Montana Fish, Wildlife, and Parks. The bull, he said, "Of all places in the region he could've picked, anywhere in the whole thing, he came to *my* backyard of my little cabin and hid there for three and a half hours." When DOL agents came to Mike's cabin and asked if he had seen the bull, he made no mention of the bull and pointed the agents in the wrong direction, saving the bull's life. As the bull left, it nodded in thanksgiving, according to Mike, and using this example to illustrate to me the relationship between BFC and buffalo, Mease said with conviction, "They bring that energy to you because they let you know that they understand that you're helping them." He continued, recounting that "I've had numerous times in the field where we've given them a heads-up to get into the woods before the DOL or Fish, Wildlife, and Parks got there, which gives them a huge advantage after the event of the day, and they didn't get caught." Mease explained that the buffalo often thank BFC activists when they tip them off to government agents: "Well later, they all came by our campfire and nodded their heads and thanked us, you know, for giving them a heads up. At least that's what I interpreted. You know, there are textbooks that say an animal only does this or that for specific scientific reasons, *but what things mean is what they teach you ... those things happen all the time out here.* It's amazing the stuff you see." Thus, from the perspective of BFC participants, the buffalo are active in the struggle for ethical renewal, recognizing that in this moral battle, the BFC is on their side.

CONTENT ANALYSIS OF ISSUE MEDIA

As a supplement to participant observation and interviews, and to better understand how the BFC's moral logic is deployed, I conducted a computational content analysis of nearly all BFC media materials. This analysis includes the full text of every newsletter published by BFC since its inception in 1997 ($n = 569$). I also collected the full text of every press releases since that time ($n = 208$). Last, I transcribed selected BFC videos from 2005 to 2013. Each of these data sources provide a slightly different picture of BFC activity. The newsletters highlight *internal* communications with BFC supporters about announcements and day-to-day happenings in the field, the press releases indicate the BFC's *external* engagement with mass media and the public, and the videos are mostly persuasive attempts to morally shock or convince viewers about the importance of the cause. To use as a comparison to these BFC materials, I collected all public comments on the 2000 Final Environmental Impact Statement of the Interagency Bison Management Plan. These are especially useful because this management plan is at the center of the bison controversy. The public comments include thousands of letters written both for and against the plan, from old-west livestock interests as well as environmental interests.

From my fieldwork and interviews I hypothesized that BFC media materials would also be saturated with moral and spiritual arguments, as opposed to the ubiquity of economic, biological, ecological, and legal discourse that permeat the issue. I created three measurable categories of meaning (Moral, Spiritual, and Science and Rationality) that capture the multiple dimensions of the issue (Table 3.1). Within these categories are subcategories that tap into more specific meanings about the issue. Using these categories I created lexicons containing hundreds of words and phrases that serve as indicators of each subcategory. For an exhaustive explanation of the methodological process involved in creating these lexicons and using them in computational content analysis, see the appendix 1.

Figure 3.11 presents findings that display the total percentage distribution of the three different categories (Moral, Spiritual, Science and Rationality). As a comparison to the BFC materials, I've included in the analysis the public comments. From the figure, it is clear that the total distribution of categories for the public comments on the 2000 bison plan (FEIS) is very different from BFC, which uses more moral and spiritual meanings and less science and rationality. For example, science and rationality makes up only 24.9 percent of the distribution of BFC newsletters, whereas it makes up nearly half for the other agencies and groups. There are similar differences for spiritual and moral frequencies. Chi-squared tests between the BFC materials and these other agencies and groups reveal that these differences are significant at the $p < .005$ level. This comparison makes the point that the BFC's internal and external discourse is more likely to be based upon moral and spiritual meanings, and less

Table 3.1: Categories of Meaning in Content Analysis

	Brief Description of Category
Moral	
Dominionism and harm	Rejection of abusive, barbaric, and brutal treatment of buffalo
Moral shock	Emotions like anger, disgust, abhorrence, horror, outrage
Greed	Claims of avarice, big money, selfishness
Rights/freedom	Claims about animal rights, deserving justice, freedom to roam
Moral duty to the future	We have a moral obligation to our descendents
Spiritual	
Aesthetic	Buffalo are beautiful, awe-inspiring, majestic, sublime, etc.
Collective history	Link to Indian ancestors, heritage, folklore
Spiritual and religious	Appeals to deity, divine, spirit, sin, sacred, creator, etc.
Science and Rationality	
Ecology/biology	Buffalo science about disease, ecosystems, grazing, habitat, etc.
Economic	Economic claims about cost, price, taxes, etc.
Rationality	Claims about facts, information, research, validity, logic, etc.

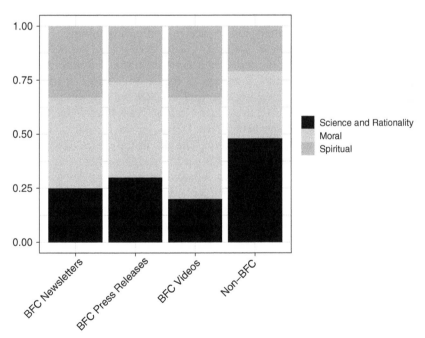

Figure 3.11: Total distributions of categories.

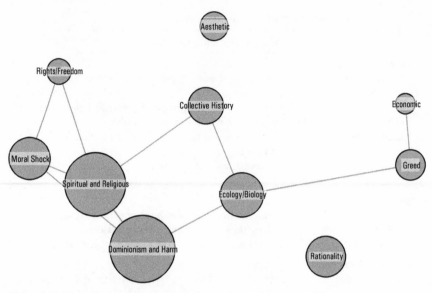

Figure 3.12: Network map of relational meanings.

likely to argue on the basis of science and rationality, than is that of other groups and agencies working on the same issue.

Oftentimes, moral, spiritual, and science and rationality meanings are used in conjunction, rather than in isolation. To dig deeper into the networks of meaning used by the BFC, I conducted a multidimensional scaling model on the BFC's internal newsletters, presented in Figure 3.12. This maps relational results of *subcategories* of meaning described in Table 3.1. The spatial distance between the different categories in the figure indicates how likely those meanings are to appear together in the newsletters. The closer the categories, the more likely the BFC used them in conjunction. The size of the circles represents the frequency with which each meaning was used in the newsletters. For example, Spiritual and Religious is used most, followed by Dominionism and Harm. The lines connecting the dyads indicate Jaccard similarity values above .10.[3] In mapping these categories in the newsletters, we see that Spiritual and Religious meanings are not only more frequent, but they are more central, by which I mean Spiritual and Religious meanings co-occur at higher frequency with other categories. What all this means is that the BFC uses Spiritual and Religious justifications in conjunction with its other categories, such as Dominionism and Harm, Ecology/Biology, Moral Shock, Collective History, and Rights/Freedom.

3 See "Multiple Meanings: Co-Occurrence of Spirituality and Rationality" in Chapter 4 for explanation of the Jaccard calculations.

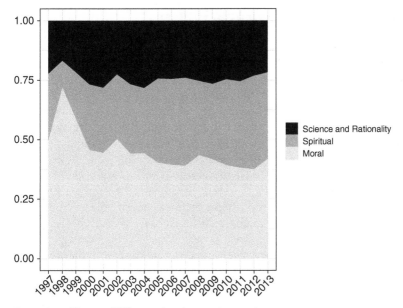

Figure 3.13: The use of different cultural categories over time.

Compare this to Rationality at the bottom right, which tends to occur in isolation from other categories. Similarly, Economic meanings, which do not occur as often (smaller circle), are neither central on the graph nor well-connected with other meanings.

How has the BFC shifted its use of these cultural meanings over time? Figure 3.13 presents an area graph of the total distribution of the the different categories in the newsletters from 1997 to 2013. This chart demonstrates that since 1997, there has been a slow trend within BFC newsletters to use more spiritual language. Because these are total distributions, this graph also shows that relative to spiritual meanings, the total distribution of moral arguments (Rights, Dominionism, Greed, etc.) declined slightly, as did Science and Rationality. These trends are not drastic, but still signal a slight shift in how BFC talked about the issue over the course of the 16 years since the group was founded.

On the whole, the results of this content analysis reinforce my overall argument that, unlike many stakeholders in the GYE who either do not recognize or actively suppress cultural and moral meanings, the BFC has made these central and public in its fight for policy change. Next I turn to examine how these moral and spiritual concepts have actually been brought to bear in public politics and the policy arena, leading to what I argue is a successful form of moral protest against approaches that tend to be locked up in more "surface-level" technoscientific methods.

Successes of Moral-Spiritual Protest

One of my central arguments is that the BFC is successful in the midst of intractable conflict because it has successfully transformed the buffalo—considered ordinary livestock by the state of Montana—into a pure and wild object infused with an incredible amount of moral force. Thus far I have focused on the BFC's process of "surfacing" purity, wildness, and virtue, making them central to the policy issue. In this section I will *show how these commitments are brought to bear on the policy conflict itself*, through expressive and aggressive moral protest.

To understand why and how the BFC is successful, we will view its tactics through the lens of what social movement scholars Jasper and Poulsen call a "moral shock"—defined as "an event or situation [that] raises such a sense of outrage in people that they become inclined toward political action" (1995, p. 498). Actions that are "highly publicized" are especially likely to morally "shock" people to take action. Since its beginning, the BFC's strategy has been to cut through GYE bureaucracy and technocratic authority with the use of morally shocking videos, images, and direct-action protest. The BFC's engagement with other environmental groups, the public, lawmakers, and management agencies (Department of Livestock and the Montana Fish, Wildlife, and Parks) is anything but cold, rational, scientific, or politically expedient, but it emphasizes uncompromising emotion and outrage. The BFC's participation in the conflict flows from an intense certainty about right and wrong about the loss of buffalo and Indian dignity, about intense fear of the extinction of an iconic and genetically pure ancestor, and about the importance of evangelizing others into the same feelings of moral outrage. The ubiquitous, and long-lasting, disputes in the GYE over the "facts" of brucellosis science, private property law, or politics can obscure what the debate is really about. In the words of Mease, "You can argue technical details until you're blue in the face... but when you *see* what they are doing to these animals, it *automatically* makes you think that we don't need to treat anything this bad."

MORAL SHOCK

The BFC is clear about its intention to morally shock. Mease has a dual degree in psychology and radio/television media because, in his words, "These subjects went hand in hand. I recognized immediately the power and manipulation of media to conform us... so I wanted to see what I could do to turn the format of television into something that could be an advocacy tool... to show the world what regular television wasn't showing us." Mease knows that with the Yellowstone bison issue all he needed to do to bring change was to open people's eyes to the treatment of this wild and sacred herd, because he believes "videos will open people's eyes enough to say, 'Look, I may not agree with their crazy tactics, but what they are doing to these buffalo is wrong.' " These tactics are

Figure 3.14: Game warden pulls skin off of buffalo killed on private land. Photo by Buffalo Field Campaign.

similar to those that contributed to a shift in public opinion during the civil rights movement: many Americans became more sympathetic upon viewing morally shocking images and videos of blacks violently sprayed with fire hoses and attacked by police dogs.

On one of the warmer days during my time with the BFC I sat on the porch and watched the sunset with an activist who had just arrived from California for a short visit. A self-proclaimed "professional environmentalist," he was well-known across the country for his participation in different movements, and was now an independent consultant for many prominent groups. Given his expertise, I asked him why the BFC has been so successful. Without hesitation he explained that unlike other groups in the area, the BFC "hits people in the heart. They recruit passionate people to their cause simply by showing a video of bison being shot or injured. A lot of the public responds to these videos, too. It cuts across political affiliations for people to see such things." Several examples of images and still shots from BFC videos that have been used successfully over the years are presented in Figures 3.14 to 3.22.

In protests at the state capitol and major landmarks around the GYE, volunteers act out shocking scenes, bringing to the surface the reality of buffalo slaughter and death. For example, at the state capitol in Helena, BFC members built a large graveyard (Figures 3.24), and in another protest they dressed up in bison costumes and lay dead, symbolizing another mass graveyard (Figure 3.23).

In addition to morally shocking media, the BFC and some of its volunteers are influenced by direct-action protest and intervention characteristic of environmentalist groups like Earth First! A handful of BFC leaders and volunteers were at one point or another connected to Earth First! networks, and thus early

Figure 3.15: Dead buffalo loaded onto flatbed with a tractor. Photo by Buffalo Field Campaign.

Figure 3.16: Decapitated buffalo heads laid out at GYE slaughterhouse in 1997. Photo by Buffalo Field Campaign.

on the BFC was more heavily influenced by direct-action strategies and tended to use more aggressive intervention tactics to prevent the slaughter of buffalo. One routine tactic is to interfere with Montana DOL efforts to capture, transport, and slaughter bison. A common strategy is to lock oneself to DOL vehicles and slaughter equipment. The following excerpt from a 1998 BFC newsletter describes an event where a volunteer locked himself to a trailer, and Figure 3.25 is an image from a separate BFC self-"lockdown" protest at the Department of Livestock

Figure 3.17: Buffalo hazed by government agencies. Photo by Buffalo Field Campaign.

Figure 3.18: Helicopter flying low to haze buffalo. Photo by Buffalo Field Campaign.

building in Helena:

> At 11:30 a.m. Thursday, [Buffalo Field Campaign] volunteer Dan Howells locked himself to a trailer getting ready to relocate the four buffalo. With a kryptonite bicycle lock around his neck, Howells, a 29-year-old non-violent protester from Michigan, stated "We must stop the buffalo slaughter. These buffalo do not belong to the Department of Livestock, they belong to the people of the United States. The buffalo should be allowed to be wild and free." Howells was cut free from the trailer, and charged with obstruction, a misdemeanor.

Figure 3.19: Department of Livestock bison head lock entrapment. Photo by Buffalo Field Campaign.

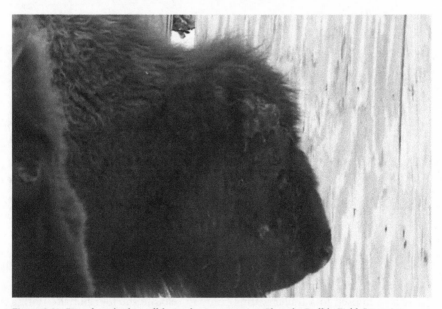

Figure 3.20: Bison horn broken off during hazing operation. Photo by Buffalo Field Campaign.

BFC volunteers have also blocked the construction of new bison traps and shut down access to important roads by constructing giant tripod and monopod structures rising 30–40 feet into the air (Figure 3.26, 3.27, 3.28). These structures are intended to block passage because they can easily fall if the beam

Figure 3.21: Baby bison with fractured leg caused by government hazing operation. Photo by Buffalo Field Campaign.

supports are touched, and thus volunteers intentionally perch themselves at the apex of the tripod, putting their lives in danger and becoming a liability for government agents who need them removed. BFC activists have occupied such tripods for months at a time for 24 hours a day, enduring grueling 40 degree below zero weather conditions, until government agencies can bring in cranes to remove the perched BFC volunteer and move forward with the planned haze, capture, or slaughter. A 1999 BFC press release describes in detail this process:

> This morning, over 20 officials including Department of Livestock agents in cooperation with Gallatin County Sheriff, Highway Patrol, and Forest Service law enforcement closed the area around the base of the tripod structures on the Gallatin National Forest, outside of West Yellowstone, MT. The blockade has been occupied by Buffalo Field Camp volunteers since January 25, 1999. One volunteer, Donald Fontenot, age 35 of Portland, Oregon, was arrested at the base of the tripods around 10:00 this morning when he tried to climb into one of the platforms. Summer Nelson, 22, of Missoula, was arrested at 3:00 p.m. after she was removed by a cherrypicker from a platform suspended from the back end of the 150 foot long blockade of 5 interlocking tripods. She was locked to the structure from her platform 30 feet in the air in order to prevent

Figure 3.22: Bison victim of hazing operation. Source: National Park Service.

the removal of the blockade until her arms were removed from the locking device and she was taken into custody by Gallatin County Sheriffs. She is being charged with maintaining an unauthorized structure and resisting arrest.

MOVEMENT SUCCESS

The BFC has achieved much success since its inception in 1997. Before 1997 there was little knowledge about, and little concern for, the treatment of the Yellowstone herd. The most successful first step was the BFC's active reframing of the issue of management as a moral (and spiritual) issue that demanded the nation's attention. Up until this point, Mease explains that the policy "used to be that they just kill any buffalo that walked out of the Yellowstone Park. That was their bison management plan." But the protests and morally shocking media turned up the heat on livestock and public land managers, and in the 2000 IBMP, these agencies instituted hazing as a friendlier alternative. Or, as one BFC leader put it to me, "I tell people, hazing never existed until we got involved with this issue! These images and videos and protests have been very successful over time, without a doubt!" Since 2000, though, the BFC has vigorously opposed hazing, and BFC field patrol images are being used more and more in federal cases against hazing. Moreover, with pressure from the BFC and other advocates in the area, the Montana Fish, Wildlife and Parks is now considering a proposal to allow

Figure 3.23: Moral protest about buffalo slaughter. Photo by Buffalo Field Campaign.

bison to roam freely on as much as 421,000 acres outside Yellowstone. This would be a monumental victory that was unthinkable just 16 years earlier when BFC began.

Since 1997 other environmental groups have jumped into the fray, but because the BFC is the only full-time group working on the issue, and the only group working in the field, it remains the unique authority. Being in the field with the buffalo, and literally recording all government interaction with the animal, puts then BFC in a powerful position vis-à-vis other environmental advocate groups. For example, in the important 2007 U.S. Congressional Oversight Hearing on "Yellowstone National Park Bison," Joshua Osher of the BFC was the only environmental NGO representative to testify before Congress. In recent years, as it has acquired more organizational resources and support, the BFC has expanded its work into more conventional legal and political arenas, in addition to its

Figure 3.24: Graveyard erected at state capitol in Helena. Photo by Buffalo Field Campaign.

disruptive and vigilant presence in the field (Shanahan et al., 2010). Courtrooms and other political halls of power are unfamiliar territory for the group, but the BFC is intent on spreading its message about the spiritual value of the buffalo into these technical arenas. Reflecting on how far it has come, Mease proudly describes the volunteers who have made inroads into the halls of power: "We now have old volunteers who went on to be valedictorians and they're just these kick-ass lawyers that are now fighting for the buffalo ... .we've had bills in the Congress that have almost passed, and we've got a guy that's out in Washington lobbying for the buffalo."

Figure 3.25: *Left:* "Lockdown" protest strategy by BFC activists at the Department of Livestock Building in Helena. *Right:* BFC activist handcuffs himself to entrance of hazing road for multiple days. Photo by Buffalo Field Campaign.

In recent years the BFC has brought its concerns to the American public through national news and entertainment networks. In addition to its very popular website videos from the field, the BFC has been the subject of several documentaries, such as PBS's *The Buffalo War*. It has been featured on ABC nightly news, and more recently the Discovery Channel's Planet Green network aired a "docu-reality" pilot (very similar to popular shows like *The Deadliest Catch, Storm Chasers, Whale Wars, Swamp People*) entitled *Buffalo Battle*, following, in dramatic fashion, the BFC during a spring season of activism. This national attention has made the BFC synonymous with the issue in the GYE. During my years of research and fieldwork around all areas of the GYE, people routinely asked me about those "crazy Buffalo people" in a polarizing tone, either praising their unique commitment or taking exception to their left-of-center beliefs and practices.

Some ally environmental groups are downright uncomfortable with the BFC's animistic spiritual rituals, zero-compromise approach to buffalo management, guerrilla tactics, emphasis on shaping public perceptions through morally shocking videos, and low-budget grassroots mentality. Mease summarized these dynamics to me nicely when I probed him about negative perceptions of the BFC from those outside the group:

> Its just like I always say, people that hate us, its just an extension of the prejudice that's being placed on the buffalo. That we don't fit your norms, we don't have our hair cut, we don't wear ties to your meetings, we're not going to kiss your ass or compromise, we're gonna tell you what we feel and that's the beauty of this country. You don't have to agree with us as long as we make you think about something you weren't thinking about. As long as we open a path to change. I mean look at any fringe movement that's made any change and they're always considered irrational radicals. But it's their persistence is what creates change, and thats what our job is to do, to be that persistent,

Figure 3.26: Monopod and tripods constructed and occupied 24/7 by BFC activists to stop trapping and slaughter. Photo by Buffalo Field Campaign.

noncompromising force that's always going to be in your face, we're going to call you out on the wrong things, and we're not going to kiss your ass, but if you do something good and right, we will recognize that and thank you for that as well.

But this approach has led some within the conservation community to question whether it's best for the BFC to continue to be the public face of the issue.

Figure 3.27: BFC protester living on monopod. Photo by Buffalo Field Campaign.

Figure 3.28: Winter protester. Photo by Buffalo Field Campaign.

Sarah Richey, a Montana resident and advocate for buffalo, appreciates the BFC's efforts but wonders if a more "rational" and subdued approach might work better, admitting that "I'm totally impressed with their energy. I think they're in a great place to gather information . . . [but] I just don't think that they're the best messenger" (Klemz, 2008).

On one afternoon I came into the cabin from cleaning up dog waste around the camp, and started talking with a BFC leader who had just gotten off the phone with a very large environmental NGO from Washington D.C. This BFC leader was maddened by the conversation with this NGO because in its press release about the transportation of 65 buffalo to an Indian reservation, the group failed to mention that three buffalo had died during the process. "These guys are like Fox News," he said. "I told them that. I said it is incredibly important that three buffalo died! And you praised the operation? I said to them, 'you are like Fox News!'" These sorts of conflicts can hinder cooperation, and as one BFC leader explained with regard to the environmental movement, "It's time we get back to community and taking care of one another and I think these are all things the buffalo are trying to teach us . . . I've been in this movement for 25 years and I've watched things dissolve over dietary issues and one thing that I think we really try to celebrate is our diversity and respecting and honoring it in a way that we're not insulting one another in our beliefs . . . because if we'd quit fighting each other . . . we could take this country back."

Indeed, conflict between seemingly allied groups is not surprising, but what is interesting in this case is the particular sources of strife: the BFC's zero-compromise stance, spirituality, and effusive emotion. In conversations about the BFC with other local environmental groups, I've discovered that its emphasis on spirituality and direct-action tactics does not sit well in a context where environmental progress is dictated by scientific proficiency, legal strategy, political expertise, and compromise. Disapproval of the BFC comes from the other side as well—from locals, who by and large are not friendly to outsiders usually seen as alarmist and idealistic "tree-huggers" who challenge the authority of long-standing old-west institutions. Moreover, the legal authorities in these areas do not take kindly to emotionalism and civil disobedience (Figure 3.29).

Mease admitted to me that he feels this pressure from other environmental groups and from disapproving locals, explaining that "people always tell me, hey 'Buffalo Field Campaign, you're too emotional.'" But these sentiments toward the BFC are exactly what Mease thinks is wrong with environmental conflict in the GYE, pointing out that "[emotion] is exactly what we need! That is what is lacking here! . . . People write off emotion because they know if we get into their hearts, and they start thinking what they're doing is wrong, then we've won. So the more we can tell stories and get into their hearts, the better." In the midst of conflict dominated by science, these "emotional concerns can fall upon deaf ears," but Mease nevertheless believes it "is our job to make people think about this stuff." As an observer, I have found that the BFC is onto something, namely, that their infusion of unconventional beliefs and tactics into the public debate has been an

Figure 3.29: BFC activist arrested. Photo by Buffalo Field Campaign.

effective way to influence policy by bringing to the surface the deeper competing moral logics that drive the conflict over bison management in the first place.

Concluding Puzzle: Religious and Moral "Muting"

To conclude I want to reflect on an interesting sociological puzzle that I continually encountered during my research. I observed repeatedly the following contradiction concerning the BFC's most important resource, its volunteers: *BFC is a moral protest movement organization with a clear moral logic derived from commitments to indigenous religion, yet I found that BFC volunteers, who sacrifice so much to be involved, were largely unaware of, and unable to articulate their personal moral and spiritual motivations.* To be clear, let me lay out the paradox in logical form:

1. The BFC is an organization with a strong moral logic, making very clear its cultural mission and religious motivations.
2. Volunteers are attracted to, and become deeply embedded within this strong moral and religious culture, paying very high costs to participate.
3. Yet, when asked, these volunteers are either unaware of morality altogether or are dismissive of strong moral claims and religious beliefs.

Why are participants who are immersed in such a strong moral and religious culture unable to recognize, much less coherently articulate, the elements of moral and religious culture that are supposedly motivating them to incur costs to travel to a remote area, live in poverty, suffer, work for no income, protest, or get arrested? Does this mean that they are not actually motivated by moral and religious commitments? This is an important question pertaining to why some people, but not others, participate in social movements like these, especially at such high personal cost. It also relates directly to ongoing debates in sociology of culture and sociology of religion about the role of culture in action, and why individuals have such a difficult time giving consistent reasons for their behavior (Mills, 1940; Swidler, 2001; Vaisey, 2009).

Let me say what I do not intend to do in this short concluding discussion. I am not proposing a theory of culture in action, of social movement participation, nor am I under the impression that we can *fully* understand people's true motivations for doing what they do. But I do think that this case study provides an example of how people's incoherent accounts of their own behavior become obscured and muted by countervailing cultural forces, despite their behavior still being motivated by deeply held commitments about right and wrong.

Two potential, and contrasting, explanations emerged. First, what I call *belonging without believing* suggests that while BFC volunteers appear to act in ways consistent with an internalized religious culture, and can parrot certain BFC talking points, their participation is not necessarily driven by internalized values (e.g., sacredness of buffalo, spiritual value of wildness) but is more likely due to exogenous pull factors that in reality may have nothing to do with internalized motives (e.g., social networks, biographical availability, a protest "personality"). Therefore, it is no surprise that they are unable to recognize or articulate moral or religious commitments because any sort of patterned motive is absent to begin with. A different and competing explanation, which I call, somewhat paradoxically, *believing without being a "believer,"* suggests that participation is indeed motivated by moral and religious beliefs about the buffalo, but for a number of reasons volunteers' own explanations about moral and religious believing are either cognitively inaccessible or are consciously muted by more powerful, countervailing cultural commitments about what it means to be a "believer" in morality and religion. The fact that they cannot articulate a coherent account does not, however, preclude them from being motivated by the spiritual value of the buffalo and the moral responsibility to protect it. While both explanations are present, I focus my attention on the second, as I found that it more accurately describes the majority of BFC volunteers and provides an opportunity to examine how moral and religious motives bump up against, and are muted by, larger narratives and habits of talk in American life.

BELIEVING WITHOUT BEING A "BELIEVER"

BFC *leaders* like executive director Dan Brister are able to reflect clearly about what they believe and how it motivated them to give their lives to this effort: "I already knew—on some level—that I needed to be an activist and to align my life with my beliefs" (2013, p. 9). Cofounder Mike Mease describes with similar ease the motivations of the group: "We're a group of volunteers that have dropped what we're doing in life to come out and stand with these buffalo, to let them know that they are sacred and we care about them." Moreover, BFC materials such as newsletters and public releases are filled with equally coherent moral and spiritual justifications.

But to my surprise, the most critical component of the entire movement—its volunteers—could not reflect with such ease, and in fact even resisted such discussions. Why? Indeed it could be that they do not buy into such beliefs and were simply "belonging without believing." For some volunteers this was the case, but these were few. Instead, I found that to best explain this conundrum we should shift our analytic focus toward understanding with more nuance what concepts like "morality," "religion," and "believing" actually mean to volunteers. For reasons that I explore below, these concepts have acquired negative connotations for many. So despite the fact that deep down they are likely motivated by profound commitments to the buffalo (e.g., wildness, sacredness, purity), which most sociologists would agree are indeed moral and religious commitments, these commitments are muted by countervailing cultural narratives rooted in the typical BFC volunteer's white, young, middle-class, liberal, and secular background.

By "muting" I mean the conscious and unconscious dampening, obscuring, and sometimes outright rejection of claims and commitments. Muting does not, however, preclude one from actively believing in, and acting on, such commitments. In fact, I argue that despite volunteers' inability to give a coherent account of their moral and religious motivations, these are nonetheless present and active among BFC volunteers. But because of these countervailing cultural forces and habits of talk, volunteers are not well equipped to make a reasoned and logical explanation of their moral and spiritual commitments. I consider two similar, but distinct, forms of muting that emerged during my analysis: religious and moral.

RELIGIOUS MUTING: SPIRITUALITY WITHOUT ALL THE RELIGION

During the late 1980s and 1990s, conservative religion in the United States became more closely linked with conservative politics, through powerful groups like the Moral Majority, culminating in the rise of the "Religious Right." Hout and Fischer (2002) argue that this alliance felt uneasy for many moderate and liberal Americans and was a major factor leading to a rise in Americans checking "none" in surveys of religious preference. This research shows that the rise in religious "nones" is largely made up of people who still believe, but choose not to be associated with what they perceive to be a hijacked and politicized version of religion. It became very clear to me during my field research that this version of "religion"—synonymous with the religious right, environmental destruction, GOP, violence, intolerance, and discrimination—colored conversations about religion with BFC volunteers.

On one particularly slow afternoon of patrol, four of us sat by the highway, watching for buffalo and engaging in a favorite pastime of these three BFC volunteers: listening to—and mocking—conservative talk radio. "There's so much fucking morality and religion on these crazy conservative radio stations, it makes me sick," bellowed Jack from the back seat of the Subaru. "No shit," moaned Pike, "but I can't get enough of it, turn it up." As we sat and listened, it was clear that "morality" and "religion" as Jack and Pike understood it, were synonymous with the far-right neoconservatism gushing from the A.M. airwaves. BFC volunteers had a difficult time distinguishing between different forms and expressions of "religion," as their perceptions were so heavily skewed by the developments within American politics during the 1980s and 1990s. Religion was not something they did. Or, as one long-time volunteer explained to me, "You know, its just that any form of religion scares people nowadays... I'm very apprehensive about any kind of organized religion."

The feeling that they ought to mute and distance themselves from this perceived version of religion created a complicated relationship with the BFC's own commitment to native religious beliefs and practices. On one hand, volunteers are more comfortable with native forms of religion because they emphasize "spirituality," a concept that is much more comfortable, and even attractive to BFC volunteers who, like many young (white, middle-class, liberal) people in America, tended to classify themselves to me as "spiritual but not religious" (Roof, 1999). Moreover, this move away from organized religion pushes people into a spiritual marketplace where, as seekers, they pull from different sources and traditions. In this case, volunteers pull from native spirituality, blending it with their commitments to their own "spiritual" view of nature. Thus, volunteers could comfortably use particular spiritual talking points about the sacredness of the buffalo, or tell native stories, poems, and songs—as we did after every nightly meeting—that would often have spiritual dimensions, stirring emotions, and bringing many to tears. On the other hand, this adopted form of native "spirituality" was often so vague and open to self-interpretation that it bordered on meaningless and, at worst, was an idealized and patronizing appropriation of native religion by white, young, middle-class, and ostensibly secular volunteers. One BFC leader told me that he warns young environmentalists to remain sober in their seeking of these idealized forms of native spirituality, because they easily fall under the "spell believing that 'oh, all natives are great. Their religions are great and pure'. But they are human too, and there's just as many fuck-ups in natives as we have fuck-ups in white people. So when you idolize people and their faith, you're gonna get burned."

BFC executive director Dan Brister gives some insight into religious muting with a story highlighting BFC volunteers' discomfort when these nebulous and idealized forms of native spirituality materialized into concrete and communal religious practices. After a particular rough day where six buffalo were killed by the Department of Livestock, BFC co-founder Rosalie Little Thunder recommended that everyone go outside as a group and form a prayer circle. Brister explained that "volunteers were uneasy with the idea of an organized prayer circle," especially for "middle-class white kids reared in the materialism of our culture" (Brister, 2013, p.48). At this point, the native spirituality that had for many volunteers been a vague source of justification for their beliefs about the sacredness of buffalo was abruptly put into concrete religious practice. Many volunteers at first objected, feeling uncomfortable with such overt religious ritual. These knee-jerk rejections gave way, however, as Brister describes, "Rosalie's suggestion and her offer to lead the prayer were greeted with downcast eyes and silence. In the end, though, even those who had initially been opposed to the idea came outside and joined hands." Circled around the cabin, as the sun sank low behind the towering Madison Range, every volunteer said a prayer out loud. Below are a sample of three different volunteers' prayers for forgiveness, strength, and the courage to evangelize the world about buffalo injustice:

> May we be more effective next time in protecting the buffalo. Let them one day walk where they choose without being harassed for crossing meaningless lines that they cannot see.

> Help us forgive the men who pull the trigger out of ignorance, sending the buffalo to their needless deaths. Forgive the one we met in the snow who taunted us with his proud boasts of having killed so many.

> Please help us share the buffalo's story with the world, with clear and strong voices. Give us the courage to face the trials of many winters and the strength to stand beside the buffalo until they are free.

After all volunteers had spoken prayers, many were in tears, and Brister explained that despite the initial discomfort with religious practice, "The prayer ceremony was an introduction to a different possibility... it helped us connect with the buffalo in a more meaningful way."

This story exemplifies the complicated relationship BFC volunteers have with religion. Mease, who is aware of his organization's paradox, explains that "you have to remember, that a lot of these people grew up in white neighborhoods and aren't comfortable [with religion]." There is a sense that even at the BFC, volunteers treat religion as a taboo topic not discussed publicly—just as they might mute politics and religion back home with friends and coworkers.

That volunteers may be "apprehensive... and have different feelings about the ways that they choose to mourn or pray" does not, in Mease's eyes, mean that they are not fully committed to the BFC's ideals. So while they believe in the cause of the BFC enough to sacrifice their lives for an animal that they take to be deeply meaningful, they nevertheless have difficulty coming to terms with, and talking about, the fact that they are indeed participants in a moral protest movement motivated by religious commitments. And while this was evident in my conversations with volunteers about morality and religion, it was especially visible when they were confronted with overt and public religious group practices, when they could no longer hide their commitments within a vague and idealized form of native spirituality. But like the story of the prayer ceremony, with enough scratching beneath the pervasive impulse to mute religion, one can, like Rosalie Little Thunder, uncover the deep spiritual meanings and commitments that led many of these people to volunteer in the first place.

MORAL MUTING: RELATIVISM AND INDIVIDUALISM

Volunteers often waffle between a prereflective gut reaction of moral outrage about how the buffalo are treated and cooler, more rational responses that tend to relativize and mute moral claims. For example, one afternoon while Leyna and I watched videos from hazing operations in the field, she blurted with disgust, "Ugh, I remember the first time I saw that helicopter over the bison. It was like a conversion experience. It was shocking, and I was like 'how in the hell can anyone think this is not wrong?' "

But during more relaxed conversations—driving to town, over coffee, or doing dishes, *I found that volunteers were more guarded with their strong moral claims about right or wrong, and instead relied on culturally appropriate language that individualized and relativized their own perspective.* In doing so, they would go to great lengths to mute strong truth claims. For example, the next day, Leyna and I discussed whether the DOL hazing was in a real sense "morally wrong." She reflected for a moment, and observed, "I mean, I wouldn't say it was 'wrong' per se, because I feel like it's their norms, from *their own perspective.* I obviously disagree with hazing, but that's just because I was raised to care for the environment."

I had countless conversations that proceeded in similar fashion, where volunteers were either dumbfounded about strong claims to right and wrong, or would relativize their view with phrases like "I feel like from my own background... " or "I'm not one to judge the ranchers" or "From my perspective." My claim here is not that these volunteers are moral relativists—indeed, I have demonstrated quite the opposite throughout this chapter, and shown how their commitments have led to successful moral protest. Their slower and more deliberate responses were incoherent and contradictory because strong moral claims are dampened by habits of talk that are part of larger cultural narratives of relativism and individualism. In other words, the volunteers who *talk like* card-carrying moral relativists are the same individuals who are enduring 40-degree below zero conditions, living in poverty, getting arrested, and forgoing the perks of a comfortable middle-class life.

Just as the influence of relativism and individualism complicates BFC volunteers' accounts of their own behavior, it can complicate *the moral beliefs themselves*. In conversations with volunteers I often asked why buffalo are "sacred." For many volunteers, sacredness is in the eye of the beholder, not a natural or universal trait inherent to the buffalo. But BFC leaders like Mease, Brister, and Rosalie Little Thunder rely on a more stable definition of sacredness that is linked to native spirituality, and Mease explained to me that while most volunteers are motivated by a core belief that the buffalo are sacred, the reasons for this sacredness vary greatly:

> Well, I think all volunteers have *their own feeling* of why they're sacred, or they wouldn't have dropped everything in their life to come here and volunteer to be part of this campaign. But just because they don't pray the way others pray *doesn't mean they don't think they're sacred*. Doesn't mean that they don't have their own way of honoring them, and that's what we're about. Not saying that there's only this way, and the native way to honor these buffalo. There's your own way and so that's what I think is very important. I think for natives to understand that too, that look, we're a very mutt oriented people that come from all over the globe, that you know are mixed with Germans, and English, and you know whatever, and we're still trying to find our own roots and our own culture. That doesn't necessarily mean that it's your culture, you know. And so that's the beauty of it is bringing people from all walks of life here to unite for one cause, the buffalo, and learn about all the different perspectives in that time.

Volunteers are careful not to make claims that favor their perspective over another individual's perspective. They talk about the sources of their moral claims—such as sacredness—in deeply personal, emotive, and individualized ways. This is especially important because with regard to the environment and the buffalo, an individual's moral education often happens through personal experiences in nature.

For example, in describing his moral education, one volunteer explained to me that a person does not learn about sacredness through instruction or in a book, but "in nature, because here [in nature] what things mean is what they mean *to you*." In response to a similar question a few days later, a different volunteer concluded that "out here you get a lot of your education by having experiences with the buffalo and then *interpreting what they mean to you*." Moral meaning and moral education is a process of individual self-discovery and exploration. Thus, moral muting occurs because volunteers hesitate to force their own individual experience on others who may have had different life experiences and thus learned different moral lessons.

There were counterexamples, however, like volunteers such as Neil, a 25 year old, who came to the BFC from his Native American community in Minnesota. Neil was a spiritual leader in training for his tribe, and being bound to this community meant that he came to the BFC with a clear purpose and could articulate his motivations with ease and clarity, "Being a Native American, I came here to protect my relatives." He continues, "We have a contract between the buffalo and my people. They are relatives, and they are being treated wrongly." On a warmer afternoon as the snow started to soften, we sloshed along on cross-country skis for what seemed like an entire day, and for two and a half hours Neil described in great detail his religious traditions. As we went along, Neil was collecting buffalo hairballs to take back to his elders, frequently stopping to pray along the way. Another volunteer with us, who was normally very talkative, became visibly intimidated and abruptly silent as Neil and I talked explicitly about his religious commitments, and as Neil stopped to engage in his religious rituals. "Protecting the buffalo is a spiritual experience for me" he said, "It's something I can't really explain, it's sort of beyond words, I guess." After seeing videos on the BFC's website and reading more about the issue, Neil said "I knew I had to come do something to protect my relatives. What [outsiders] are doing is wrong, and needs to be stopped. My relatives deserve to roam free, as they have since the beginning of creation." As part of an organized religious community, Neil had a clear set of cultural resources upon which to draw when talking about why the buffalo are sacred, and he could articulate with ease strong moral claims rooted in his religious beliefs. While many of the other activists hold roughly similar moral convictions about the buffalo, Neil could provide a clearer account of his behavior because his own reasoning about his actions were not as susceptible to the strong cultural winds, and habits of talk, characteristic of religious muting and moral relativism.

Conclusion

The analysis above shows that, despite the fact that many hot-button issues in the GYE are subsumed by intractable biological, ecological, or economic disputes, the infusion of moral and religious meaning can disrupt the technorational status quo and bring to the surface nonmaterial and nontechnical evidence that can influence policy. I have demonstrated that the BFC, through its clear moral logic and in its aggressive (and controversial) form of moral protest, has indeed shaken up the intractability of this long-lasting conflict, by clearly and emphatically making the issue a matter of moral and spiritual obligation. In addition to this empirical and substantive argument that the BFC has been successful because it has brought the moral and spiritual logic of the issue to the fore, I also use this case to argue that these deeper commitments can, for many volunteers, come under the control of larger cultural narratives about American religion, moral relativism, and individualism. This, I argue, results in a moral and religious muting, and can complicate activists' relationship with native religion. This process of muting, while sometimes suppressing and making it difficult to observe moral boundaries, does not, nevertheless, abolish the deep commitments guiding activists to sacrifice their lives protecting the purity and sacred legacy of America's last remaining buffalo herd.

4. Between Good and Evil: The Science, Culture, and Polarization of Wolf Conflict

On January 12, 1995, at the iconic northern entrance of Yellowstone Park, President Clinton's secretary of the interior, Bruce Babbitt, proclaimed a triumph of modern conservation biology to hundreds of fervent spectators and national news media: "This is a day of *redemption* and a day of *hope*... we're showing our children that restoration is possible, that we can restore a community to its natural state" (Fischer, 1995, p. 161). Babbitt was referring to the reintroduction to Yellowstone Park of 31 wolves, an animal that once numbered over 2 million (Madonna, 1994) but by 1930 was exterminated from the Rocky Mountains and nearly all of the contiguous United States—a systematic effort fully supported at the time by the U.S. government, wildlife biologists, and even most conservationists.

As the story goes, the long road to reintroduction in 1995 was the result of 20 years of careful scientific research about the wolf and its complex relationship to ecosystems. Biologists expanded our horizons about the animal itself, moving us beyond irrational folk knowledge, superstition, fear, and hatred, toward more logical and scientific knowledge about taxonomies, physical characteristics, pack organization, mortality, and dispersal patterns. Similarly, the science of ecology expanded our knowledge about how the wolf impacted the environments in which it lived, again dispelling myths about the animal, in favor of new scientific knowledge about its positive role in ecosystems as an apex predator. With this new knowledge, a growing belief among biologists, ecologists, managers, and environmentalists emerged that without the wolf, the Yellowstone ecosystem was biologically "incomplete." Managers were under a legal directive to use the best available science in the management of our nation's natural resources, and scientific evidence demanded the wolf's return. The wolf was *the* missing *ecological link* that could make one of the world's last and largest ecosystems *biologically whole* again. At the same time, however, there was vitriolic opposition that marshaled its own broad base of scientific research. Anti-wolf advocates used their own ecological and biological expertise to combat "phony zealot biology," arguing that wolf reintroduction would be harmful to other wildlife, and to human communities around Yellowstone. They focused most intently on population models that forecasted many detrimental effects of wolf predation on the northern range elk herd. This natural science was supplemented by complex economic research that warned of the costs of wolf reintroduction for local GYE ranchers, whose cattle would likely become a target of prey for wolves.

Wolves were eventually reintroduced in 1995, but only after nearly two decades of intense social strife—easily the most bitter and long-lasting conflict in GYE history. Conflict between these two warring sides involved 120 acrimonious public hearings, more than 160,000 public comments, bomb threats, executive directives from six U.S. presidents, debates by dozens of congressional committees—costing $12 million for scientific research alone (USFWS, 1994; Wilson, 1997).

The eventual restoration of wolves also brought little resolution to these scientific and technical disagreements. Instead, it poured gasoline on a fire of social conflict that continues to blaze today. The two highly polarized sides in the conflict continue to develop new scientific knowledge to use as ammunition in a war that, on the face of it, concerns objective facts. Anti-wolf groups point to the exorbitant costs of reintroduction, the ecology of a declining elk population, and the financial costs to area cattle ranchers. Pro-wolf interests, with the help of ecologists and biologists, churn out masses of scientific research papers to justify the wolf reintroduction, by showing the positive environmental effects of wolf recovery on the Yellowstone ecosystem: how wolves regulate prey numbers, regenerate aspen and willow trees, improve habitats for dozens of other species, promote stream bank recovery, reduce disease transmission, improve water quality, and so on (Mech, 2012).

My broader objective in this chapter is to understand the causes of this conflict. *Why, with all of this political, legal, and technical energy and expertise, did this conflict escalate to such heights, and why does it still remain so intractable today?* My main argument is that within this complex institutional context (e.g., bureaucratic, legal, academic, economic, scientific), the deeper cultural, moral, and spiritual motives of each camp were knowingly, and unknowingly, pushed beneath the surface of the policy debate. Because these deeper cultural commitments remain beneath the policy-making surface, the debate over wolves became—for those involved—about the scientific facts of the issue, rather than the presuppositional starting points in which different groups place their trust in the first place. I have argued throughout this book that these presuppositional cultural starting points can make all the difference, and by displacing them, these groups are merely fighting at the outskirts of the deeper differences themselves. Thus, the issue is gridlocked, in large part because opposing stakeholders persistently, and somewhat obsessively, marshal abstract, analytical, rational evidence, despite the fact that this evidence is meaningful only within the context of these underlying (and incommensurable) beliefs about nature and humanity.

There are two basic parts to my argument. The first is that deeper, and identifiable, cultural codes structure and motivate each side of the conflict. The second is that these cultural mechanisms went unrecognized, were ignored, or were actively suppressed beneath the technorational institutions charged with policy making. I focus in this chapter almost exclusively on the first part. My reasons for doing so are largely theoretical. There is an immense body of work spanning sociology, philosophy, history, and religious studies about the processes of disenchantment and rationalization, and Western institutions' post-Enlightenment attempt to deal with nonrational aspects of human behavior (e.g., values, religion, emotion, and other features of culture). These questions have been explored, in different ways, in the work of intellectual giants like Marx, Weber, Durkheim, Habermas, and Rawls. They are especially relevant here pertaining to questions about the inclusion (or suppression) of moral and spiritual arguments in democratic deliberation, and the bureaucratic and legal aspects of policy making more generally. Indeed, one might examine how wolf activists deliberately suppress explicit appeals to spirituality in bureaucratic or legal contexts, out of fear that such nonscientific appeals will be less effective or, worse, seen as absurd (e.g., see Shields (2009) on the Christian Right). For example, some anti-wolf advocates described to me how they were "coached to suppress emotion and properly follow the steps of administrative law." These sorts of institutional pressures intensified with the development of ecology in the 20th century—a scientific field that provided environmental institutions with a much-desired objective measuring stick for making policy (see chapter 1 for more on this historical development of the "biocentric" worldview). This had an effect on which arguments were now seen as valid (e.g., ecology, biology) and which were no longer authoritative (e.g., romanticism, spirituality), without the necessary scientific evidence. Indeed, I examine below how pro-wolf advocates still deploy moral and spiritual claims within the hyperscientific context of the wolf policy debate—but while interesting and important, this analytical approach is not the main focus of the chapter.

Instead, I contend that, just as important to understanding how aspects of culture are received and affected by technorational institutions, is understanding the elements of culture *themselves*. This relates to the first part of my argument above. Thus, my focus here is more narrow, in that I rigorously investigate the moral order of anti-wolf and pro-wolf stakeholders, seeking to uncover and understand the moral and spiritual commitments themselves, rather than the processes by which they are influenced by the legal and bureaucratic processes of environmental management. This approach has received far less attention, in part because, as members of modern society, actors and observers often fail to recognize or ignore these deeper cultural dimensions, and secondly, because a rigorous, in-depth analysis of moral order and boundary making "in the wild"

(Hitlin and Vaisey, 2010) can require researchers to devote considerable time and effort moving beneath the findings of large-scale surveys and experimental laboratories, toward the messy ground-level complexities, in order to uncover the more subtle social structures and codes shaping what people find sacred, good, and meaningful in life at a most basic level.

With this approach in mind, we must step back from this conflict and return to the questions posed above about what ultimately propels the obsessive flood of scientific research on the wolf issue. Is it about the honest effort—on both sides—to build new knowledge about wolves and ecosystems? Maybe so. But this exclusive, surface-level focus on scientific knowledge obscures deeper, and potentially more interesting and important questions: *How do we decide what is worth researching in the first place? What facts are worth knowing, and why do they matter?* These basic, and *prescientific*, decisions about what is worth studying (and why) are not instrumentally rational, but concern at a deeper level *morality*—what we find truly good and why. What seems worth studying, what scientific knowledge is relevant, and why we should spend millions researching this but not that—these questions are propelled by deeper starting-point desires, beliefs, and commitments about the innermost sense of who we are, why we are, what we want, and how we should act. That is, why should we care about the survival of wolves in the first place? Are humans part of nature or above it? Does "untamed" nature have any sacred or intrinsic value, beyond its instrumental utility for humans? And why should we prefer a biologically whole ecosystem to an incomplete or less natural one? The foundational faith in a set of beliefs— that a healthy ecosystem is better than an unhealthy ecosystem; that there is a natural hierarchy of human dominionism over nature—is the *cultural* basis from which all these scientific, political, and legal efforts are generated and sustained. They inform what is worth fighting for in the first place, and thus this interminable conflict is not, as it would appear, entirely about practically rational or factually scientific matters, but it is about basic assumptions and beliefs that themselves are often incommensurate and cannot be adjudicated with evidence from some objective or otherwise independent body of biological or economic facts.

Thus, in what follows, I set out to empirically uncover, and rigorously examine, the competing moral orders that motivate the ongoing war over the wolf in Yellowstone. In doing so, I demonstrate along the way the influence of moral commitments, and the drawing of moral boundaries by these polarized factions. As I describe in the introductory chapter, who we humans are, and what we want, is not universal, but is socially constructed from alternative narratives and sets of desires, beliefs, and moral commitments. This explains why, as one Wyoming rancher told me, "Wolves are much more than an animal; they are a powerful symbol of wildness for some, and evil for others." Recognizing that this is an extremely polarized issue, I split my empirical analysis into two separate parts, focusing first on the shared moral order of anti-wolf advocates, and second on the shared moral order of pro-wolf advocates. By separating these two groups, I am able to focus in more detail on the ways in which each relies on socially constructed views of the wolf, nature, and humanity. My analysis concentrates on "protest discourse" about the wolf issue, by which I mean "explicit criticism of other people, organizations, and the things they believe or do" (Jasper, 1997, p. 5).

These data include discourse from local town hall meetings, public rallies and protests, transcripts of partisan documentary films, culturally meaningful images, meeting transcripts, newsletters, and nearly 11,000 public letters written to the U.S. Fish and Wildlife Service. While the pro-wolf analysis relies more on these public letters (because the pro-wolf movement is more national in scope), both sections draw heavily from ethnographic fieldwork and in-person interviews I conducted between 2011 and 2013.[1] I use these data to sketch the moral order of each side, identifying and classifying major sets of moral commitments that are embedded within different cultural narratives, and showing how groups bring them to bear on the conflict by drawing moral and spiritual boundaries.

Uncovering the Anti-Wolf Moral Order

Early American hatred of the wolf was part of a social context where utilitarian meanings about nature and the instrumental value of wildlife was stable and widely shared. The wolf was primarily an economic threat as a predator of livestock and a competitor with early hunters and trappers for big game. Extirpation of the wolf from the American West, then, was primarily motivated by economic interest. There was even agreement among government leaders (including President Theodore Roosevelt), conservationists, and leading wolf biologists that the wolf was "a menace to human life" (Mech, 2012). But times have changed. With the arrival of the new-west economy, the GYE has seen the decline of ranching (see chapter 2). *Thus, in real economic terms, the wolf today does not pose the economic threat to the Western economy it once did.* Nevertheless, most academics, journalists, and stakeholders involved in the conflict still rely heavily on this economic theory to explain why the conflict persists.

I contend, however, that even though economic arguments have been central in the surface-level debates over reintroduction and subsequent management of wolves (e.g., USFWS 1994), they mask deeper, more determinative, cultural meanings and motivations. One good indicator of this is the fact that alleviating economic concerns *has not* changed anti-wolf attitudes. Consider that in the final report leading to wolf reintroduction, the USFWS cites research asking

---

1 See the appendix for more information about the data and methods used in this chapter.

ranchers whether they would change their mind about wolves if certain financial conditions were met (e.g., if ranchers were compensated financially for livestock losses, keeping livestock losses to less than 1 percent, and containing wolves in the park and surrounding wilderness areas), concluding that "most respondents who do not favor reintroducing the wolf would not change their opinion regardless of the [financial] options presented to them" (Bath 1989 quoted in USFWS 1994, p. 358). Some ranchers even refused financial compensation after wolves killed their cattle, claiming they were motivated "for principle's sake," and viewed compensation as a tool used by environmentalists to pacify deeper cultural objections ranchers had to the wolf (Urbigkit, 2008, p. 277).

In an interview about the economic threat wolves pose to ranching, I spoke with one prominent rancher from Sublette County who vowed that he and his anti-wolf allies would continue to fight, but that economic interest had little to do with the reasons why:

> The majority of ranchers are not willing to give up the fight [against wolves]. People have a lot more reason for being involved in agriculture in the West than the economic benefits offered by it. As you know, their private ground, and ranches, are sometimes worth millions of dollars, and yet they scrape by, operating within a narrow margin on their yearly income from livestock grazing. They could easily sell and be instantly wealthy. But it's their love of the land, and love for this western landscape that keeps them going.

What's more, many people associated with the anti-wolf movement are not ranchers, and are not at all financially burdened by wolf reintroduction. Ed Bangs, the head of wolf reintroduction for the USFWS, puzzled at the rancorous reactions to the wolf, given its small negative economic impact, commenting that "the remarkable attention that people give wolves is particularly striking given the minor impact wolves have on the physical lives of modern people" (Nie, 2003, p. 110). Yet despite all of this, the central surface-level (bureaucratic and legal) argument from anti-wolf advocates is still an economic one: wolves are hated because they threaten the livelihood of ranchers. But again, to give a sense of the actual minimal economic impact, consider that between 1996 and 2006, the average annual compensation for all wolf livestock kills totaled only $27,000 (Duffield et al., 2006). Then compare this sum to the revenue wolves have brought to the regional economy, when visitors from outside the GYE who come specifically to see wolves spend $35.5 million additional dollars *annually* (Duffield et al., 2006). Anti-wolf advocates' perceived economic interests are a relevant piece of the puzzle, and I do not deny the costs incurred by some ranchers in the region. But in the bigger-picture conflict, these costs are minimal, and thus it is not surprising that economic "compensation has not reduced the intensity of the conflict over wolf reintroduction ... [and] has not stopped the development of an entire industry of anti-wolf activists in the region" (McBeth and Shanahan, 2004, p. 323).

Table 4.1: The Moral Order of Anti-Wolf Opposition.

Rugged American Individualism
Antifederalism
Private property rights
Ecological "outsiders"

Human Dominionism
Theological authority
Natural hierarchy
Misanthropy
Fear and hatred

Simple and Sacred Heritage
Sacralizing work
Recreation practices
Distrust of outsiders
Lived knowledge

Something more profound is going on. Looking closer and digging deeper, I found that anti-wolf discourse about reintroduction actually has little to do with economic interest and much more to do with the ways that the wolf—and the symbolic politics of reintroduction—violates the boundaries of an anti-wolf moral order. For many people in the GYE, wolves have become a symbol of deeper cultural anxieties, threatening three main pillars of a weakening old-west moral order which I define as *rugged American individualism, human dominionism,* and *simple and sacred heritage.* In what follows I empirically describe and explain how the elements of this moral order are derived from larger contextualizing narratives, and how its beliefs, commitments, and desires give moral meaning to the conflict and propel anti-wolf politics. Table 4.1 outlines the contents of this moral order and provides the framework for the analytical description and explanation that follow.

Rugged American Individualism

Remember my theoretical approach, which observes that the substance of our most important human beliefs and moral orders derives from narratives in which our lives are embedded. These fundamental stories tell us what is significant, who we are, why we exist, what we do and should want, and why it all matters. Three particularly important—and overlapping—narratives emerged in my research (table 4.1 above). They serve to organize more specific elements of resistance toward the wolf. The first is the *rugged American individualism* narrative that goes something like this:

> Once upon a time early Americans living in the East dreamed beyond their immediate horizons, looking West in hopes of gaining private property and carving out new lives far from urban congestion and federal government influence, where the ideals of liberty and self-sufficiency could be enjoyed. Countless pioneering individuals blazed their own trail westward, settling rough-hewn landscapes. Against all odds they bravely succeeded through individual will, perseverance, with limited government interference and holding fast to their private property rights. But now the federal government and its out-of-touch environmentalist allies threaten this progress by imposing heavy-handed restrictions, locking up public lands, trampling on private property rights, and violating states' rights. All westerners should remain vigilant in their opposition against these ideologies and actions that further threaten the legacy of liberty, private property, individual conscience, and local control of private and public lands.

The rugged American individualism narrative involves three key substances: antifederalism, private property rights, and ecological "outsiders."

ANTIFEDERALISM

By "antifederalism" I mean a strong aversion among anti-wolf advocates to the imposition of federal laws and policies from outside the GYE, by federal agencies such as the USFWS, the National Park Service, and far-off "DC" judges who rule from thousands of miles away. Antifederalism has profoundly shaped the dominant culture of the American West, and is an important frame giving meaning to the wolf issue. The wolf is a political symbol that challenges these most sacred beliefs, desires, and commitments. As one prominent anti-wolf advocate remarked about the wolf debate, "This is a battle for every *believing* patriot to be engaged in." Because a federal agency (USFWS) was responsible for planning and carrying out wolf reintroduction, the wolf itself became a political symbol representing the threats of federal power. Two GYE environmentalists I spoke with reflected on the symbolic nature of wolves, separately remarking:

> Looking at wolves, they see the federal government. It is one and the same.

> It's a surrogate for the feds. Its a symbol of government intrusion.

Anti-wolf advocates talked frequently about feeling like they are under siege from the federal government, commonly referring to the animal as "federal wolves" to reinforce the idea that reintroduced wolves are the imposition of an overbearing U.S. government. Four representative quotes from anti-wolf residents, from speeches at anti-wolf rallies in 2011 in Montana and Wyoming,

Figure 4.1: Anti-wolf protest in Jackson Hole, WY. *Sign 1*: "Feds are trampling on states rights." *Sign 2*: "Delist Wolves Now!" Photo by Rebecca Watters.

for example, along with Figure 4.1, express how this played out in the midst of public protest:

> The intent from Ed Bangs [USFWS manager of reintroduction] from the very beginning was to shove these wolves down our throat. Here it is Idaho, Montana, Wyoming, you're going to have this wolf and whether or not you like it, it doesn't matter. That was their agenda.
>
> When people come to me and they give me their wolf story—and everybody's got a wolf story across this country—each story is the scariest and each one is proof positive that the federal government really believes that they can intervene in every avenue of our lives and control us 24/7.
>
> So we have an issue here that basically does pit county, state, federal government. It's a triangle of turmoil. This is the time, this is the place, for a [local] sheriff, if any sheriff was ever going to really take a stand, and uphold his duty, this is the time and place to do it.
>
> The government has no right to come in. Wolves are government-sponsored terrorists.

After viewing a 2011 anti-wolf documentary film about the wolf reintroduction, viewers had an opportunity to respond to express their feelings about the wolf issue. These two quotes are representative of how many viewers voiced their concern:

> Just as so many issues are federal usurpation of states rights, so is this farce of wolf reintroduction. We need state government with the backbone to stand up for us.
>
> We need to stand up for our rights and our heritage Montana, and stop being pushed around by D.C. and corrupt environmental groups!

This connection between antifederalism and wolves extends beyond environmental policy, becoming for many politicians in the GYE an opportunity to link the issue with larger hot-button issues in national politics. In the spring of 2011, for example, a gubernatorial candidate in Montana, Robert Fanning Jr., made the wolf issue central to his campaign platform, leveraging it to link the federal government with concerns about social class warfare:

> We are in a crisis situation... I am not proud of the fact that food for poor people was fed to wolves. I am not proud that the United States government was targeting the middle class, ranchers, and hunters—and actively trying to violate their civil and constitutional rights. So if you agree with me, today is the day that you decide to make a difference with your life, and please, to become active in this or in whatever you think is necessary to preserve this great country that is in a time of trouble.

The link between a commitment to antifederalism and wolves was stated most clearly by one rancher I spoke with, who lives just south of Yellowstone. She said that she, and a lot of her friends and family who hate wolves, "see them as more of a symbol than a reality. For a lot of us, they symbolize the federal government."

PRIVATE PROPERTY RIGHTS

The government "invasion" of the wolf also threatens sacred boundaries around public and private property. Because wolves do not adhere to the boundaries of designated areas like Yellowstone Park, they often venture onto private land in search of food. When wolves were first released, federal regulations forbade landowners to kill a wolf even when it came onto their own private property (these regulations have since been loosened in all three states). In addition to feeling helpless in the symbolic defense of sacred ideals about autonomy, self-control, and private ownership of land, many private landowners felt helpless to defend their property and their families. The leader of a powerful anti-wolf coalition described to me in an interview that the wolf is used as a "bioweapon," contending that "with stolen money and collusion, this is a criminal conspiracy by government officials to attack the Fifth Amendment rights of 30,000 ranchers... these zealots are using the wolf as a bioweapon!" He continued, raising his voice in frustration:

This is a conspiracy where the government is going after a specific group of Americans, and going to destroy their private property rights, and use wolves as a bioweapon to achieve their political ends. This is not biology you're talking about. This is political strategy.

These feelings were also viscerally expressed publicly in town hall meetings and public comments about the issue:

We're prisoners on our own property because I can't go out there and take care of the problem.

I need help ... I need protection for my family, for myself and for the property I'm entrusted to take care of.

The time to stop the destruction caused by wolves is long passed. The federal government must return control of state resources to Wyoming where it rightfully belongs ... If we don't have the right to protect ourselves and our property then we have no rights. A government that outlaws the inherent right of self-defense and the right to protect our property is a government that has overstepped its authority. The people of Wyoming must be granted permanent control of the wolf now.

NO PROPERTY RIGHTS AND CONTROL!! Like the rancher said we might as well be in Russia or China!! GOD HAS NOT GIVEN US A SPIRIT OF FEAR. 2 TIMOTHY 1:7. It is time we take a stand against tyranny! When you place animal rights over Human rights, something is badly wrong.

All will have to stand before God one day to be judged of their works and how they treated others. Boy am I happy that I was not involved is this ever so wrong act that infringed upon the rights and privileges of the people, landowners, and once stewards of these states. The damage will never be made up in many generations to come.

The statement about this not being about the wolves is correct, it is about our government taking away our rights once again.

There is a sense among many ranchers and sheepherders that wolves are simply a surrogate issue to destroy private property rights and eventually remove sheep and livestock from public lands. One cattle rancher vented to me that "I absolutely am convinced that wolves are a surrogate issue for wanting to rid the public lands of livestock grazing. It's funny, because you can go on several Internet forums and see postings that will start out being about pro-wolves, and then it turns to the need to get rid of the range maggots [cattle and sheep]." Another rancher from Montana expressed frustration that "wolves are being used to help accomplish the goals of environmentalists to restrict rights ... this has absolutely happened already, even though the planning process for wolves did not call for that at all!" Still another rancher and local community leader from Montana told me proudly: "I will stand on national TV and state that there is no other human being in the USA that has a greater understanding and knowledge of the wolf reintroduction programs than I do, and I will state that the wolf is used as a weapon to destroy the American peoples' rights. At the end of the day, it's about Machiavellian intent, it's about controlling our rights!"

ECOLOGICAL "OUTSIDERS"

Anti-wolf advocates blend deeply held commitments to antifederalism and private property rights with scientific arguments about the origins, characteristics, and taxonomy of reintroduced wolves. I call this the "ecological outsider" argument. Because wolves were extirpated from most of the United States by 1930, the U.S. government purchased wolves from the Canadian government for reintroduction. These are, in strict terms, nonnative wolves. Thus, according to this view, not only has the federal government forced wolves down the ranchers' throats, but even worse, it did so with nonnative, "immigrant" wolves. As one rancher describes it to me, with a great deal of frustration in his voice:

This is the perfect role model for federal government shoving something down the throats of local people. Rather then letting nature take its course, or helping nature along in a certain direction, it was actually, you know, go to Canada, capture some wolves and then plop them down in Yellowstone, and that was not nature, that was the feds.

The fact that these wolves were from Canada exacerbates the feeling that they were, as several anti-wolf advocates described to me, "dumped on us from the outside," "plopped down on our landscape," and "shoved down our throats." Foreign wolves do not sit well with many westerners who, along with having suspicion of the federal government, also have deep suspicions of outsiders in general. Anti-wolf advocates routinely expressed these views, both privately (to me) and publicly at protests:

They're a nonnative species… It was never native to this area, so they were right from the outset and the ruling in Wyoming will probably create a lot of tensions between the two judges and just continue the politics of this whole fight and we need to stop that, we don't need to manage these wolves, we need to remove them.

The point of it is, this wolf was dumped on us. The original wolf that was here, the one that I told you I had the study on from 1984 that these guys had actual numbers and accounts of in Central Idaho. We didn't have a problem with that wolf.

The first violation of the Lacey Act, wolves were imported illegally into the United States and they were purchased with stolen money.

I'd love to let polar bears go in Golden Gate state park except they would be non-native and defeat the purpose of reintroduction. I do know that

Figure 4.2: Anti-wolf protest. *Signs:* "This is our state we decide!" "Thank You U.S.F.W.S.: Non-Native Canadian Wolves." Source: Toby Bridges, Lobo Watch.

Washington D.C. was built on filled-in swamps, should we bring back malaria? It was there first!

Human Dominionism

Narratives often tell us about the supposed natural order of things—about our natural capacities, and where such capacities place us in relation to other living things. In my observation, interviews, and discourse-analysis, I found a *human dominionism* narrative shaping the beliefs, commitments, and desires of anti-wolf advocates. It runs something like this:

Long ago, humans were created with the physical and mental capacities to rule over the rest of nature. This natural hierarchy guides humanity's ethical relationship to the environment. Because humans are at the top of this natural hierarchy, they have a greater right to exist and flourish than do plants and nonhuman animals. As Americans moved westward in pursuit of prosperity and the spread of liberty, they exercised their natural capacity, right, and duty to modify nature to suit their needs. Through adversity, hard work, and human ingenuity, our western forebears wrestled unyielding landscapes into submission and bravely destroyed nonhuman threats—like wolves—that terrorized human enterprise and control. There are plenty of natural resources left for us to use, and access to these resources on public lands should be expanded. Nevertheless, antihuman beliefs and policies have recently come to threaten human beings' status in this natural hierarchy. All who believe in the proper distinction between humans and nature—who resist pantheism and misanthropy, and labor for human progress through the wise use of natural resources—should remain vigilant and oppose these antihuman threats.

There are four related dimensions of the human dominionism narrative: theological authority, natural hierarchy, misanthropy, and fear and hatred.

THEOLOGICAL AUTHORITY

The human dominionism narrative is influenced by a certain interpretation of Protestant Christianity's emphasis on God transcending the created world, standing at a distance from a disenchanted and desacralized but usable nature. A good example of this type of interpretation is a 2011 full-length, anti-wolf documentary, *Crying Wolf*. This documentary about the Yellowstone wolf reintroduction has become influential in anti-wolf circles, winning conservative-Christian film awards. The Montana-based director was "inspired to make the film by his religious convictions," to expose the "extent and significance of the impact that wolves have on wildlife and western culture ... on shaping ways of life," and in the end it is his hope "that this [film] will be more than a movie. That it will be an awakening to the truth. The truth in environmental stewardship, the truth in government, and truth in the heart and soul" (King, 2011b). The central premise of the film is that, with the Yellowstone wolf issue, humans have strayed from the biblical mandate of "taking dominion over nature." The trailer for the film starkly frames the issues at hand:

> This nation was founded on Judeo-Christian ethics, commonly called Christianity, and if you study the Bible, the one thing you understand is that man has dominion and man has a stewardship responsibility.
>
> In an age of radical environmentalism comes a cry for dominion.
>
> Because they rejected the creator they had to worship the creature [the wolf]. [Alluding to the Book of Romans, Chapter 1]

Thus, not only does God provide humans the authority for dominionistic beliefs and practices, but, even more, God demands it. To not exercise this duty is to "reject the creator and worship the creature." In interviewing a leading anti-wolf activist, I asked, "How did you get involved in the wolf issue?" And without a pause, he shot back a surprising response, "Well, because I believe in God!" Such an outlook was also expressed, sometimes very explicitly, by other anti-wolf advocates:

> Whether people agree with it or not, we all are under the law and sovereignty of God. By His standards all things will be measured... Without this authority, without this frame of reference, then there is absolutely nothing wrong with elevating wolves, or any other animal, or any other object to a high place. If wolves are majestic, and ought to be protected, then so be it. If a pile of rocks is majestic, and ought to be protected, who is to stand in the way? However, under the logic and laws of a Christ-centered universe, man has been given responsibility and authority to dominate all the species.

> Giving Glory to God for His creation, and recognizing that He has given authority to man over all creatures ought to be commended.

> They [pro-wolf advocates] despise the rancher who would feel disgust that the government has told him that he cannot legally protect his land or livestock. These New Age Adam and Eves have fallen to the same trap that the serpent used in Genesis. They don't like God's plan that all flesh must die and want to become as gods themselves deciding what and who is good and evil outside the confines of their own hypocrisy.

> It is truly sad to see our country deteriorate and be overtaken by people who are so disconnected with reality, nature, and Christianity.

> Without a foundational belief in God, a vacuum is always created. Man will always fill that vacuum with something. That something for the progressive left is "Mother Earth." You won't find any Christians worshiping at the alter of the environment... If these folks believed in God, this whole deal is a non-existent issue. Faith isn't a "bent" on the issue, it is the core of the issue.

I found a somewhat more subdued expression of human dominionism in my conversation with a sheepherder from Montana. She described the spiritual duty she has to protect her sheep from wolves, linking it explicitly to her own purpose as a Christian:

> I think that for some people, our duty to watch over land and animals is spiritual. For me, my lifetime being a shepherd out here has deep biblical meaning to me. And that is the feeling that I have about my livestock, about my sheep and my responsibility to tend to them and to protect them from wolves. I know that my fellow ranchers, my neighbors here, have similar feelings; a cow to them is not just, you know, a certain dollar amount walking around out there.

NATURAL HIERARCHY

The human dominion narrative presupposes the existence of a natural hierarchy that is fundamental to reality. This hierarchy is often rooted in theological authority, but it need not be. It can just as well be rooted in a Darwinistic perspective about natural selection and the evolutionary capacities of humans to enforce their will on the rest of the natural world. Whether rooted in God or not, the commitment to a natural hierarchy came up frequently among anti-wolf advocates. For example, Dean Kleckner, the president of the powerful American Farm Bureau, expressed his concern over pro-wolf challenges to the "natural hierarchy" in an op-ed, arguing that "concern for wildlife *should not overshadow concern for people*. So to the Defenders of Wildlife, we admit that your distorted ads, messages and threats are disconcerting. But we are not intimidated. We'll see you in court" (Urbigkit 2008, p. 232; emphasis added). Similarly, western historian J. Frank Dobie reminds us that the wolf issue is about negotiating this hierarchical relationship between humans and wolves: "If you peeled away the layers of this onion, the core issue was clear: were people willing to share the land with a fellow predator? At one extreme, people said that human needs must come first. At the other, people held that wolves should come first" (quoted in Fischer 1995, p. 125). But concern with violating the boundaries of a natural hierarchy is summed up most clearly in a speech by a local anti-wolf leader, speaking at the 2008 Idaho Anti-Wolf Coalition meeting:

> These people [pro-wolf environmentalists] are eco, wolf-hugging terrorists. They will do anything to achieve their goal of keeping wolves here. They'll do anything. *The government and environmentalists have elevated these wolves to a godlike status!* I think the lady that I had the confrontation with probably would like an alpha male wolf as a boyfriend. And now, that may sound absurd to you but it's a factual truth.

MISANTHROPY

For many anti-wolf advocates, promoting the status of wolves in the natural hierarchy constitutes outright misanthropy—a mistrust of, and hatred for, the human species. It is a turning-of-one's-back on fellow humanity and, at its most extreme, expresses the desire for the human race to no longer exist. At a 2011 anti-wolf protest in Jackson Hole, WY, for example, a pro-wolf counterprotestor held a large sign: "Humans are the Pest" (Figure 4.3). These sorts of provocations violate anti-wolf moral boundaries and deeply held cultural commitments about the highest value of human beings. They routinely came up in conflict discourse and fieldwork conversations. For instance:

> They [environmentalists] will never be happy until humans are gone and only animals are left.
>
> *Question from man in audience*: To get back to what she asked, [is] the original reason they introduced wolves just so they could file a lot of lawsuits?
>
> *Answer from rally speaker*: Well, that's part of it. The other part is these environmentalists have this pipe dream about getting rid of all of us. [Q&A at a 2011 Freedom Action Rally.]

Figure 4.3: Argument between anti-wolf and pro-wolf advocates at anti-wolf rally in Jackson Hole, WY. Source: Scott Rockholm, Rockholm Media.

But really it's unbelievable. I've heard of liberals or environmentalists that, you know, people say that they don't care about anybody just whatever their passion cause is at the time—animal or plant or whatever—but I didn't really believe until I was almost killed by a wolf. To me they really don't care about human life. That was plain as can be through my experience, I mean just vicious. And I just hope that God softens their heart and gives them some human compassion.

I have debated against the culture of Earth First! and Animal Liberators for years. Humans are always the parasite that should be eradicated from the earth. They hate humanity.

FEAR AND HATRED

Human emotions are very good indicators of our moral assumptions, and their appearance can reveal the boundaries that form our moral orders. When these aspects of shared moral order are violated, they often elicit emotional reactions that we can use to trace back to, and identify, the moral beliefs themselves. Fear and hatred are two emotions that are particularly salient in anti-wolf moral discourse. Humans have a long history of both fear and hatred of the wolf, and these emotional reactions played an important role in its eradication (Coleman, 2004). Other than the snake, perhaps no species has elicited negative emotions quite like the wolf. But today the wolf does not seriously threaten the economic well-being or physical security of most in the American West, as it had in the past. It has morphed into a symbolic threat, challenging the reign of human mastery and control. I found that anti-wolf advocates keenly felt these emotions and, more important, knew when to use them—as their ancestors did—as a political tool to oppose and destroy the wolf.

Even though wolves do not seek out and attack humans, anti-wolf advocates recurrently tell exaggerated, fear-filled stories about the threat that wolves pose, especially to women and children. For example, in one interview, an anti-wolf advocate framed the matter as an issue of public safety:

> In Mammoth Hot Springs, there's an elementary school, and wolves literally pack up and rendezvous right above the school, and it's just amazing that this is allowed to happen. I mean, not only are the elk being decimated, now there's a public-health issue.

A woman I interviewed in Sublette County, WY, described how fear of wolves affected her family's sleeping patterns:

> There are just a lot of side effects [to having wolves]. Our general lifestyle has changed. You're just really having to be a lot more alert and wary when you're out... really watching and looking for signs. And then doing things like sleeping with your window open in the wintertime so that you can hear what happens at night... it affects your sleep patterns, for sure.

One Idaho woman told a story about her experience with wolves on her property:

> [rubbing nose and crying] I remember thinking how bad their teeth were gonna hurt. And I had a wool coat on and I was hoping that it would protect me from the bites, but in reality I knew that there's no way I could fight four wolves. I just remember praying to God that it would go quick, and if this was my time to go and this was God's will that it just go quick. I've never had to, you know, face death like that. I revisit that part of that thinking that you're on the edge of death, the most savage death you could possible die from. And wondering, you know, and I've even googled it. Do people die instantly, or does it make them go unconscious quickly or are they just enduring this whole thing? I didn't really find anything. I found some gruesome stories but I didn't find anything [on wolf attacks]. Maybe they just don't know because nobody lived to say. That was the hardest part, you know, wondering how long it's going to take, knowing that they were going to be ripping at me before I wouldn't feel it and that was my biggest concern just make it go quick. If this was it, then make it go quick.

This same woman recounted the same story at a 2011 Idaho public hearing about wolves, testifying that wolves are indeed a public health threat, and we have good reason to fear them:

> Well I think more than anything, I think the public needs to know that we are
> under attack and that this is a very real thing. Some day, some time, you're
> going to get called out to go do a report where there's gonna be somebody's
> child at a bus stop that's going to be attacked and killed, just like the gal in
> Alaska that was killed. Just like Kenton Carnegie in Canada. These are real
> things, these are real problems, it's not a political thing anymore, this is a true
> danger to the public.

Fear of the wolf is associated with outright hatred and demonization, whereby
the wolf is designated as an *immoral* animal. Thus, opposing the wolf becomes
a morally worthy and honorable task. The history here is long. In 1904, for
example, prominent conservationist William Temple Hornaday wrote in his book
of natural history, "Of all the wild creatures of North America, none are more
despicable than wolves. There is no depth of meanness, treachery or cruelty
to which they do not cheerfully descend" (Fischer, 1995, p. 16). A Montana
newspaper, the *Dillon Examiner*, eulogized the passing of a wolf in 1921, calling
it "the master criminal of the animal world... the death of the cruelest, the
most sagacious, and most successful animal outlaw the range country has ever
known... [it] struck terror in the hearts of ranchers... it was not merely a wolf,
but a monstrosity of nature... possessing the cruelty... and the craftiness of
Satan himself" (Fischer, 1995, p. 18).

Modern anti-wolf advocates cast wolves in the same immoral light. Yet what
is interesting for our purposes is that the economic motive for these sentiments
is largely gone, with the decline of the old-west economy. Moreover, public
opinion has shifted, with the majority of Americans now favoring the existence
of wolves, and even viewing them with positive emotion (Coleman 2004). Thus,
what remains in the GYE of fear and hatred toward wolves is on the whole not
linked to economic realities, but I suggest is propelled by moral commitments to
human mastery, control, and domination. These feelings are on visceral display
at anti-wolf rallies, represented by this selection of representative quotes from
speakers at two anti-wolf rallies in 2008 and 2011, respectively:

> So the point is, these animals, if the devil had an animal, it would be Canadian
> wolves. And I've been in the meetings where people have jumped on me, "Well
> aren't you a Christian? Don't you think everything has a place in nature?" You
> know, I do. But I don't think an animal that absolutely kills everything else has
> a right to be here... now people say, how are you going to kill them? I don't
> care—maybe dynamite carriers—don't care how they kill them, I just want
> them gone. The only wolf we want left in Idaho is one in the zoo in Boise.

> There is a good reason to have wolves. They are good for target prac-
> tice... they're worse than cockroaches, I can tell you that. But, at least you

Figure 4.4: Popular anti-wolf apparel. Source: http://www.nowolves.com.

can spray for cockroaches. But there's things you can do for wolves too. But we've got our work cut out for us. We really do. There is not a magic wand.

Elected officials have also not been shy about declaring war against wolves. In 2007 the governor of Idaho, C. L. "Butch" Otter, declared, over a roaring crowd: "I'm prepared to bid for the first ticket to shoot a wolf myself!" Anti-wolf advocates even convey fear, hatred, and violence by symbolically linking the wolf with America's post-9/11 adversaries. For example, the four images in Figure 4.4 are popular t-shirts that convey these sentiments. In other cultural artifacts around the GYE, such as bumper stickers, the wolf is referred to as "The Saddam Hussein of the Animal World" and as "Government-Sponsored Terrorists!!" These images and sentiments make wolf opposition a patriotic duty and ordain those who oppose and kill wolves as morally worthy of honor and esteem.

Simple and Sacred Heritage

Narratives also often reveal how communities represent and transmit their most meaningful experiences into a "way of life" or a "culture." The wolf poses a symbolic threat to the beliefs about, and commitments to, a particular way of life that, as the third element of the anti-wolf moral order, I call the *simple and sacred heritage* narrative. It can be told something like this:

> Once upon a time, people in the old-west ranched and farmed on small parcels of land. Work was hard, but they labored diligently because it was honorable and their duty. Through tireless physical labor on parcels of land—running the plough, herding cattle, digging wells, fencing property—they developed a special connection to the land that became part of who they inherently were. Over the generations, they developed a storehouse of skills and practical knowledge that could only be gained through these experiences. They hunted for elk, deer, and moose, and went fishing in the local lakes and streams. Today we proudly teach our children to do the same. Families lived in tight-knit communities and passed down our simple, yet sacred, culture to future generations. But now these simple traditions are under attack from people who define our culture as ecologically evil, and view our practical knowledge as primitive and unscientific. Today we must stand up to out-of-touch environmentalists, arrogant urban elites, the oppressive federal government, and other sophisticated outsiders who seek to destroy our beloved way of life.

SACRALIZING WORK

This narrative sacralizes the human work one does *in* nature, as well as the workers *themselves*. It connects the act of physically mastering nature for useful purposes to much larger narratives about the traditional (Protestant) valuation of hard work and self-made men. It also sacralizes work done in nature by fostering deeply affective bonds with particular parcels of land that go well beyond simple material or economic dependence, which can define the core identity of a family or community. As one rancher told me in an interview, "It's not about the money, it's about a way of life." In an interview about wolves, a local sheepherder south of Jackson Hole describes in rich detail this connection:

> I think that we just have a special feeling for the land. And sometimes it seems like it's a specific piece of ground, or a general region because, it's an interesting thing, if you talk to people who live out and work on the landscape, the landscape means more to them than just a combination of soil and vegetation and everything that it is. They have a sense of history, often even if it wasn't their family, they know the history of that land in the area and they know that these game trails have been used for hundreds, if not thousands, of years. And it's the same trails. You know migration of wildlife

through here seasonally, those pathways have been used for eons and now livestock use those same migration paths and we realize that it's a shared landscape. And I think that's a lot of the attachment besides the family histories and stuff. When you walk out to the land you realize that yours is not the only boots that have been out here on the ground, but you know it was the Indians, you know the Native Americans, the early trappers and explorers, the early immigrants that came through with their wagon trains and livestock and you get a real sense of that, and it really provides a perspective on your place in that landscape.

Another rancher explained how he and his family know every cow by name, including "their quirks and personality traits, their mothering ability, their personal history." He continued, "A lot of other ranchers would tell you the same thing, that we have a deep affection for these animals that goes beyond simply making their living from them. And I think this same view applies to the landscapes in which we live and work as well." Many anti-wolf advocates feel that the deal their grandparents took to come out West to homestead land, to graze cattle, and make a living on the natural resources is now being revoked in bad faith. For example, Sherry, a family rancher from Gallatin County, MT, lamented that "the prospector and miner, the user of timber, the user of the range, the user of water had a contract when they came west to be able to live this lifestyle. This was the deal... so all of this new environmentalist stuff—the wolves especially— is bad faith dealing. Our ancestors put their blood, sweat, and toil into it, and now they want to revoke our contract with the land?"

Many anti-wolf advocates perceive wild wolves as a threat to these deep and cherished connections to the land. For example, at a Wyoming Wolf Coalition rally in January 2010, protestors lined the steps of the Wyoming state capitol, holding signs reading "Protect our Heritage and Way of Life!" The main speaker at the rally, a sturdy man in a large cowboy hat and jeans, introduced himself as part of a proud heritage of outfitters, but now, he said, with the reintroduction of wolves in 1995, this way of life is at risk for future generations:

> I'm an outfitter with my wife and our family in Lander, WY. I started guiding hunters in 1970. My granddad was an outfitter. I knew that when I grew up I wanted to be an outfitter, and I was lucky enough to live that dream. But in 1995 [the reintroduction] they changed the rules of the game. [cheers and applause]

RECREATION PRACTICES

Because of the breakdown of the old-west economy, the primary beliefs, commitments, and desires that undergird the *simple and sacred heritage* way of life no longer live through ranching and farming, but through meaningful recreational practices, especially hunting. These practices are even experienced as spiritual for some. One anti-wolf advocate noted in response to seeing the *Crying Wolf* documentary, "Ya I gotta say hunting with bow and rifle definitely brings me much closer to God, nature, and makes me feel more like a man than just about anything."

Wolves are more than just a symbolic threat to these hunting practices. In the years since their reintroduction, wolves have contributed to the precipitous decline of the prized Yellowstone elk herd—the most important game for local hunters. In the early 1990s, this Yellowstone elk population hovered around 20,000 in number. But since the wolf reintroduction, elk numbers have decreased by almost 80 percent to just over 4,000 in 2012 (Brown, 2011; Finley, 1999). Like the attack on, and eventual decline of, old-west work practices, the wolf is in the same way an attack on one of the last remaining cultural practices linking anti-wolf advocates to their old-west heritage: hunting. So at a 2011 protest and rally on the steps of the Idaho state capitol building in Boise, the president of the anti-wolf organization Save Western Wildlife stood up to address the crowd of reporters and anti-wolf advocates:

> There's a lot of people here that don't buy into the crap that we've been sold over the last 15 years. One thing that we need to realize is that we funded nongovernmental [environmentalist] organizations to kill our game. The game that we already paid for. [Environmentalist organizations] have figured out a way to tweak the system to work in their favor and they take millions and millions of [government] dollars to destroy what we have built in 80 years. For 80 years we built this elk herd and these people need to be stopped at the non-governmental level … *They're using it to destroy us and our culture.*

In an interview this same speaker explained his motivates for founding Save Western Wildlife:

> I was reluctant to do so at first, but I realize it's my duty, not only as a citizen of Idaho, but as a father, and as a person that wants to continue the heritage of hunting for many generations to come. I just felt it to be a duty and I started the organization.

Such a feeling that a foundational part of their heritage is under attack was pervasive among anti-wolf advocates. It showed up routinely in field observation and discourse, as evidenced by these representative quotes:

> The wolves have now destroyed the sportsmen's culture by wiping out the big game.

> Hopefully people will understand that it isn't about the wolf at all, but the ecoterrorists using the wolf to end hunting in the United States as we know it.

> Sure, I mean they want us off the land. They want nature to balance itself and they don't want humans here. They're anti-hunting. And that's a big part of it too. They want to put an end to all sport hunting. They don't believe in our

way of life. They're different. They're a different breed than we are. Back when I first started Lobo Watch [an anti-wolf nonprofit] I tried to be a little nice sometimes, but finally one day I just said to hell with it, and from that point on I get a chance I was going to the jugular every time. I try to keep it somewhat professional, there's been times I've crossed that line too.

What we need is dead wolves, period. Our elk can't take it. Most of the hunters were asleep but now that they've had part of their hunting season taken away from 'em, now that they've gone hunting for a few years and seen more wolf tracks than elk tracks . . . we've lost our lives.

Hunters and ranchers have been unfairly punished by wolves and they have borne a disproportionate burden of the wolf experiment.

Don't forget that these animals are eating game herds that are the property of the people of the sovereign states of Montana and Idaho and Wyoming. This is your property, this is your food and so feeding your food to federal wolves is especially offensive to people that live in rural places.

DISTRUST OF OUTSIDERS

These unhappy feelings are exacerbated by the fact that it is "outsiders" who, from this perspective, are orchestrating and carrying out the attack on the locals' beloved heritage. For example, in my sample of pro-wolf public letters below, only 4 percent were written by people living in the GYE. This means that 96 percent of written support came from people across the country and the world, the majority living in urban areas. It is bad enough that anti-wolf advocates feel powerless to stop the federal government intrusion of wolves, but it is especially infuriating to them that the voices of cultural outsiders like urbanites, elites, and environmental groups are so vocal and influential, deceiving people with what anti-wolf advocate described as "Madison Avenue emotional hooks."

Jerry, a heavily involved anti-wolf activist from Idaho, sees a particular outsider "religion" as the problem in the wolf issue. He explains that outsiders have impressed

> their extreme "religion" from the far left wing. The closer you get to Moscow and Beijing, the larger the segment becomes . . . they want to turn the American West back into prehistoric times . . . that's their utopian religious view. Wolves are just part of it. These outsiders have starry-eyed visions of unicorns and rainbows, of the utopian forest that will be just like it was before Adam and Even fucked it up.

The suspicion of outsiders—whether it be wolves from Canada, bureaucrats from Washington D.C., or "religious" ideologies friendly with Moscow and Beijing—was routinely brought to the surface in private conversations with people like Jerry.

One environmentalist who has now lived in the GYE for 20 years described how he still feels like an outsider in the area, because, as he put it to me:

> Outsiders get sized up out here in the GYE really quickly. Are you a real cowboy? Or are you an environmentalist?... These people came out here long ago to be left alone. They came with deep distrust of big government and of outsiders... and wolves are an outsider attack on their skills, on what they are good at. Its all going by the wayside. Their power is weakened because of wolves. Their influence in the area is slipping, along with their way of life.

Lou Jackson, a long-time rancher from Idaho, and an active participant in the anti-wolf movement, gets especially frustrated when, as he describes it to me, "well-intentioned, do-gooder outsiders, become emotionally intoxicated over western issues." He gives a hypothetical example of "an average woman in her middle ages from an urban area. Maybe she's a nurse or a government worker or something. Because she is childless, she decides that she's going to protect, you know, use her mothering instincts, to protect wolves. Urban people like her have been intoxicated by environmental organizations."

In 2012 Wyoming legislators themselves protested outsider control of the region by proposing a bill to reintroduce wolves to Central Park in New York City. The bill, written by Representatives Allen Jaggi and Donald Burkhart and Senator Kit Jennings, stated:

> A JOINT RESOLUTION requesting Congress to acquire the area commonly known as Central Park on Manhattan in New York City on behalf of the federal government; urging the United States Congress to declare Central Park to be a wilderness area and to prohibit any further improvement or development of Central Park unless authorized by an Act of Congress.

Later adding:

> WHEREAS, in the event Congress authorizes the creation of the Central Park Wilderness, the state of Wyoming shall donate a breeding pair of grey wolves to begin the re-colonization of the grey wolf to Manhattan, an area, like Wyoming, encompassing the grey wolf's historic range.

The bill goes on to argue, in the same way as the 1995 reintroduction of wolves to Yellowstone, that Manhattan was very long ago an intact ecosystem that contained gray wolves, and thus Wyomingites would like to manage New York's Central Park as a wilderness area, restricting multiple uses and returning native animals like the wolf to the area. Of course the bill was not successful, and wolves were not restored to the middle of Manhattan. But the symbolic point, about outsiders minding their own business, was made.

LIVED KNOWLEDGE

One of the reasons anti-wolf advocates are so suspicious of outsiders is because they wield forms of ostensibly disinterested technical evidence that are purported to be more authoritative than the lived knowledge that is so central to the *simple and sacred heritage* narrative. By "lived knowledge," I mean the practical skills and expertise built up over generations of physical interaction with, and recreation on, particular lands. An Idaho rancher just west of Yellowstone talked at length about this form of knowledge:

> There is absolutely a form of traditional knowledge that comes from the connection to the history of a landscape. It is passed down from one generation on a ranch, to the next people who are out there working on the land. They learn things about certain wildlife, but not the kind of knowledge that is a documented scientific thing. I think there's actually a term for it; it's called traditional ecological knowledge. People often associate it with Native Americans, but the same holds true for us pastoralists. If you talk to people here that remember talking to their dads or granddads from years ago, about the history of wolves that were here in the late 1800s before they were killed. They knew of where some of the den sites were and the areas wolves were using. Again, its not really a documented thing, but it's just something that the locals know.

A farmer from Wyoming worries that lawmakers and environmental groups "do not even know that this traditional form of knowledge exists." As a result, he says that "these agencies and groups think that this [wolf issue] is a mechanical or technical issue, but it's not quite this simple kind of mechanical thing."

In my fieldwork and in analyzing discourse I found that anti-wolf advocates appealed more to this "purer" form of practical cultural knowledge than to the "out-of-touch" technical science used by federal agencies and environmental groups. Consider, for example, these representative quotes:

> Don't listen to the politicians and city dwellers. If you want to know the truth, go talk with the people who have to live everyday in these areas. You will find that the fantasy stories are not the case. The "great wolf" is nothing but a killer with no respect for the ecosystem.

> That is the problem with all city people they have no common sense, also no ability to make good judgment calls about anything because they have other people doing it for them.

> Let local people take care of the local animals that live there. If local people are mistreating animals, then let local people take care of that. The problem is when a bureaucracy in D.C. or an enviro group hijacks an issue like stewardship, they never understand the issues like the locals do. The locals should be left to handle things like animals the way they know is best.

I guess you just have to *live here* to see the difference.

In contrast to technical knowledge that is perceived to be disconnected from practical realities, lived knowledge is a supposedly purer form of knowing that cannot be reduced to technical studies and numbers. I am not suggesting that anti-wolf advocates oppose science—actually they rely on it quite heavily to document the declining elk population, for example—but they are very conscious of the ways that science is used against them in wolf politics. First, they perceive that claims to "unbiased" and "objective" science about wolves and ecosystems is a commonly used tool to push environmentalists' biased ideologies and interests:

> There is just so much practical knowledge that doesn't get weighed into the wolf equation.

> They plug 'em into a computer program and similar to what happened with Wall Street and the debacle that happened there, that was all based on a computer model, similar to what the Fish and Game is employing right now and everybody just states this as fact, one after another, when it's not.

> These [pro-wolf] people take these numbers and throw them around like it's nothing, kind of like what the federal government does with billions and trillions [of dollars].

> They're counting cow/calf ratios, they're mixing these numbers up ... this is not science, they developed a way to use a computer model that tweaks it so the outcome is certain. Yes ma'am.

By contrast, according to many anti-wolf advocates, everyone needs to grant more legitimacy to the "lived" knowledge built up through generations of practical local experience with the ecosystem. This solution is often framed as bringing "common sense" to the wolf issue, as evidenced over and over again in U.S. congressman Denny Rehberg's 2010 and 2011 speeches to anti-wolf advocates:

> With help from the SCI with the help from the elk foundation, with the help from other fishing and hunting organizations, and with the help from the farm bureau, farm union, and all the rest of the organizations, we're going to have an opportunity to bring some *common sense* ... we've got to bring some *common sense* to the endangered species act. (emphasis added)

> If we could go down memory lane a little bit, when the Republicans were in control of the house of representatives a number of years ago, we passed the first reform to the endangered species act to try and bring some *common sense* back to the act ... we must reform it because there has to be some *common sense*, we cannot continue to address these issues in the court. And it was interesting because at my wolf hearing, people would stand up and say well we don't think congress ought to be involved, sound science ought to be. *Well really? Define sound science.* We had quite a bit of debate in congress of trying to define it, because the interesting thing is, and I could use many examples,

whether its (sic) global warming or the endangered species act there are many different definitions and you can find the sound sciences over here and sound sciences over there and eventually you got to come to a conclusion, you got to come to a resolution, there has to be a final chapter and it seems like in the wolf issue, *common sense* would dictate ... we've met the threshold ... and so why can't the court make a determination that they have been reestablished under the Endangered Species Act? *Common sense* would tell you. (emphasis added; capitalization as in original)

Furthermore, many anti-wolf leaders who do not have formal scientific training also feel that wildlife agencies and environmental groups are arrogantly condescending, looking down upon lived knowledge and presuming that anti-wolf advocates are ignorant about the hard facts of natural-resource management. For example, consider testimony at a recent anti-wolf meeting in Idaho:

The upper level people at Idaho Fish and Game went to Washington D.C. and took a seminar to understand this game better than anybody, because they were a part of wolf introduction to begin with ... And they chastised us and told us we need to go home and study like them. They're basically saying that we didn't know what we were talking about. This is a public official talking to us.

Do you like that, do you enjoy knowing that people actually think you're stupid people?

SUMMARY OF THE ANTI-WOLF MORAL ORDER

If, as I have argued, it is not about "the facts" but about what different groups find meaningful, put their faith in, and believe worthy enough to defend—then what sorts of deeper motivations animate anti-wolf activity? I found that the vociferous opposition to the wolf is, in contrast to prevailing economic theories, motivated in large part by cultural threats to *rugged American individualism*, as operationalized in my fieldwork by long-standing commitments to antifederalism, private property rights, and defining the reintroduced wolf as an ecological outsider. I found that a related set of commitments pertain to *human dominionism*, the belief that humans sit atop a (sometimes God-ordained) natural hierarchy, thus giving humanity certain rights and duties vis-à-vis nonhuman animals. Pro-wolf advocates often talked about a transvaluation that would subordinate humans in this hierarchy, and thus crossed sacred boundaries, leading to anxiety and outrage among anti-wolf advocates. Last, I found that the wolf symbolized for anti-wolf advocates a declining *simple and sacred heritage* that sacralized physical work on the land and recreation practices. For many anti-wolf advocates, the wolf is a symbol of the new-west changing of the guard, devaluing a heritage that values lived experiences and practical knowledge—what for generations many anti-wolf advocates have relied on to define their place in the world.

Uncovering the Pro-Wolf Moral Order

Environmentalists and natural resource managers framed the reintroduction of wolves in scientific terms: it was quite simply an ecological solution to an ecological problem. Decades of new research about wolves and ecosystems lifted the veil of ignorance about the wolf. With clear-eyed judgment, park managers relied on sound science to carry out the reintroduction. Sixteen years later, in today's equally contentious sociopolitical context, wolf management continues to be, on the face of it, a purely scientific and technical enterprise. For example, in a 2013 op-ed, a local environmental journalist reflected back on the original motivations for wolf reintroduction, reminding readers not to lose sight, in the contemporary contentious milieu, that the action was, and always should be, about ecological science. He wrote that we needed "wolves back in the West because they're an integral part of the region's wildlife and wildness... scientists hoped their return would enable those ecosystems to function fully and more efficiently. *It was not a matter of sentimentality... bringing wolves back to function as predators in the wild was a smart decision biologically; it had nothing to do with wolves' moral value*" (Dax 2013, emphasis added).

But I contend to the contrary that wolf reintroduction has *everything* to do with wolves' "moral value." Like all other humans, technical experts are embedded in certain cultural narratives and are committed to certain moral beliefs that, whether they realize it or not, determine what is worth researching in the first place. Environmentalists similarly start from presuppositional assumptions that inform why we should care in the first place about the survival of the gray wolf (or any species), and why "whole" ecosystems are better than fragmented ones. As I demonstrated above, the arguments of anti-wolf advocates appeared on the political surface to be about economic concerns over cattle loss and biological concerns over elk predation. But by probing deeper we see that, in reality, the wolf provokes anxieties around the violation of shared moral commitments to individualism, human control, and a proud heritage in decline. In the following pages, I will present results from a comparable analysis of the moral order of pro-wolf advocates.

In my fieldwork, analysis of discourse, and historical study on the issue, I discovered a guiding narrative that defines for pro-wolf advocates what is significant about the issue, what role they play in the larger story, and why it all matters in a cosmic sense. This broad story, which I refer to as the *moral and spiritual redemption* narrative, frames my empirical analysis of the pro-wolf moral order. It goes something like this:

> Once upon a time, the United States was populated by an estimated 2 million wolves that freely roamed untrammeled wilderness and thrived as rightful members of intact ecosystems that were pure, wild, and free. But bloodthirsty humans mercilessly and greedily exterminated wolves. In response to this

shameful wrongdoing, environmentalists fought successfully to restore these sacred animals to their home in the Yellowstone area. This was a watershed moment of redemption, atoning for blatant wrongs of our past and committing ourselves to a more enlightened relationship with nature. Nevertheless, hatred for the wolf still abounds, and today Yellowstone wolves are threatened by hunting, trapping, and related pursuits of human domination and greed. We must remain steadfast in this battle against instrumental utilitarianism, holding tight to our deeply held commitments to this majestic animal, and more broadly to intrinsic values of wilderness and the goal of protecting and restoring wholeness to our most treasured ecosystems.

ANALYZING PRO-WOLF LETTERS

In addition to relying on thick description from interviews and fieldwork with local pro-wolf advocates, I also operationalize pro-wolf moral and spiritual justifications using computational content analysis of thousands of letters written to the USFWS about its 2011 proposal to remove the gray wolf from the endangered species list in Wyoming. I describe in more detail the methodology of such an approach in the appendix. In short, and following Ghaziani and Baldassarri (2011), these methods are especially useful to capture the *simultaneous* meanings used by wolf advocates. These unique and original data also allow me to capture a more representative sample of pro-wolf advocates, which is much more national in scope than is anti-wolf activism.

These letters were written in response to the most contentious action proposed by the USFWS since the reintroduction of wolves in 1995, proposing to turn the management of wolves over to the state of Wyoming and to allow hunting and trapping of wolves within the state. This alarmed many environmentalists who feared that the state of Wyoming would not manage wolves humanely. Following the National Environmental Policy Act of 1969, an important part of the proposal process involved soliciting comments on the issue from the general public. These comments, or public letters, are very important because they provide an opportunity for people to express their agreement or disagreement with a proposal, and to provide explicit evidence and justifications as to why their position is correct. They are a primary way through which the general public participates in the policy-making process.

But what can these data tell us? What sorts of meanings do they contain? These letters have a definitive genre, by which I mean the intent of the letters is straightforward: for pro-wolf advocates, it is to critique the proposal to remove the wolf from the endangered species list in Wyoming, and to make a convincing argument about why their position is justified and should be adopted. Thus, the ultimate motive behind writing a letter is to *persuade* the USFWS to change its course of action. The qualities that constitute a successful letter are clearly laid out by the USFWS. In the solicitation for public comment, the

USFWS requests that letters be based on "the best scientific and commercial data available," and thus *the focus of these letters is meant to be technical, economic, and scientific.*

The agency goes so far as to guide public letters toward six specific and highly technical questions, ranging from "(1) Is our description and analysis of the biology, population, and distribution accurate?" to "(6) Is it reasonable for us to conclude that Wyoming's approach to wolf management is likely to provide for sufficient levels of gene flow (either natural or human assisted) to prevent genetic problems from negatively impacting the Greater Yellowstone Area's population or the larger Northern Rocky Mountain meta-population in a manner that would meaningfully impact viability?" Thus, writers letter were asked to address technical and scientific concerns—a directive that defined what a "successful" letter would look like in the eyes of the USFWS. These letters are thus biased in this way. This hyperscientific context provides a good opportunity to examine— in a rigorous test—whether deeper cultural meanings indeed lay beneath the surface, and if so, how they might manifest themselves in the reasons pro-wolf advocates give to the USFWS for not removing wolves from the endangered species list. The letters allow me to examine these questions in a way that is both fine-grained at the level of the individual letter and is all-encompassing of the national population of written arguments made to the USFWS.

I use thick description from fieldwork and interviews to supplement the quantitative analysis that follows, where I ask the following questions: How often do different pro-wolf advocates use moral and spiritual justifications in these letters? How does their frequency compare to technical and rational justifications (e.g., ecology, economic growth)? Do different arguments cluster together, co-occurring in proximity? If so, what type of moral commitments (e.g., aesthetic, spirituality, intrinsic rights) tend to co-occur with different types of rational justifications? Does spatial context matter? That is, does proximity to Yellowstone influence the types of arguments pro-wolf advocates make?

Features of the Pro-Wolf Moral Order

Table 4.2, which emerged from this qualitative and quantitative approach, describes the categories of meaning that make up the moral order of pro-wolf advocates. The third column provides illustrative pro-wolf quotes from different people to describe how advocates actually make these different moral arguments. This table of the pro-wolf moral order is especially important because it structures the analysis in the remainder of the chapter. In looking at the table, some of these categories are seen to be issue-specific, such as "Ranch Compensation," while others represent broader moral concerns about the pollution of greed or the ruin of human dominionism.

Table 4.2: Features and Examples of the Pro-Wolf Moral Order.

Category of Justification	Concise Definition and Context	Sample Quotes: Why should wolves remain on the endangered species list?
Moral and Spiritual		
Aesthetic	Appeal to the beauty of wolves.	The gray wolf is a **beautiful** animal worth saving.
Collective History	Appeal to historical value of wolves.	I plead with you to consider the impact this plan would have on our American culture and **heritage.**
Disgust	Rejection of policies based on intuitive emotions of revulsion, moral shock, abhorrence, etc.	I am writing as a concerned citizen who finds it **appalling** that the US would allow for the hunting of wolves in Wyoming.
Duty to Future Generations	Appeal to shared responsibility to ensure future enjoyment of wolves.	Stop the slaughter, will my **grandchildren** only be able to see wolves in the zoo?
Greed	Rejection of ulterior motives of big money, corporate interests, and related lobbyists.	Don't let **big money** dictate what species to eliminate!
Human Dominionism	Rejection of abusive and barbaric practices of humanity, especially hunters, ranchers.	**Man is killing** everything in its quest for taking over everything.
Intrinsic Morality	Appeal to the inherent rights of wolves and ecosystems to be protected.	Wolves have an **inherent right** to live here, to roam free and to breed.
Spirituality	Appeal to creator/creation, nature as a wild sanctuary, and spiritual experiences.	Wolves are creatures of **God**, do not **desecrate** our national park **sanctuaries.**

Table 4.2: Continued

Category of Justification	Concise Definition and Context	Sample Quotes: *Why should wolves remain on the endangered species list?*
Technical and Rational		
Ecology	Appeal to specific ecological concepts and evidence.	I urge you to heed the scientifically established importance of **apex predators** in **ecosystems** and the many benefits they provide to other species.
Economic Growth	Appeal to the economic benefits of wolves.	**Wolf Tourism** now brings in a huge amount into the states that have healthy wolf populations.
Ranch Compensation	Appeal to programs in place that reimburse ranchers who lose cattle to wolves.	Ranchers are **repaid** for any losses to livestock as a result of wolves.
TechnoRationality	Rejection of irrational evidence and call for use of hard facts, science, logic, experts, data, etc.	This is not **wise** animal conservation, which should be based on **science**, not emotions!

To provide a sense of a typical pro-wolf letter to the USFWS, consider these representative full-length examples (caps in original).

From a concerned man from the D.C. area:

It is appalling to think that these beautiful animals that have every right to exist, as they always have, will once again be threatened with extinction because of a bunch of sick yahoos who don't care about anything but making money and shooting things for "sport." Find another way to protect your sacred cows or better yet, find another way to make a living!

A woman from Westmont, IL, expresses her outrage:

What is Wrong with you allowing killing wolves or any wildlife in National Parks? This is NUTS! Thats NOT what NATIONAL PARKS are for. It is to keep our wild land beautiful for ALL AMERICANS to enjoy. And that includes SAVING OUR WILDLIFE FOR EVERYONE. It is our Country's original Natural resources. WILDLIFE LIKE WOLVES WERE OUR ORIGINAL ANIMALS LIKE THE BUFFALO. I AM REALLY UPSET WITH ALL OF YOU FOR EVEN CONSIDERING THIS.

A concerned woman from Virginia writes:

I OBJECT TO THE REMOVAL OF THE WOLF FROM ENDANGERED SPECIES STATUS IN WYOMING. Wolves are responsible for less than ONE PERCENT of livestock mortality. Ranchers have profited by claiming wolves as attackers of their livestock, but when injured livestock have been examined, the finding has REPEATEDLY been that wolves were NOT involved. Not only that, there are scientifically validated, HUMANE DETERRENTS that are available, so the low predation that does occur can be avoided. Brutal deaths are clearly not the answer! Furthermore, more than 90 percent of that low predation can actually be PREDICTED by location factors! The wolf population has just started to gain strength. We worked so hard to build the population back up. MORE THAN HALF OF IDAHO'S WOLF POPULATION IN ONE HUNT SEASON! More than half! I DEMAND all parties to not delist Wyoming wolves! You hypocrites supposedly WORK FOR ALL CITIZENS NOT JUST BIG MONEY!! How do you sleep at night knowing you are traitors to the heritage of OUR country!? I IMPLORE YOU TO NOT REPEAT THE UNNECESSARY, INHUMANE AND IRREVERSIBLE ERRORS COMMITTED IN OTHER ROCKY MOUNTAIN STATES AND TO INSTEAD USE SCIENCE AND REASON IN THIS MATTER. Please follow Alaska's laudable lead and use science.

A native Wyomingite now living in Chicago argues:

I am a native of Wyoming and speak as someone intimate with the wildlife and geography of the place. I cannot believe we would be foolish enough to remove the Gray Wolf in Wyoming from the Federal list of Endangered and

Threatened Wildlife. Similar removals in other states have been DISASTROUS and cruel—resulting in the needless (and strangely blood-thirsty) slaughter of a necessary predator. Under no circumstance should Wyoming follow the brutish idiocy of other western states. I hope we are smarter than that. A naturally selected wolf population is a necessary part of the health of Wyoming's ecosystem. Without it, there is an overabundance of large and small herbivores that do more damage to the ecosystem than wolf-packs could ever do under any circumstance. As we have seen in other western states, when the wolf is removed from this protected list, people seem to go crazy with aerial (and other types of wolf) killing sprees. Keeping the Wyoming Gray Wolf on this Federal list is probably the only way to keep this predator alive and in its necessary place in Wyoming's ecosystem. Be SMART! KEEP the Wyoming Gray Wolf on the Federal List of Endangered and Threatened Wildlife! I would like a response to this email. I would like you to respond in favor of the wolves. That is the smarter Wyoming way.

What is particularly important to note about these letters, and this method of analysis, is that because words and phrases are the unit of analysis, I am able to document multiple expressions of meanings in a sentence, paragraph, or letter.[2] To illustrate this point, consider this sentence from a letter:

I am sickened that humans want to kill everything for their own economic benefit. Listen to the voice of reason, not greed!

The computational content analysis method can simultaneously measure these varied justifications protesting the USFWS proposal: Disgust ("sickened"), Human dominionism ("humans want to kill"), Greed ("economic benefit", "greed"), and Technorationality ("listen to the voice of reason"). This is the major payoff for computational content analysis. Not only can we assess how often different justifications occur in huge bodies of texts, but more powerfully, we can also assess whether and how these meanings co-occur and examine how categories tend to cluster together (or not) by proximity. I also geocoded each letter based on the home address of the letter writer, and calculated the euclidian distance of the authors from Yellowstone Park. Figure 4.5 uses these geocodes to display the spatial distribution of the individual letter writers. The map demonstrates that, even though this USFWS proposal affects policy only within the state of Wyoming, the response was indeed national in scope, primarily coming from locations far from the GYE.

2 See the appendix for more on this method.

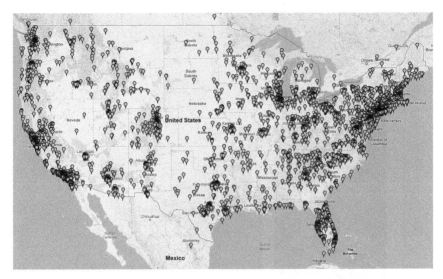

Figure 4.5: Spatial distribution of U.S. letter authors by zip code. Map data © Google, Sanborn.

The Primary Role of Morality and Spirituality

The first question I sought to answer is: Within the hyperscientific context of the USFWS proposal and request for public comment, do pro-wolf advocates even appeal to moral and spiritual meanings? That is, does the contextual pressure from the USFWS to use technical and scientific evidence suppress deeper moral and spiritual motivations? Figure 4.6 displays the total distribution (in percent) of science and rationality categories versus moral and spiritual categories (combined from the expanded view presented in Table 4.2). As a comparison, I have included a computational content analysis on the USFWS proposal itself (more than 43,000 words). In contrast to the proposal (76 percent science and rationality), and to the larger scientific context in which the letters were presumed to be written, a greater percentage of public letters expressed moral and spiritual language (57 percent) than science and rationality (43 percent). This broad comparison demonstrates that, in contrast to what one might expect, these deeper moral and spiritual elements of culture are actually used *more often* than science and rationality in pro-wolf efforts to justify the opposition to removing wolves from the endangered species list. This is surprising, given the fact that the USFWS explicitly asked letter writers to focus on science and technorational aspects of wolf ecology.

In my fieldwork I found at times that despite the underlying motivation of moral and spiritual sentiments, some environmental group leaders—in contrast to letter writers—were uncomfortable using such justifications in legal and bureaucratic contexts. They operated in a different context than public letter

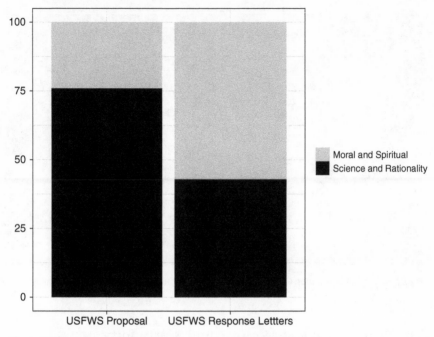

Figure 4.6: Total distribution of categories for letters and USFWS proposal.

writers, and felt that they had more to lose. Thus, in contrast to groups like the Buffalo Field Campaign, which were successful with the overt use of moral and spiritual sentiment, there were pro-wolf professionals who worried that overt use of such sentiment would harm the effectiveness of the movement. For example, in one conversation a board member of a pro-wolf environmental organization in the GYE explained that despite the deeper spiritual inspirations of many pro-wolf advocates,

> It costs us for wearing too much emotion, too much of your heart on your sleeve. That's why I never speak about my spiritual moments out there with wolves, you know, when I'm addressing politicians. It was "I'm a business owner, this is my business, and this is hurting our economy when you kill wolves." You can't have any of that sentiment in there, as much as it drives you, and you know there's so much value to spiritual emotions, but it's just very counterproductive to come in with a tie-dye and pony tail and wave a flag and throw yourself on the steps. You have to talk dollars and cents with them. It's the language they speak. You know, you wouldn't go to Polynesia and hope to get your point across in English. You have to speak the language, and theirs is money.

One pro-wolf activist who works both in the GYE and on Capitol Hill similarly explained the importance of context for morality and spirituality, despite admitting their underlying importance for the cause:

> When I came out of the backcountry with the wolves, and went to talk to people in Washington D.C., I had to cut the beard, cut the hair, get a suit, and you know, tone down the rhetoric. You know, we're concerned about the wolves' spiritual well-being, but for bureaucrats its about commerce, you know. I'm going there to play *their* game. Some people showed up with their favorite "Save the Wolf" t-shirt and yoga pants, tie-dyed bracelet or whatever, and they're going to speak with senators. But save that for the wolf rally, you know, when you have like-minded people together—put your wolf tails on and dance around and talk about positive spirituality, but to make change we need to be on their playing field.

In turning our attention back to the letters, a breakdown of the findings from the broad categories above into their different features will be helpful. Figure 4.7 charts the percentages of the total frequency of all categories introduced in Table 4.2. Ecology—a form of science and rationality discourse—makes up 22.2 percent of all expressions. In the proposal itself (figure not displayed), Ecology accounted for 62 percent of discursive expressions. Pro-wolf letters referring to Human Dominionism make up 13.9 percent, and Spirituality makes up 13.2 percent, followed by Disgust (9.3 percent), Intrinsic Morality (7.4 percent), and Technorationality (7.2 percent). It is striking that Ranch Compensation and Economic Growth show up so little, given the centrality of both concepts in the USFWS proposal itself. This is consistent with my larger argument that, despite the overwhelming presence of economic arguments in the surface-level debates (as we would certainly expect in legal and bureaucratic settings), these deeper moral and spiritual categories of meaning are present and powerful.

But because *multiple* categories can be present in a single letter, another way to understand the distribution of the categories is to examine in what percentage of letters the different categories show up. Figure 4.8 charts the percentage of letters in which each category appears. Ecology is used in 40.6 percent of letters. For example, one woman writes: "I disagree with the culling of wolves in the State of Wyoming, as they form part of the *natural ecology*. There must be a balance to maintain." Another advocate argues, "This *wildlife corridor* helps to maintain *genetic variety* in *wildlife populations*, which is essential for *healthy wildlife*." But it may be surprising to some, given the scientific context, that Ecology does not appear in an even higher percentage of letters, especially given the fact that half of all letters appeal to either Human Dominionism (25.5 percent) or Spirituality (24.2 percent).

How does spatial context influence these findings? I found that the most useful comparison is not incremental distance from Yellowstone Park (based on the

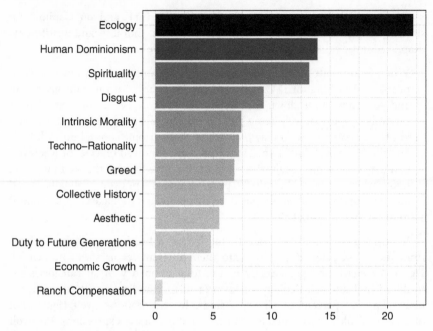

Figure 4.7: Total frequency of all categories.

letter writers' latitude and longitude), but instead with a dichotomous measure comparing advocates who live in the GYE versus those not living in the GYE. The assumption here, based on my fieldwork with local residents, is that living in or not in the GYE makes a bigger difference than whether someone lives 750 miles or 2,000 miles away. Table 4.3 presents this binary comparison of pro-wolf letter writers, with percentages indicating total distribution of categories by column. As this table demonstrates, pro-wolf advocates living in the GYE were significantly more likely to appeal to Ecology, Technorationality, Economic Growth, and Ranch Compensation. Pro-wolf advocates from outside of the GYE were significantly more likely to appeal to Spirituality, Intrinsic Morality, Aesthetics, and Duty to Future Generations. In broad terms, living in the GYE yielded more scientific and rational justifications, and living outside yielded moral and spiritual appeals.

This is consistent with my fieldwork, where I found that non-GYE advocates were further removed from the material and scientific pressures that tend to drive moral motivations beneath the surface. One woman from Sublette County described to me in an interview how "attitudes about wolves can become much more complicated when you actually live with wolves on the ground." In other words, pro-wolf political arguments at the local GYE level are heavily influenced

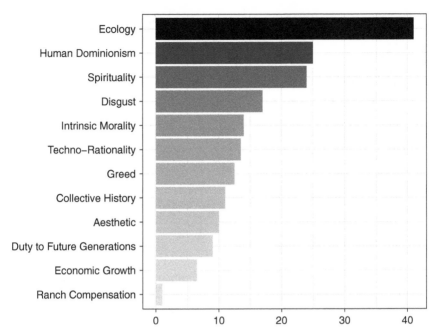

Figure 4.8: The percentage of letters in which each category appears.
Note: Unlike Figure 4.7, this chart allows for multiple categories to show up in a single case. Thus, the total percentage exceeds 100.

by a more direct, and less idealized, experience with the wolf. Another woman, from Gardiner, MT, affirmed that "people who live outside of this area are more vocal. I mean, it's pretty polarized locally, and pretty extreme. But it seems that the loudest voices, in you know, media and letters to the editors, seem to be the people who don't live here. So I guess wolves definitely have an effect on them." In this local context, pro-wolf advocates are more familiar with wolf ecology, and are aware that in this scientific context, moral and spiritual arguments, while important, only go so far politically without more objective evidence from ecology or economics. Locals also learn and recite the handful of popular scientific "talking points" and scripts. That is not to say, however, that local pro-wolf advocates are not motivated by these deeper moral and spiritual beliefs, but simply that these local GYE advocates are more likely than non-GYE advocates to mute these arguments amid their hypertechnical context.

On the other hand, because non-GYE advocates have less direct engagement with the day-to-day life co-existing with the wolf, they tend to express themselves in more emotional and symbolic ways. I spoke about this issue with a local wildlife photographer who lives just north of Yellowstone Park and, reflecting on the passion of pro-wolf advocates, he explained that "people in cities love

Table 4.3: Comparing Geographic Locations of Letter Writers.

Category	GYE (%)	Non-GYE (%)	Chi²	p-value
Ecology*	28	22	15.479	0.000
Human Dominionism	14	14	0.102	0.750
Spirituality*	10	13	4.347	0.037
Disgust	7	9	1.851	0.174
Intrinsic Morality*	3	8	13.787	0.000
Technorationality*	11	7	14.120	0.000
Greed	8	7	1.576	0.209
Collective History	8	6	3.167	0.075
Aesthetic*	3	6	6.634	0.010
Duty to Future Generations*	2	5	8.586	0.003
Economic Growth*	5	3	7.855	0.005
Ranch Compensation*	2	1	8.375	0.004

*Significant at the $p < 0.05$, $p < 0.005$, or $p < 0.001$ level (two-tail).

buying my wolf photographs because it represents something wild to them. They may work in their cubicles in downtown Chicago, and you know, they want that photo of a wolf—that wild symbol—hanging in their home or their office. Everybody has something inside them that relates to the wild." Non-GYE advocates feel less political pressure from the local material and scientific context, and when they reflect about the wolf—through photographs, stories, personal experiences—they are less likely to mute these deeper moral and spiritual meanings, beliefs, and desires, which define to them why the wolf is "good" in the first place.

Multiple Meanings: Co-Occurrence of Spirituality and Rationality

Thus far I have demonstrated that moral and spiritual meanings are an important source of motivation for pro-wolf advocates. But we know that in most cases our distinct beliefs and commitments, and their expression, are not mutually exclusive. In the messiness of explanation we often simultaneously mix and match, piecing together different sorts of evidence and arguments to make the best case we can. For example, in one conversation a pro-wolf advocate from Chicago explained to me why "wolves belong back in Yellowstone" by drawing on several different justifications (categories annotated in the text):

Well, I'd say they belong for several reasons. They were here first, they're indigenous, and simply deserve to exist here [intrinsic morality]. Another is that they balance the ecosystem. When you eradicate a predator like this, it affects all other wildlife populations [Ecology]. Of course, all of the hunters liked this because now they had bigger elk bulls and over 20,000 elk to shoot [Human Dominionism]. But we can't let the groups with deeper pockets, the ranchers and outfitters, pump a lot of money into fish and game for their own interests [Greed]. Wolves are just so integral you know, including to our economy through ecotourism [Economic Growth]. And, um, we've already talked about the soul-stirring experiences wolves give people. You know, that sort of heartfelt spirituality they bring to everybody, more than a lot of other animals [Spirituality].

In addition to my interviews, I also expected multiple meanings like these to appear in the letters written to the USFWS. To capture this quantitatively, I examined the proximity and co-occurrence of different categories with one another. I calculated co-occurrence similarities using the standard Jaccard similarity coefficient ($a/(a + b + c)$) where a represents cases where both items occur, and b and c represent cases where one item, but not the other, is found. Equal weight is given to matches and nonmatches. I calculate co-occurrences within each letter, as opposed to more narrowly focusing on smaller textual units such as paragraph or sentence, because I am interested in how individual letter writers wield multiple meanings. Table 4.4 is a similarity matrix presenting Jaccard coefficients for every category co-occurrence. A Jaccard coefficient of .08 (i.e., Aesthetic and Collective History) means that, of all letters containing either one of these categories, 8 percent contain both. As another example, of all the letters containing either Spirituality *or* Ecology, 26 percent contain both.

Because these data are relational, these coefficients are most easily interpreted visually, and Figure 4.9 presents a multidimensional scaling model of these Jaccard proximity values. In this figure, the lines connecting a dyad indicate Jaccard values above .10 (from Table 4.4). On the map the spatial distance between all categories indicates how likely those items are to appear together in a letter. In other words, the closer categories are to one another, the more likely pro-wolf advocates are to simultaneously use the categories in their letter.

A few important points are demonstrated in Figure 4.9. First, toward the bottom right, Ranch Compensation, Aesthetic, and Economic Growth tend to occur in isolation from the rest of the categories. They also occur in isolation from one another. Economic Growth and Ranch Compensation are economic arguments, and thus it appears that these types of justifications stand alone in the minds of pro-wolf advocates who make these arguments. Second, Ecology is more likely to co-occur with a wide variety of arguments, as indicated by its centrality on the map and the number of dyadic connections linking Ecology to most other categories. Third, identifiable clusters of categories exist in proximity with one another, especially at the bottom left and the top middle. To better illustrate this point, I have included a dendrogram (Figure 4.10), which uses these same Jaccard similarity coefficients to illustrate hierarchical clustering among categories. Ranch compensation, aesthetic, and economic growth

Table 4.4: Similarity Matrix, Jaccard Coefficients.

	Aesthetic	Collective History	Disgust	Duty to Future Generations	Ecology	Economic Growth	Greed	Human Dominionism	Intrinsic Morality	Ranch Compensation	Spirituality	Technorationality
Aesthetic	1.00											
Collective History	0.08	1.00										
Disgust	0.13	0.24	1.00									
Duty to Future Generations	0.10	0.32	0.22	1.00								
Ecology	0.12	0.19	0.23	0.14	1.00							
Economic Growth	0.08	0.06	0.07	0.06	0.09	1.00						
Greed	0.11	0.10	0.16	0.06	0.17	0.11	1.00					
Human Dominionism	0.14	0.12	0.19	0.08	0.30	0.08	0.21	1.00				
Intrinsic Morality	0.09	0.26	0.21	0.26	0.15	0.04	0.08	0.11	1.00			
Ranch Compensation	0.01	0.01	0.02	0.01	0.02	0.03	0.03	0.02	0.01	1.00		
Spirituality	0.15	0.11	0.14	0.09	0.26	0.07	0.14	0.27	0.10	0.01	1.00	
Technorationality	0.08	0.11	0.20	0.07	0.21	0.10	0.20	0.17	0.08	0.04	0.13	1.00

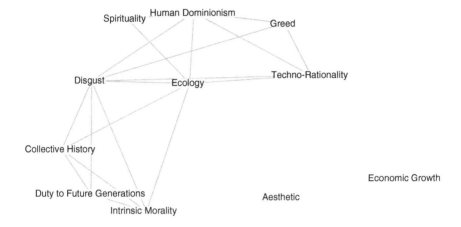

Figure 4.9: Mapping the network of relational meanings.
Note: Multidimensional scaling of categories. The closer categories are to one another, the more likely pro-wolf advocates are to simultaneously use the categories in their letter.

were dropped from the diagram because they do not cluster with other categories. This dendrogram reveals three broad clusters of meaning.

The first cluster, *Duty to Future Generations/Collective History/Intrinsic Morality/Disgust*, describes a broad orientation toward concern about the inherent rights of humans and wolves: wolves inherently deserve to survive, and human cultures *deserve* to have wolves as part of their future. The letters simultaneously express disgust that these rights have been violated by the proposal of the USFWS. For example, consider this representative example of how pro-wolf advocates concurrently express these feelings:

> It is reprehensible that you would consider decimating the wolf population that we have worked so hard to help for so long… please do the right and just thing rather than the expedient. Do not allow indigenous wolves to fade from our children's, children's, children. We have an obligation to them and ourselves, to keep all species alive and well.

A second general cluster is *Ecology/Human Dominionism/Spirituality*, which describes a broad orientation against human disruption and destruction of the ecological health of creation. As we saw in Figure 4.9, these three are the most frequently used of all the categories, and thus they co-occur with many other

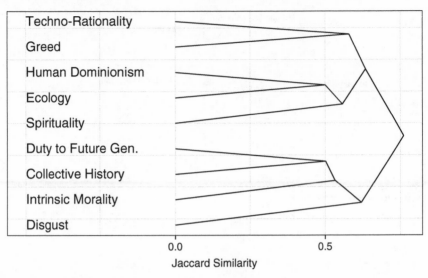

Figure 4.10: Dendrogram displaying clusters of meaningful categories.

categories, but even taking into account their frequency, they tend to co-occur in this cluster of three, as illustrated by this representative example:

> The wolves are very important to the ecosystem... Predators help maintain healthy populations of game animals... God gave us the planet to protect, not to destroy but it seems like we're doing a great job at destroying this place and its animals.

Anti-wolf advocates would often express frustration at the fact that Human Dominionism and Spirituality were linked to the personification of the wolves themselves. For example, one anti-wolf politician from Montana complained to me that "emotionally influenced wolf lovers will build intimate, personal relationships with these animals. They actually think that wolves reciprocate these personal relationships [laughter]. Environmental groups exploit these people because they aren't thinking straight—because they are so emotional about these animals." Some pro-wolf advocates I spoke with expressed frustration at those within their own movement who publicly expressed fawning emotion like this, fearing that it would harm the cause. One woman who is active in a pro-wolf environmental organization was especially troubled at "eye for an eye" reactions to Human Dominionism, telling me:

> I get notes from pro-wolf people who want wolf hunters to have body parts cut off, or be castrated, and on and on. While I appreciate their passion, there's got to be a better outlet. You know, people talk about laying their lives down

for a wolf, jumping in front of a bullet, you know, or chaining themselves to stuff and spreading their urine on trails. But sometimes I shudder because, even though I am on board with the passion, this stuff can play right into the hands of anti-wolf people who already believe that we are a bunch of wacko, left-wing, tree huggers.

The third cluster is *Greed/Technorationality*, which describes a feeling among many pro-wolf advocates that USFWS decision making has strayed from the purity of reason and science because of the lure of greedy special interests. Of course, Greed co-occurs with several categories (e.g., Human Dominionism and Disgust), but this cluster shows that pro-wolf advocates are especially upset at the polluting influence of money at the expense of rational decision making, as described in this representative example:

> All changes to laws regarding the environment and wild animals should be made based on sound scientific investigation and studies, not politics, profit margins, and private gain!

ECOLOGY AS MEANINGLESS?

Ecology is the most frequently used category, tends to co-occur more with other categories, and as the map seen in Figure 4.9 showed, does not occur in a vacuum like some other categories (e.g., Economic Growth or Ranch Compensation). Consistent with the broader theoretical and empirical claims of this chapter, these data show that *Ecology as a form of scientific or moral justification is not inherently meaningful on its own, but requires externally given moral and spiritual categories to give it meaning.* Intentional or not, pro-wolf advocates rarely make Ecology arguments in isolation, but rather pair them with deeper meaning-making categories. Thus, instead of examining Ecology on its own terms, we should pay particular attention to proximate moral and spiritual justifications *co-occurring* with Ecology. Figure 4.11 graphs the proximity values for Ecology to all other categories. As this graph shows, opposition to the USFWS generated responses that paired Ecology not with economic arguments (at the bottom are Economic Growth or Ranch Compensation), but with deeper moral commitments and narratives about de-centering humans from the top of the natural hierarchy (Human Dominionism), protecting God's creation (Spirituality), and instinctive and affective feelings of right and wrong (Disgust).

Conclusion

The preceding analysis leads me back to a simple statement that I heard over and over again in my fieldwork and interviews: "It's not about the wolf." Indeed, this conflict is not about the wolf. At its root, it is not all about wolf science,

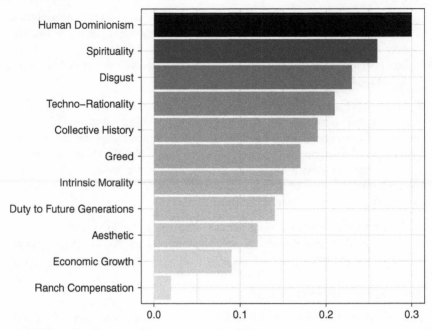

Figure 4.11: Proximity value of "Ecology" to all other categories.

ecosystem dynamics, or economic threat. I argued at the beginning of this chapter that the primary fuel source for this conflict exists beneath a heap of technical knowledge, research, and reports. There is no doubt that technical knowledge plays a crucial part, but it is merely evidence in the service of larger, more meaningful goals. To get to the heart of the issue, and to understand why this conflict remains so intractable, we must ask different, and perhaps more difficult and complicated questions: What motivates all the scientific activity? Why do pro-wolf advocates even care about wolves in the first place? If it's not really all about economic interests, then why are wolves feared and hated so vigorously by some people? Why does an "intact" ecosystem have higher value? Should we care if future generations get to "experience" wolves? The current mass of technical knowledge cannot, in the end, answer questions like these, because such answers require deeper moral and spiritual commitments to give them meaning. I have shown that such commitments come from larger cultural narratives in which the lives of anti-wolf and pro-wolf advocates are embedded. These contrasting narratives and commitments propel intractable conflict because they are at times incommensurable, and thus it becomes difficult to even see opportunities for collaboration, especially in a context where moral meanings rarely rise to the surface of the debate.

In the first section of this chapter, I showed how the anti-wolf moral order, and vitriolic opposition to the wolf, is influenced by *rugged American individualism*, involving commitments to antifederalism, private property rights, and the wolf as an ecological "outsider." I also found that a complex set of cultural factors relating to *human dominionism* fueled fear and hatred for the wolf, because it literally and symbolically challenged a "natural hierarchy," which for many people is divinely ordered. Finally, I found that the wolf also symbolized anxieties about, and threats to, the devaluation and decline of a *simple and sacred heritage*. Taken together, this moral order explains, in large part, how most anti-wolf advocates have understood their place in the world, and the cultural resources upon which they draw in the conflict over wolf policy.

In my fieldwork and content analysis of pro-wolf letters, I found that beneath the obsession with ecology and technical expertise lay deeper cultural, moral, and spiritual attachments to the wolf. These are moral and spiritual commitments that, for many, go far beyond the wolf, to the natural environment more generally. This explains why, despite requests from the USFWS to keep these letters about science, they nevertheless express thicker, more meaningful arguments that delve much deeper than mere scientific logic and rationality. These moral arguments happen in complex ways, and I explored how pro-wolf advocates simultaneously draw upon multiple meanings that tend to cluster together. For example, Ecology was the most frequently used category, but more surprisingly it was one of the least likely to be used in isolation. I demonstrated how ecological arguments were perceived to be most powerful when they were paired with more basic appeals to Human Dominionism, Spirituality, and Disgust.

Also interesting was the fact that there were significant differences between local GYE letters and nonlocal letters. Locals were more likely to appeal to Ecology, Technorationality, Economic Growth, and Ranch Compensation, but because nonlocal writers are disconnected from the everyday concerns about the wolf—much of which is roiled by scientific and technical debate—they were significantly more likely to appeal to Spirituality, Intrinsic Morality, Aesthetics, and Duty to Future Generations. These substantive differences between anti-wolf and pro-wolf commitments are stark, and this goes to show that even though their concern is with the same animal, in the same ecosystem, these groups rely on radically different social constructions about what the wolf is "good" for, how it fits into their moral narrative, and what it all means for their vision of the future.

With that said, in the midst of intractable conflict, some similarities also emerged. First, both sides rely on a spiritual connection to the land, albeit in different ways, and for different purposes. Remember that an important part of anti-wolf heritage is a spiritual connection, cultivated on the land and with the land, which shapes each group's views of private property rights and human dominionism. Pro-wolf advocates similarly express a spiritual connection to all that is "wild," to "soul-stirring" untrammeled wilderness, and, explicitly and implicitly, to "creation." Thus the redemption of the wolf represents ecological, as well as spiritual, renewal. Second, both groups believe in a moral duty to future generations. Anti-wolf advocates view the wolf as a threat to their ranching and hunting traditions and fear that their children will be shut out of these historically meaningful practices. Pro-wolf advocates similarly express a duty to pass down their soul-stirring experiences of wolves to their children and grandchildren, so future generations can enjoy nonconsumptive wolf-watching experiences, but also because of a larger sacred duty to the perpetuation of biodiversity and intact ecosystems.

As the decades-long battle about the wolf continues to rage, stakeholders would do well to pay closer attention to these deeper cultural, moral, and spiritual motives that undergird the conflict and ultimately define why the wolf is important in the first place. Natural resource managers and policy experts talk frequently about the need to be more aware of environmental "values." But I have attempted here to push the conversation even further to the *sources* of values themselves—to the deeper narratives that orient stakeholders' lives within an identifiable shared moral order, informing what they want, what is "good," and why it all matters. For the foreseeable future, it seems, the gray wolf issue will continue to serve as a stage upon which these deep, conflictual, and sometimes incommensurate, moral commitments will be acted out.

5. Drilling Our Soul: Moral Boundary Work in an Unlikely Old-West Fight against Fracking

Why are some parts of nature treated as more special than others? Why do we draw strong moral boundaries around areas that supposedly deserve more protection, yet other areas we neglect with the ease of indifference? These questions involve (1) how, and why, we value nature, and (2) the social and political conditions under which collective action about these values actually takes place. This chapter investigates the intersection of these two important questions.

These questions bubbled to the surface in what became one of the most important, but puzzling, cases of environmental activism in the GYE. The conflict was over a plan to drill 136 natural gas wells in the Hoback Basin area of the Wyoming Range (a national forest area about 70 miles south of Yellowstone). This plan to drill a modest number of wells was not out of the ordinary, given that Wyoming is a national leader in energy production, and 136 wells was merely a drop in the bucket to the more than 30,000 wells in the same county and around the state. The puzzle had to do with *who* was engaging in activism against this proposal, and the reasons *why*.

The conflict that ensued was anything but business as usual: natural gas drilling in the Hoback was permanently shut down, and the activists largely responsible for this outcome were not the typical environmentalists but the very types of people who have historically opposed environmentalists and have actively supported (and participated in) gas drilling just down the road. Instead of endorsing this energy proposal, a large group of old-westerners reversed course, and launched one of the most successful environmental movements in GYE history. People who, for generations, had relied on and *vigorously defended* extraction industries (e.g., coal, oil, gas, minerals, ranching, farming), from environmental regulation, were now organizing against their own way of life and economic interests. Perhaps most surprisingly, they were collaborating with environmentalists to do so. But what explains such counterintuitive behavior?

In other words, why did some miners, ranchers, outfitters, and other old-westerners act against their own economic and cultural traditions, and become environmental activists?

The first place we should look to explain this puzzle is the rich body of research within sociology and political science about the emergence and organization of collective action. Findings from this work shows that collective action tends to emerge when people become aware of their grievances, when they assemble enough resources to take action, and when the larger political opportunity structure becomes favorable to change. Similarly, environmental justice research on "not in my back yard" (NIMBY) movements highlight the importance of resources such as social capital for explaining when people might successfully take collective action (e.g., Bullard 2008). Other, more basic explanations might point us toward the supreme power of economic self-interest, or to variation in the scientific literacy or ignorance of the pool of potential participants.

Any attempt to explain this case of unlikely activism must take into consideration these important theories. Certainly, in some cases, these organizational and economic theories can adequately explain phenomena in question. But in other cases, such as this one, the conditions for action may not have clear organizational or economic explanations, and can beg deeper questions. In response, I argue that sometimes lost in organizational and economic accounts are cultural experiences relating to the social sources of why, and how, we value nature. I will show how closer attention to such experiences will improve our sociological understanding of collective action in cases like this. In doing so, I am *not* rejecting these prior explanations of collective action, nor am I ignoring the power of economic self-interest and scientific knowledge to explain behavior. Nor is it my goal to present a full-fledged theory of social movement emergence and success. With that said, I take these factors into serious consideration throughout this chapter, but I focus my investigation on a slightly different and, I believe, much needed level of analysis.

I argued in the introductory chapter that while useful for determining the value of most tangible commodities, economic approaches pose limits for explaining behavior about that which is morally objectionable. That which is morally objectionable is related to what humans value—and what humans value is rooted in different communities' "sociohistorical experiences with particular natural sites, landscapes, or wildlife" (Fourcade, 2011, p. 1725). These different "sociohistorical experiences" define nature's ultimate "worth" and exert real causal power in social, political, and legal processes. Extending this line of work, and consistent with the larger argument of this book, *I start at this deeper moral-philosophical level, to uncover and explain the causal cultural mechanisms pertaining to the different narratives, emotions, and place-based experiences that create moral boundaries and structure social reactions to natural gas drilling in the first place—thus providing a cultural basis for understanding why old-westerners acted in such counterintuitive ways this time, but not in the myriad other times companies drilled nearby.*

An introductory example will help. Over dinner in a rustic tavern between Jackson and Pinedale, Dan Smitherman—the leader of this unlikely coalition of old-west activists known as the Citizens for the Wyoming Range—explained to me the motivations behind the surprising opposition to "fracking the Hoback area." As we washed down our dry roast beef sandwiches with cold beers, Smitherman talked in his slow deliberate drawl, characteristic of a Wyoming cowboy, describing the history of the issue, and how he, as a retired Marine, hunting outfitter, political conservative, and self-described "antithesis of a tree-hugger," led a successful environmental movement against this proposed natural gas development. I interrupted, "But why oppose drilling *this time*?—especially during an economic recession?" Continuing, I pressed further, "And how is this case any different from the 30,000 other natural gas wells nearby that people benefit from, and overwhelmingly support as central to their way of life?" Smitherman paused, and with his eyes welling up with tears, he reflected with sincere emotion, "I'm *not* anti–energy development, you see. I'm *not* antifracking. I just don't want drilling *here*, because this land is just *too special*... The connection Sublette County residents have to this land is unexplainable. The wildlife, the beauty, the uniqueness. People just don't understand what this land means to us. Its incomprehensible. Its about, what do you call it, intrinsic value? It can't be quantified into dollars and cents. It's part of our soul."

So I return to the question at the heart of the puzzle: Why would a group of people who have a deep-seated distaste for environmental regulation, and rely on mineral extraction for their economic well-being, actually fight to oppose drilling here, *but not anywhere else*? Over the course of my research *I found that the intense negative reaction to drilling in this area, but not others, is caused by a violation of strong moral boundaries linked to old-west place attachment.* By "place attachment" I mean a deep emotional, and sometimes spiritual, bond with particular landscapes that forms over time, within larger narratives, and shapes one's sense of self, community, and connectedness with the natural world. Such attachments cannot, in the end, "be quantified into dollars and cents," as Smitherman articulated. Place attachment can structure parts of a moral order, creating within people a feeling of moral responsibility, leading them to draw moral boundaries and protect areas to which they are meaningfully connected.

But old-west place attachment involves a very different connection to the land than that experienced by the typical GYE transplant who moves to the area and joins an environmental movement against fracking.[1] Instead, and perhaps unique

---

1 "Fracking" is a popular colloquial term used by participants to refer to hydraulic fracturing, a powerful process of drilling and injecting a highly pressurized chemical mixture of liquid and sand into the ground, fracturing rocks and releasing natural gas.

to this context, it is a connection rooted deeply in one's familial dependence on particular landscapes. It is less an abstract idealism and more about generations of embodied utilitarian and nonutilitarian interaction with these physical spaces. For Smitherman, it is about a deep intimacy with the landscape, "knowing every nook and cranny, every peak and valley, from, my years on horseback in the Wyoming Range." For others, it is the long tradition of annual hunting and fishing trips with children and grandchildren. Still, for others, it is farming and ranching the same soil that their great-grandparents homesteaded long ago. Place attachment is so emotional and so influential because it is cultivated by generations past and bestows upon the present the moral responsibility to preserve place-based bonds for future generations.

Place attachment also provides clues about how—in contrast to most other GYE policy issues—old-westerners and environmentalists were able to collaborate. As I demonstrated in previous chapters, these two groups would most often (knowingly and unknowingly) disagree about the intrinsic value of the natural environment. In this case, however, old-west place attachment generates a supply of intrinsic value that is compatible with environmentalists working on the issue. The incommensurable is made commensurate. In other words, long-time conflicting groups are now able to establish trust based on common moral ground—or a common moral currency—about the intrinsic value of this particular landscape. While the source of old-west intrinsic value is rooted in different narratives and experiences, it nevertheless creates a common language, meaning, and set of values upon which these groups can base cooperation.

But this cooperation was not without much cultural discomfort. While my main aim in this chapter is to show the relationship between place attachment, moral boundaries, and an antifracking movement, I am also interested in the influence of this movement on the participants themselves. Many people in the movement are first-time activists, who go to great lengths to distance themselves from people they perceive to be extreme and idealistic "tree-huggers." How do these old-west activists make sense of this new identity as converted environmental activists and the perceived moral baggage that comes along with it? How do they attempt to align their activism with their traditional cultural narratives described throughout this book (e.g., individualism, pragmatism, manifest destiny, antifederalism)? I briefly examine these questions, *arguing that old-west activists engage in a process of moral "boundary work" to assert their old-west identity, over and against environmental groups that do not share "Wyoming values," and thus are regarded as less virtuous.*

It will be helpful here to provide a general roadmap, and to clarify my approach. Beginning with the next section, I describe in more detail the history of the policy issue in Wyoming. This is especially important as comparative evidence to understand how unusual it is that old-westerners opposed fracking in the Hoback, but nowhere else. From here I focus on the the unique cultural dynamics of the movement to save the Hoback (Citizens for the Wyoming Range), and consider how it achieved such a successful policy outcome. I then briefly consider, in more depth, the alternative explanations I touched on above about why the social movement emerged and gained such an unlikely coalition of participants. I demonstrate that, while insightful, previous theories do not take into account the cultural complexity on the ground, and therefore do not provide the fullest account of the moral boundaries that structure relationships to fracking in the Hoback. I end by reflecting on how the participants themselves engage in moral "boundary work" to make sense of their unlikely conversion to environmental activism.

A State of Mining

To understand just how surprising it is that old-west Wyomingites mobilized against drilling, we must first grasp just how important oil, coal, and natural gas mining is to Wyoming's economy and way of life. A very important point in my overall argument is that place attachment, and the drawing of moral boundaries, is not present in the same way throughout Wyoming as it is the Hoback. As I will show, there is even considerable variation in place attachment in Sublette County itself (home to the Hoback). But I begin here with the state of Wyoming as a whole, before narrowing my focus to the Sublette County and the Hoback area.

State income from mining continues to dwarf all other industries, making up 26 percent of state GDP in 2012 (Bureau of Economic Analysis, 2012). Despite the rapid growth of new-west services and tourism across the GYE (see Chapter 2), mining is still king throughout the rest of Wyoming. Within the GYE, mining is most important to Sublette County, the site of our case study. In fact, mining in Sublette County makes up over 30 percent of the county's total annual income. Figure 5.1 compares income from mining in Sublette County to the GYE, Wyoming, and the entire United States. This chart not only shows how important mining is to Wyoming, but also shows just how uniquely important it is to Sublette County, especially over the last decade with the dramatic rise in natural gas development.

But this economic reality has been overshadowed by a persistent belief in the myth that the state was built by pioneering ranchers and other agricultural cowboys who symbolized ideals of rugged independence. One Wyomingite I spoke with summed up well this cultural phenomenon of fierce Wyoming individualism and antifederalism, jesting that "the federal government could offer every citizen of Wyoming a million dollars for free, and their first response would be a cynical 'Why? We don't need handouts, especially from the feds!'" Perception was, and still is, that the state of Wyoming was built by ruggedly independent farmers and ranchers. Nevertheless, the economic reality is that agriculture (crop and

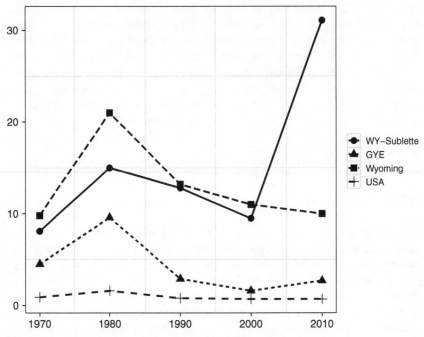

Figure 5.1: The growth of mining industries in Sublette County, Wyoming. Percentage of annual income from mining industries. Source: Bureau of Economic Analysis (2012).
Note: In 1997 the BEA implemented a new classification scheme, switching from the long-standing Standard Industrial Classification (SIC) scheme to the North American Industry Classification Scheme (NAICS). Data include both schemes, and thus data from 2000 and 2010 are based on the NAICS. I followed Yuskavage (2007) in converting industry data for the 20 counties of the GYE across this time period.

animal production) played a somewhat minor role compared to mining.[2] By the 1970s crop and animal production accounted for less than 5 percent of employment in the state, and by 2012 accounted for only 1 percent of the state GDP (Bureau of Economic Analysis, 2012). Perception is reality, however, as the veneration of cowboy ideals (e.g., the state's iconic cowboy symbol, and nickname "Cowboy State") has allowed the ranching industry, and the associated values of individualism and antifederalism, to exert inordinate political influence in local government.

Thus, despite the popular legends of ranching and pioneering cowboys, mineral production has actually sustained Wyoming's economy since the beginning of statehood in 1890. Early explorers to the Wyoming Territory reported evidence

---

2 But this is not as true in the other 19 counties in the GYE, where ranching and farming played a more important role in building the old-west way of life, as I demonstrate in Chapter 2.

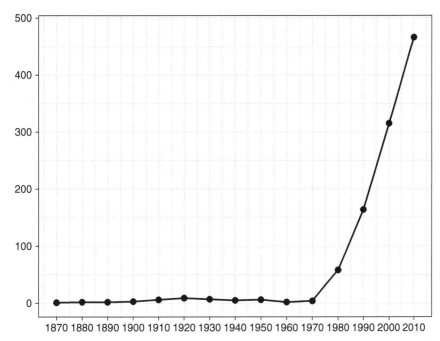

Figure 5.2: The historical growth of "king coal" in Wyoming (thousands of tons). Source: Wyoming State Geological Survey.

of oil, drilled the first well prior to statehood in 1884, and by the 1920s the industry was going strong, eventually peaking nationally, and in Wyoming, in 1970 (Roberts, 2012). Many refineries closed in the 1970s and 1980s, partly because the boom in production had taken its toll on Wyoming oil reserves. While it is no longer at its peak, oil development in Wyoming still ranks in the top 12 of U.S. states in annual production. In 2011, over 400 different companies produced 54 million barrels of oil from 879 fields and 10,600 different wells. Two of Wyoming's top three oil-producing counties are Sublette County and Park County. Both of these counties are part of the GYE—and in fact, 53 percent of Yellowstone National Park is contained within Park County.

Even more significant than oil is coal mining. Wyoming has been the nation's leading coal producer since 1986, and today 40 percent of America's coal is mined in Wyoming. The state produced an astonishing 440 million tons of coal in 2011. To put this in perspective, consider that Wyoming produces nearly four times more coal than the second leading producer, West Virginia, and more than the next top six states combined (West Virginia, Kentucky, Pennsylvania, Illinois, Texas, and Montana). Additionally, Wyoming contains 9 of the nation's 10 largest coal mines. Figure 5.2 provides a look at coal production in the state of Wyoming from 1865 to 2012.

Figure 5.3: Black thunder coal operation in Wyoming. Photo courtesy of EcoFlight.

Some 99 percent of Wyoming's coal is produced using a method called "surface mining" (including related "strip mining" and "mountaintop removal") where, in contrast to traditional underground mining, companies use heavy equipment—earthmovers and dragline excavators—to scrape away layers of the earth (rock, soil, other ecosystem elements) to get to the coal underneath (Figure 5.3).

Alongside oil and coal, Wyoming has also experienced, in recent decades, a natural gas boom. The state ranks second in the nation in proven natural gas reserves and third in annual production. In 2011, over 275 different companies produced a total of 2.37 trillion cubic feet of natural gas on nearly 30,000 separate Wyoming wells (Lynds, 2013). Fracking is a highly effective process of drilling and injecting a highly pressurized chemical mixture of liquid and sand into the ground, fracturing rocks and releasing natural gas. Advancements in horizontal drilling have also increased well productivity. Figure 5.4 shows the rise in natural gas production since 1978 in Wyoming, compared to oil production.

Especially important for our purposes is that Sublette County is the leading producer of natural gas in the state. Remember, too, that it was also the number two producer of oil. Sublette County is part of the GYE, home to the Hoback area, and is located just southeast of Jackson Hole and Yellowstone Park.

But before narrowing our focus to the political, environmental—and ultimately moral and spiritual—consequences of natural gas development in Sublette

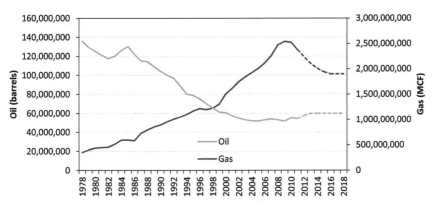

Figure 5.4: Wyoming oil and gas production. Production estimates for 2012–2018 are shown as dashed lines. Source: Graph from Wyoming State Geological Survey (Lynds, 2013).

County, I want to emphasize here my larger point from this brief analysis of mining in Wyoming. The takeaway here is that Wyoming has, since entering statehood, been a state that has subsisted by extracting its wealth of mineral riches for America's use. This is especially true in Sublette County. The people of Wyoming—and many, many more outsiders who came to take advantage of countless boom and bust cycles—have expanded energy production into every corner of their large state. With a vast storehouse of mineral riches, and with a pioneering spirit characteristic of their cowboy myths, Wyomingites plowed forward unfettered by political and environmental restraints, transforming their state—and its natural landscapes—into America's energy capital. External pressure from America's voracious appetite for energy, along with Wyoming's own hostility toward government restrictions, meant that there are now very few places untouched by one form of mining or another. With this important point in mind, I examine in the rest of this chapter the conditions under which Wyomingites might, against all these odds, actually *oppose* mining. That is, why, and how, might Wyomingites resist the tidal wave of economic opportunity that has been so central to the state's way of life and vision of progress?

Drilling in the Greater Yellowstone Ecosystem

A NATURAL (GAS) PARADISE

The southern part of the GYE is home to two of the most productive natural gas fields in the nation, the Jonah Field and the Pinedale Anticline (Figure 5.5). Both are nestled in Wyoming's Upper Green River Basin between the Wind River and Wyoming Mountain Ranges. Both are in Sublette County. With the

Figure 5.5: Drilling rig near Pinedale in Sublette County, WY. Source: U.S. Department of the Interior, Bureau of Land Management.

introduction of fracking technology to the area in the mid-1990s, the number of gas wells boomed from just a handful in 1992 to 1,347 wells by December 2000; industry and government plans to eliminate restrictions on the amount of space required between well pads could increase the number to over 3,100. This rapid expansion in Sublette County during the late 1990s and early 2000s created thousands of jobs for locals and transplants, brought record windfalls for energy companies, and injected millions into local communities like Pinedale. But economic success came at a high cost. The entire ecosystem surrounding the area has been disrupted. For example, A 2010 Bureau of Land Management study showed that energy development caused the prized Sublette mule deer herd to decline by 60 percent from 2001 to 2009. Some 85 percent of deer habitat on the wintering mesa has been lost due to new well pads and new road construction for hauling. Air and water quality have declined precipitously, and people often lamented to me that their view of the Wind River Mountains is obscured by a persistent haze that was unseen before drilling began.

The cascade of negative environmental effects—and the sense that in due time the entire state of Wyoming would be polluted by gas development—led to a bipartisan effort to limit development in the Wyoming Range. In 2009 President Barack Obama signed into law the the Omnibus Public Land Management Act, which included a piece of legislation called the Wyoming Range Legacy Act. The Wyoming Range, which contains the Hoback area, straddles the western border of Sublette County, running north to south, spanning about 85 miles of grassy valleys, towering mountain peaks, and rolling sagebrush hills replete with diverse flora such as conifers, aspens, and sagebrush that are home to deer, pronghorn, elk, moose, and countless other animals. Supported by a surprisingly broad base of Wyomingites, this act permanently shielded 1.2 million acres of the Wyoming Range from future oil and gas leases. However, companies that had leases issued *before* the act was signed, would be permitted under the law to develop their holdings within the Wyoming Range.

This brings us to the drilling proposal at the center of the conflict in this chapter. Figure 5.6 depicts the location of the proposed fracking area by the Houston based Plains Exploration and Production Company (PXP for short). PXP's leases on the now protected Hoback Basin in the Wyoming Range were still valid because they had been acquired before the Wyoming Range Legacy Act was signed into law. Thus, PXP's plan to drill 136 gas wells on 17 pads in the remote Hoback area had the initial green light. According to PXP's vice president of corporate communications, its proposal would infuse a struggling economy with jobs and "help meet our nation's domestic energy needs"; moreover, he added that PXP always emphasizes "environmental protection in all its operations" (Ostilnd, 2010).

PXP's proposal came with the standard risks associated with fracking, the consequences of which had become routine, and even an acceptable trade-off, for the majority of Wyomingites. Like the massive Jonah Field and Pinedale Anticline—or even oil and coal development everywhere else in the state— drilling in the Hoback Basin would threaten wildlife habitat and corridors, risk polluting local rivers, increase ground-level ozone (i.e., smog), blemish the landscape, and necessitate the building of new roads in roadless areas. Wyomingtes had by and large accepted the fact that being the energy capital of America requires environmental sacrifice. They understood that their "wise use" of the state's bounty of natural resources meant facing the realities of environmental risk and harm. This pragmatic way of life is rooted deeply in Wyoming's history, and accepting these side-effects is simply the cost of playing the game. This explains why the continued expansion of energy development— more coal fields, more oil pads, more fracking—has elicited relatively little public attention or concern by visitors and residents alike.

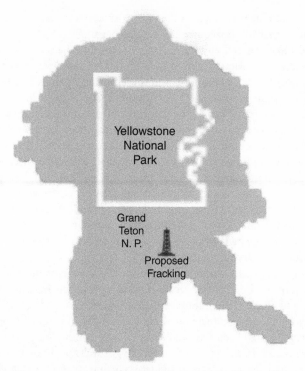

Figure 5.6: The proposed Hoback development area, southeast of YNP and GTNP.

NOT BUSINESS AS USUAL: THE OPPOSITION LED BY CITIZENS FOR THE WYOMING RANGE

Although in the apt words of Republican Wyoming senator John Barrasso, "We have never been a state that has said 'Not in my back yard,'" things were very different this time. This PXP proposal was anything but business as usual. There was an intense and demonstrative outcry, despite the fact that 136 wells was trivial compared to the oil and gas pincushion that Sublette County, and the rest of the state, had become. PXP's plan to drill became one of the most controversial and public disputes over mining in Wyoming. The Bridger-Teton National Forest office received 60,000 public comments on the plan—a record number topping any previous issue. Most plans receive a few dozen to a few hundred public comments. Jacque Buchanan, the forest supervisor, noted that some of these 60,000 comments were also from Americans outside the GYE, recognizing that this was indeed an environmental issue gaining national attention.

As we have seen throughout this book, public outcry over an environmental issue in the GYE is nothing noteworthy. What is remarkable here, however, is the fact that this record-setting uproar came from a diverse—yet united—base of local citizens opposed to drilling in the Hoback. Public outcry over wolves or

Figure 5.7: Hoback River and Wyoming Range. The primary image for Citizens' media materials. Source: Citizens of the Wyoming Range.

buffalo arose from two *opposite* sides of public debate. But here, the outcry, coming from many of the same people who are polarized about other GYE issues, was declared in agreement, with one voice, against the plan. There were old-westerners and new-westerners, wolf-lovers and wolf-haters, cross-country skiers and snowmobilers, Republicans and Democrats, miners and conservationists, millionaire transplants and long-time residents, hunters and hikers, first-time activists and seasoned environmentalists. This diverse band of people, which included several environmental groups, was spearheaded by the most active and influential coalition, the Citizens for the Wyoming Range (Citizens) (Figure 5.7). Before their leader, and spokesperson, Dan Smitherman took the helm, the group had played a successful role in the eventual passage of the Wyoming Range Legacy Act. But for people like Smitherman, there was still unfinished business—namely, the threat of PXP in the Hoback. An important feature of Citizens is that the bulk of the group is made up of old-west outfitters, steelworkers, miners, ranchers, farmers, and other Wyomingites who had built their lives on the land around the Noble Basin.

Like most members of Citizens, Smitherman is not, at first glance, the kind of guy one might expect to be the leader of an environmental movement. I met Smitherman in June 2012 just south of Bondurant, WY, to talk more about the movement, and his role in it. He pulled up in his large truck befitting of a long-time landowner and former outfitter in the Hoback area. An ex-Marine, and towering at 6-foot-4, Smitherman is fashioned right out of an old-western movie, always wearing his customary black cowboy hat, boots, and salt-and-pepper Fu-Manchu (Figure 5.8). Smitherman tells me in his slight drawl about his love for his horses, and invites me—as he does with everyone—to take a horseback ride into the Hoback area to see the beauty that he has become so intimately familiar with. As we talk about the Citizens movement, Smitherman is very quick to stress that he like most members of Citizens, is not opposed to energy development. "We recognize that a Prius isn't going to pull our horse trailers," he says, continuing, "I'm not anti-energy and never will be." While Smitherman and Citizens support oil and gas development in the state, they believe it should not

Figure 5.8: Dan Smitherman, spokesperson and leader of Citizens. Source: The Wilderness Society, Jared White.

take place in areas that are "too special to drill." He continued, "Everyone in this coalition might not agree on a lot, but the one thing we agree on is that the Hoback basin is too special to drill."

"TOO SPECIAL TO DRILL"

The phrase "Too Special to Drill" became the official slogan of Citizens. It was the group's tactical tagline at local meetings, in newsletters, in trips to Washington D.C., in written public comments, in blast e-mails to stakeholders, in phone calls to legislators, in interviews with media, and in every other strategy the group used to bring attention to the issue. In all of this, Citizens' claim was simple and pragmatic: as Wyomingites we support energy extraction but recognize that we should protect small gems like the Hoback basin because they are just "too special." The group was very effective at using digital media to get its message out. It produced several very short videos of everyday old-west residents beseeching their neighbors to get involved. For example, an avid local hunter declared in one video, "I cannot be in [the Hoback area] without feeling a deep, abiding respect and reverence for it. This is not a place for oil companies. Please get involved." In another video, a local steelworker declares:

> Yes, we are an extraction state. There are places to drill, to get that energy out of the ground, for our nation and for our Wyoming tax base. But there are places where we shouldn't drill. This is one of them... We need to hang on to at least a little piece [of Wyoming]. And when we have the opportunity to hang on to a little piece of special land, we should.

In a poignant plea, Dan Smitherman fears that the old-west legacy that he experienced in the Hoback area would be gone forever. Welling up with tears, Smitherman reflects: "I've ridden this ridge a thousand times... never had to worry about what is going to happen if they drill that... All I could think about, was to be able to tell Jace [a young kid, rodeo rider], that he hadn't lost it. And, to be able to tell Carl [local miner], that he hadn't lost it." Another local resident expresses a similar, common, sentiment that the heritage that he knew would be gone forever: "I've hunted this land for 52 years, and I'd like to pass this legacy on to my children and grandchildren." Another hunter, dressed in his camouflage shirt, and looking across a sweeping valley in the Hoback area, urged his fellow "home-grown" Wyomingites to consider the limits of drilling:

> I feel that there are places here in America that we can't just go in and, you know, just rape the land for the riches of it. To me the riches of it are the way it is right now... there was a lot of home-grown type people involved in this to a high degree. You know, who took this on. They made this part of their *life*. You know, as their life. If we group together in numbers, we do have power to do things like this.

In August 2011, Citizens held a "Rendezvous for the Wyoming Range" community barbecue in Daniel. While it was open to the public, a star-studded cast was in attendance—a who's who of Wyoming politics. Former governor Dave Freudenthal led the list as the guest speaker. Others in attendance included members of the public, Forest Service supervisors, representatives from current governor Matt Mead's office, the Wyoming Game and Fish Department, the Wyoming Department of Environmental Quality, and local politicians. To this diverse crowd—from miners, ranchers, hunters, environmentalists, to the states' political leaders—the former governor pledged support to the vision of Citizens because, despite Wyoming's commitment to drilling, there are just some places where we shouldn't conduct economic activities. He encouraged participants to be vigilant in protecting these places, affirmatively declaring:

> We have to till the field, sow the seeds, so that someday we'll be able to harvest the preservations of great parts of this country. Keep the faith! But remember this country is an amazing place, and America is filled with amazing people. But we have to keep our eye on the ball. *And that is: there are places where we have economic activity, there are places where we don't.* And where we have economic activity we can make sure it's done right to preserve the kind of lifestyle that we want, but you gotta be vigilant. Hang in there, don't give up, and God bless you.

As the leader of Citizens, Smitherman made clear to me that the group is intentional about practicing "pragmatic activism" in accordance with "practical Wyoming values." This approach is in contrast to many environmental groups he (and others in Citizens) perceives to be "zero-compromise idealists," all about "money and careers." Citizens did, however, team up with "down-to-earth" conservation groups such as Wyoming Wilderness Society and the Wyoming Outdoor Council, which, according to Smitherman, "have more credibility because they are mainstream, and have roots in the area." This strategy proved successful, because many of the more than 1,000 participants in Citizens had been turned off by environmentalist stereotypes, and had thus never taken part in any sort of politics beyond the ballot box. Smitherman laughed and said, "You know, some of these old boys had to go into town and buy their first necktie to wear to the different public meetings." But it is this sort of group culture that made first-time activists feel comfortable enough to take action.

Leading the charge against PXP, Dan Smitherman and Citizens focused their efforts on convincing PXP to sell the leases back to the people of Wyoming. This pragmatic approach recognized and honored PXP's legal right to drill, but insisted that the people of Wyoming (through conservation organizations) were willing to pay fair market value to the company, if it agreed to turn over its leases. Over the course of about seven years, Citizens rallied local Wyomingites' support for this solution and put continual pressure on PXP to consider this buyout option. Part of this process involved convincing the U.S. Forest Service (which must approve PXP's plan) that this area was indeed too special to drill. Citizens was able to slow the drilling exploration, ultimately buying more time to drum up support in local Wyoming communities, fly to Washington to lobby, meet in person with PXP, and use the Web to generate a broad base of national support. For example, the group mobilized over 30,000 e-mails to PXP. In addition to these e-mail blasts, the group estimates that about 100,000 letters were written by citizens over the years of this long campaign.

Recognizing the unified opposition against drilling in this area, and happy with the practical approach taken by Citizens, PXP finally agreed on October 8, 2012, to sell its 58,000 acres worth of oil and gas leases. Wyoming governor Matt Mead and former Wyoming governor Dave Freudenthal were in attendance at the announcement of the deal in Jackson Hole, along with dozens of environmentalists, and scores of what one activist described as "old boys in cowboy boots, who were foot soldiers getting this thing done." This was a monumental victory for Dan Smitherman, the thousand-plus participants in Citizens, and the supporters across Wyoming and the United States. In the words of Smitherman, the success "really represents Wyoming people solving Wyoming problems." Working with the Trust for Public Land and a handful of other conservation organizations, Citizens had to raise $8.75 million by December 31, 2012, to purchase the leases. Donations poured in from over 1,000 different individuals, some donations as small as $10, and others into the millions. One of the largest donations came from Joe Ricketts, a notoriously conservative benefactor and former CEO of financial giant TD Ameritrade, who now lives in Jackson Hole. Ricketts is well known for pouring millions into conservative political action committees, and thus his generosity in this case again shows how this was not a typical left-leaning environmental effort but was a broad base of people opposed to energy development in the Hoback. Shortly after December 31, 2012, the deal was closed with PXP, and the oil and gas leases were officially handed over, thus ensuring the land's protection forever. The deal secured one of the most unusual and successful conservation victories in Wyoming history.

Considering Alternative Explanations

What led so many people—who support the oil and gas way of life in Wyoming—to change course and join a movement to forever restrict the development of a lucrative source of domestic energy? Why did they choose to defend *this* particular space, but not any others nearby in their county, or throughout their state? My aim in this section is to cast doubt on more conventional answers to these questions, as they relate to explanations about economic self-interest, scientific knowledge, and predominant theories in the study of social movement participation. In doing so, I attempt to clear room for my alternative approach, which I believe more fully explains, at a deeper level, the motivations behind the emergence of this movement. It is not my intention to ignore or reject these alternative explanations. Indeed, they have a lot to offer. I consider their explanatory value but, at the same time, demonstrate how they are incomplete, because they fail to take into consideration the deeper cultural dimensions of the humanity's relationship with natural environment.

ECONOMIC SELF-INTEREST

Often times the best explanation for human behavior is simple: follow the money and/or follow the distribution of power. This has certainly been the case in the long history of energy extraction in Wyoming. But sometimes human behavior can be more complex, and looking beneath economic self-interest we can sometimes find more complex human motivations at work. This case presents a unique opportunity to do just that, especially in light of the self-sacrifice by old-west activists that I discovered during the course of my research. They voluntarily forfeited the economic benefits of drilling, sacrificing time and money to sustain a successful movement and, in a more subtle sense, became culturally vulnerable by setting aside longstanding claims to old-west power and identity (e.g., manifest destiny, utilitarian use of nature, limitless growth) that have hindered collaboration with environmental groups.

To understand why this movement, and participation within it, was *not* motivated predominantly by economic self-interest, it is first important to understand the economic benefits of fracking for local communities. The well-known Wyoming historian Ann Chambers Noble, a Pinedale resident intimately familiar with natural gas development in Sublette County, writes about the economic benefits of drilling in the Jonah Field and Pindale Anticline, just to the south of the Hoback:

> Positive impacts from the successful drilling in the Jonah Field and Pinedale Anticline were immediate and far reaching. Millions of tax dollars have been collected as a result of the natural gas production in Sublette County, which have been used for improved infrastructure and community resources. Thousands of jobs have been created for local residents and for those willing to relocate to the area. Industry has also been very generous in volunteering time and donating money to organizations that serve the community (Chambers Noble, 2011).

Furthermore, the 2010 Draft Environmental Impact Statement for the PXP plan, published by the U.S. Forest Service and Bureau of Land Management, reiterated the importance of continued natural gas drilling for the health of Sublette County's economy. In considering the economic benefits of this proposal, they reminded stakeholders that "the oil and gas industry has provided a majority of the tax base and has been a principal industry affecting the economy of Sublette County for the past 50 years… the significance of oil and gas revenues to the region's economy has increased and is expected to grow," continuing with the conclusion that "Sublette County is dependent on minerals as a source of tax revenue… over 90 percent of the county's assessed valuation in 2007 was from minerals."

In mobilizing against drilling in the Hoback, members of Citizens were aware that their actions thwarted the economic interests of the communities in which they lived, and the industry on which many of them continued to rely. During my fieldwork I encountered miners who would talk at length about the unique economic sacrifices people made on this particular issue. One multigenerational miner from Rock Springs explained:

> Well, I'll tell you that I know of no other similar movement where people that make their living in the oil fields, some for their entire careers, stand up and say NO! They say this is too special, you can't drill here, when it would benefit them financially, you know, immensely to have that area developed. I've got a cousin who is married to a guy here in town that has a trucking company that hauls frack sand and water and drill mud, and that's their livelihood. They would benefit from that by millions of dollars, but they were totally against it.

Remember that this is not a group of faraway environmentalists who can more easily disregard people's subsistence on natural resources, but is instead a group of local people who rely on natural gas to put food on the table, but still choose to reject the benefits of PXP's drilling operation (which scientists predict would be very successful because of the amount of gas thought to be in the Hoback).

According to one miner, there were "many, many people who went against their own interests. I mean, there are landowners who would have made millions of dollars if they allow access for the company to get in there, and they said 'No! You're not coming through my land to get to this to ruin it.'"

One potential objection to this line of thinking is that drilling is not all that beneficial because there are social side-effects on local communities, characteristic of traditional "boom and bust towns" (e.g., Pinedale, WY) (Berger and Beckmann, 2010; Fuller, 2007). While these concerns are indeed serious, and warrant consideration, they are not as relevant in this case because the Hoback area does not rival the magnitude of the Jonah Field or Pinedale Anticline, which are two of the larger gas fields in the United States. These two massive fields are just to the south of the town of Pinedale, whereas the Hoback area is smaller and more remote, and thus would not carry the same *social* side-effects. It would, however, carry similar environmental effects, and these could potentially harm the bottom line of the handful of people who benefit economically from hunting. Nevertheless, in my research I found that these arguments about the economic side-effects of fracking were largely set aside in favor of a cultural approach that I discuss in the next section.

Moreover, for the most involved members, participating in Citizens' opposition to PXP meant not only giving up economic benefits but also contributing time and money. I will describe these personal contributions in more detail below, but suffice to say that organizing local involvement, traveling to meetings, writing letters, and participating in the daily grind of the movement for upwards of seven years requires voluntary obligations that I found are motivated by something deeper than economic benefit.

Movement participation also involved, in a more subtle way, sacrificing certain parts of a closely held, and comfortable, identity rooted in narratives and commitments about manifest destiny, limitless progress, and environmental deregulation. It was difficult for some activists to set these aside, and in one sense can be seen as a sort of cultural sacrifice for the goals of the movement.

What is also interesting about this movement's relationship to economic self-interest is the process by which the group was able to shut down drilling. It was not through more common strategies such as litigation, or successful political appeals to federal agencies to forbid it; rather, it was, as described above, through an offer to purchase the leases, at fair market value, from PXP. Citizens was intent that PXP had a right to develop these leases, and instead of challenging PXP's leases through political or legal channels, it convinced the company to let those who believed in the cause to incur the costs themselves. As I describe below, we see in this strategy traces of old-west rugged individualism and antifederalism—but ironically, this time it is in the service of environmental regulation. In the end, then, more than 1,000 different individuals, over the course of three months, donated a total of $8.75 million to stop a project that was, for many of them, in their own economic interest to let move forward.

SCIENTIFIC KNOWLEDGE

Another potential explanation for why this movement emerged against drilling here, but not in countless other places, is that old-westerners were uninformed about the science of fracking. As this line of thinking goes, once an ill-informed public is brought to the light, and learns of the objective "facts" of an issue, they will act rationally in accordance with these facts. Thus, in this case, once old-westerners were informed of the scientific facts about the negative impacts of drilling, they would organize to oppose drilling, based on this new information. This general approach to explaining human behavior was commonplace throughout my research and in my interactions with natural resource managers (National Park Service, U.S. Forest Service, etc.) and environmentalists.

Here I briefly present two general points about why this explanation is insufficient. First, if it is really about scientific knowledge regarding fracking, then Wyomingites would, in theory, oppose natural gas drilling on the 30,000 other wells across the state, would mobilize against coal strip-mining (elementary scientific knowledge is all that is needed to know that this tears whole ecosystems out of the ground), and, last, would have long ago put the clamps down on oil development. The point here is that scientific knowledge about the harmful effects of these mining practices is well-known in Wyoming, and this knowledge often does little to change people's behavior. As described above, most Wyomingites have embraced their role as America's energy provider, and have accepted the price to play the game. In the case of PXP, it is not as if Wyomingites were all of the sudden brought into the light that fracking raises ozone levels, invites methane pollution, uses vast amounts of water resources, and scars landscapes from pads, roads, pipelines, and industrial infrastructure. They witnessed this firsthand just miles down the road in the Jonah Field and Pinedale Anticline. If scientific knowledge of these effects were enough to push people to mobilize against their own economic interests and way of life, it would have likely happened years ago, in these and countless other mining sites across the state. But it hasn't, and the state continues to lead the country in mineral extraction; thus there is something different about people's connection to the Hoback *itself* that might explain this unique case of old-west opposition to drilling.

Second, if, in reality, scientific knowledge was the basis of this movement, then Citizens would have placed more emphasis on technorational evidence in their tactics. Indeed, science played a role in the public conversation concerning the environmental effects of drilling in this particular area, but as I will show shortly, science played a very minor role compared to the campaign promoting old-westerners' cultural attachment to the Hoback. Thus, as I have argued throughout this book, conflict over natural resources in the GYE is not first and foremost about technoscientific knowledge, but about what makes this technoscientific knowledge meaningful. What makes it meaningful are the cultural and interpretive frameworks through which the scientific knowledge becomes enfleshed with meaning.

MOVEMENT RESOURCES AND OPPORTUNITIES

Social scientists studying why a social movement emerges, why it attracts participants, and why it is successful (or not), have focused most intently on the importance of movement resources and the macro-level political opportunities that make certain social contexts ripe for change. Resources such as an economic support base, media connections, and alliances with powerful institutions all figure in the emergence and success of a movement (McCarthy and Zald, 1977). Work within environmental sociology on "not in my backyard" (NIMBY) movements similarly highlight the importance of community resources, such as social capital (Bullard, 2008). No doubt, resources are essential ingredients, and are a good place to look to potentially explain why Citizens successfully shut down drilling in the Hoback. Much more could be said here about analyzing this movement from the perspective of resources. But, as useful as this approach is, it does not explain why people react with deep emotion in the first place, and why they feel the need to do something. There is a growing sense within the study of social movements that such initial "grievances" relating to identity and culture have been lost because of an overemphasis on the importance of resources (Effler, 2010; Polletta, 2009; Swidler, 1995). I agree. So, while I could fill an entire chapter about Citizens' strategic use of movement resources, a new and important question, at a different level of analysis, concerns the moral genesis of the movement—namely, what cultural resources structure the sense of injustice, or moral outrage, that leads people to want to make change in the first place?

Beyond resources, the most significant explanation of social movements to date concerns the role of "political opportunities" (McAdam, 1982; Meyer and Minkoff, 2004). This approach focuses on how a political context is or is not vulnerable to challenge. More emphasis is placed on the macro-level political and economic context, rather than a movement itself, for explaining whether or not a movement will emerge and goal-oriented social change will happen. This theory formed in opposition to the prevailing view that collective behavior was the result of irrational mobs of protestors and was not a rational way to resolve legitimate grievances. While this approach is indeed helpful for shifting our focus to the larger social context of a movement, it tends to be overly broad and abstract, and it does a poor job of theorizing the mechanisms that give rise to, and sustain, movement opposition. Political opportunities can explain a lot about why Citizens was successful, especially in the wake of the doors that were opened by the Wyoming Range Legacy Act. But this approach is limited when it comes to explaining the counterintuitive behavior of old-westerners in this case.

Similar to resource mobilization theory, political opportunity theory does not fully explain the cultural substructure of old-westerners who actually *promote and uphold* the dominant economic and political context, despite engaging in a one-time act of opposition here, but not elsewhere (in other cases of drilling)—where the same economic and political context exists for promoting social change. In other words, the same political opportunities have existed elsewhere in Sublette

County, with the same issue (fracking), the same people, but with a different outcome. The outcome here is that there was no organized resistance to natural gas drilling, and actually, quite the opposite: widespread support. Thus, we should look beneath opportunities and resources, to more particular cultural dimensions, for clues about why things turned out so radically different in this case.

"Too Special to Drill": Place Attachment and Drawing Moral Boundaries

Some areas are "too special to drill," and some areas are not. Some ecosystems we plunder with impunity, and some ecosystems lead us to pause and reflect on repercussions. Some ecosystem wildlife we vigorously protect (e.g., elk, bears, wolves), and others we comfortably destroy (e.g., rodents, snakes). *But what makes something more "special" than something else?* Where do these moral boundaries come from? And why do people sometimes do everything in their power to protect them? Remember that these questions are best understood in the context of lived experiences that are shaped by narratives that tell us most fundamentally who we are, why we are, what we should do, and why it all matters. They are the sorts of "whys" that inform what people find sacred, good, and meaningful. We rarely think about them explicitly, but these deep narratives and commitments that are inscribed in our identities and cultures inform what we judge to be *more* "special." We then erect moral boundaries around that which is held as special, protecting it with purpose and, in some cases, "extreme strictness," in the words of Durkheim. These moral boundaries include specific prohibitions that separate the "too special" from the everyday—explaining why it would be morally wrong to drill one place, but not another.

Throughout my research, I found that drilling in the Hoback area would violate intense moral boundaries that old-westerners had drawn around this particular area. These boundaries are not as strong in other ares of Wyoming and, perhaps more surprisingly, vary within Sublette County itself. Stated differently, my argument is that fracking was *allowed* in most places in Wyoming and most of Sublette County because these moral boundaries were not erected and protected. *Thus, to understand the cultural motives behind the moral outrage of Citizens, we should pay particular attention to the influence of place attachment for the emergence, and subsequent defense, of moral boundaries.* This, I argue, is the best explanation for why an unlikely group of old-westerners would team up with environmentalists and vigorously oppose drilling here, but nowhere else.

Before jumping into the narrative profiles of three different activists, it is helpful first to flesh out in more conceptual detail the notion of place attachment, and how it relates to the construction of moral boundaries. As noted above, my working definition of place attachment is a deep emotional, and sometimes spiritual, bond with particular landscapes that form over time, within larger narratives, and shape one's sense of self, community, and connectedness with the natural world. Indeed, we ascribe meaning to places, imbuing them with emotion and feeling, making them much more than the bundles of matter that they are. The individual attributes of a space emerge into something much more culturally meaningful: a neighborhood becomes the self-identity of a people; a national park becomes for some visitors a lasting source of positive emotional attachment; a farm becomes more than fields and crops, but the site of family ritual, passed down to future generations. A wide-reaching, and cross-disciplinary, body of literature spanning community planning, geography, leisure studies, and psychology has made good use of this concept. This literature distinguishes between two related, yet distinct, types of attachment: community attachment and place attachment (Trentelman, 2009). Here I focus primarily on Citizens' place attachment—namely, members' connection to the *biophysical* attributes of the Hoback space, rather than to the local human communities surrounding the Hoback area. In the profiles below, I draw on the narratives and experiences of activists to show how place attachment is influenced by three factors: *family heritage, labor on the land*, and *wilderness experience*.

Through these processes of place attachment, the land can became, for some people, intrinsically valuable. By intrinsic value, I mean that the land is valuable in and of itself, for its own sake, and not because it provides some economic or other instrumental benefit. It is an end in itself. A few examples might help. At the celebration of the deal to stop drilling in the Hoback, the current governor of Wyoming, Matt Mead, exclaimed:

> This is historic... Someday, there will be a grandfather out there with his granddaughter or grandkids, and there will be a point where that grandchild will see their first eagle, or first deer, or first moose, or have a chance to go fishing there for the first time. *I can't place a money value on that, but I know that it is invaluable.* (Koshmrl 2012, emphasis added)

Similarly, the former superintendent of the Lewis and Clark National Forest, Gloria Flora, spoke to a crowd in Jackson Hole about the intrinsic value of the land, connecting it to meaningful recreation with family: "When you look back on your life and think of what this forest has given you, are you going to count the number of [wooden boards] you took for your back porch? No, you are going to remember the time you watched your granddaughter catch her first fish from a forest lake" (Pioli, 2010). She contrasts a utilitarian or instrumental value (boards from trees to build a porch) with an intrinsic value (priceless family experiences). But intrinsic value can also be generated from an instrumental or extrinsic use of the land—such as, in this case, the invaluable experience of watching your granddaughter catch her first fish. These experiences, in addition to other forms of place attachment, such as narratives about family heritage, or generations of labor on the land, increase the intrinsic value of a place.

Figure 5.9: Dan Smitherman looking out over Cottonwood Creek in the Wyoming Range. Source: The Wilderness Society, Jared White.

A particularly important attribute of place attachment to the Hoback area, in contrast to some other areas, is the perceived uniqueness of the natural landscape. The Wyoming Range is considered by many to be among the most aesthetically beautiful landscapes in the GYE (e.g., Figure 5.9). It contains numerous lakes, rivers, mountains, valleys, and grasslands, all mostly undeveloped. But beauty alone does not generate place attachment. One can have a positive aesthetic response to a place, but such emotional responses may, in some cases, be fleeting. One may like to look at mountains and lakes, but this does not mean that this person will have a deep, meaningful, positive, or lasting attachment to such mountains and lakes. Instead, the sorts of place attachments that I argue are beneath the Citizens' movement to stop drilling combine aesthetic beauty *and* narratives and experiences about family heritage, labor on the land, and wilderness.

But, interestingly enough, beauty is also in the eye of the beholder. Some people living in central or eastern Wyoming may prefer flat landscapes and endless horizons over towering mountain ranges. They may prefer the wildlife of these arid ecosystems to the popular bears, elk, or wolves that inhabit the Wyoming Range. In a conversation with Dan Smitherman, I asked how Citizens can base its opposition to drilling on the assumption that the Hoback is too special to drill, when folks living in other parts of Wyoming might believe that

Figure 5.10: Beautiful to some? Worthy of protection? Arid north central Wyoming near the town of Buffalo. Photo by Ildar Sagdejev.

their landscapes are just as beautiful, and just as special. He responded, conceding my point, and letting me in on a similar conversation he had with the governor of Wyoming: "I said, Governor, we both know that the Hoback area is just too special.' And the governor responded, 'Dan, you know, there are a lot of people in central Wyoming who think that their land is pretty special too.'" Visitors to, and residents of, other areas of the state might find just as much beauty in the flat, arid plains, pictured in Figure 5.10.

Not only may these landscapes be as aesthetically beautiful to some people, but they are, in the same way as the Hoback, complex ecosystems teeming with their own unique plants and animals. Thus, there is no prima facie reason why these ecosystems are not too special to drill, in the same way as is the Hoback. With that said, Wyoming's history of oil, coal, and gas development has not been kind to areas viewed by some people as less desirable. Figure 5.11 shows one example of how ecosystems like these have been transformed across the state of Wyoming. People, especially old-westerners, have not stood up to preserve these sorts of places like they have in the case of the Hoback area. While the governor might be right in theory, the history of energy development in Wyoming suggests that place attachment is weaker in these areas, and thus the moral boundaries against drilling not as strong.

The lines distinguishing right from wrong, good from bad, virtuous from virtueless, are sometimes difficult for social scientists to observe. My approach

Figure 5.11: Natural gas development in Sublette County, WY. Photo courtesy of EcoFlight.

here has been to uncover these moral boundaries by comparing why, in the same political context (Sublette County), Wyomingites organized around the belief that drilling is wrong in this part of their backyard, but not in others. This point is central to my argument in this chapter. Moral boundaries start to come into focus when we dig deeper into the differences that might contribute to this inconsistent behavior. My argument here is that, for reasons I will explain below, old-westerners developed stronger positive place attachment to the Hoback than other nearby areas. Implicit in my argument is that the strength of moral boundaries (and sensitivity to violating such boundaries) increases as positive place attachment increases. When PXP set out to develop energy leases, it breached boundaries that were woven deeply into the fabric of this particular culture and moral order. I've included a diagram of the logical process (Figure 5.12), to make the presentation of this argument even more straightforward. Thus far I have focused on the right side of Figure 5.12; in the remainder of the chapter, I will provide evidence from my field research about the narratives and experiences (far left side) that cultivated in old-westerners a feeling of positive place attachment. This cultural process best explains why they would organize an environmental movement in this case (and against their own local interests and an established culture of environmental deregulation), but not others.

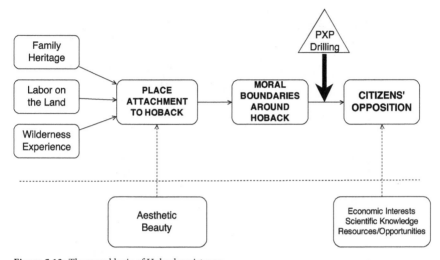

Figure 5.12: The moral logic of Hoback resistance.
Note: The dashed lines and arrows represent other factors contributing to activism. While these are important (and often sufficient for explaining other social movements), I argued above that they neglect important cultural dimensions operating in this case and do little to reveal the moral boundaries drawn around the Hoback in the first place.

Three Profiles of Old-West Environmentalists

Each participant in Citizens has a story, and each story can tell us a lot about why they, under unlikely circumstances, joined a movement against energy development. In what follows I present in-depth cultural profiles of three important activists in Citizens'. These profiles highlight three different, but interrelated, ways in which activists developed positive place attachment to the Hoback, providing the cultural ingredients necessary for moral outrage, and eventual political engagement: *family heritage, labor on the land,* and *wilderness experience.*

JOE BATISTA AND FAMILY HERITAGE

"My legacy is up in them Hoback mountains. My father told me when I was a young child that these mountains are my mountains. He said, 'Take care of them like I have, and like your grandfather did'" For the first time in his life, Joe Batista stood up and spoke his feelings in a political setting, laying out, with great emotion, his attachment to the Hoback area. In his camouflage hat and black canvas jacket (Figure 5.13), and catching the attention of everyone at this town hall policy meeting full of concerned citizens, politicians, business owners, and natural resource managers, Joe expressed his outrage about the proposal to "destroy these mountains" that his father had passed down to him, and that he

Figure 5.13: Joe Batista speaking for the first time in a public meeting in Pinedale, WY, against PXP's plan. Source: Citizens of the Wyoming Range.

had the responsibility to protect. Joe's address, which has since been admired as an important point in the movement, made no mention of science, economics, or politics—it was simple: his family's legacy is tied to the natural purity of the Hoback, and drilling violated strong moral boundaries that had been established and passed down by his grandfather, father, and now through Joe to his children. Joe explained to me that as he grew up, "The mountains were all my grandfather and father had. It was the only thing that they had to pass down to us. This is why we love and respect the Hoback so much."

Joe comes from a long tradition of Wyoming miners. His grandfather came to Wyoming from Chihuahua, Mexico, and worked most of his life in the local mines south of the Hoback, in Rock Springs, WY. Joe's father worked on oil rigs, and Joe is proud to carry on this legacy, telling me, "I followed in my father's footsteps and I worked on the oil rigs. That was going to be my life, and I really liked it." But after getting married and having children, Joe and his wife looked for something with better hours. Joe stumbled upon a local newspaper ad hiring for the local Trona mine. This mine has particular sentimental value, because it was the same mine from which his grandfather had retired. "I took a huge pay cut for this job, but you know, money isn't everything," Joe concluded. In discussing his long family history of mining, I wondered if, like some ranchers and farmers, his life of mining cultivated a special connection with the natural resources. Not for Joe, because, as he describes it, "I look at being a miner as just a paycheck. It's a way for me to make money for my family, so we can have a house to live in. You know, I don't feel any connection between my work and the mountains at all."

Throughout my research I found that activists like Joe, who either spent their lives in the mines and oil fields or lived in areas surrounded by them, view the Hoback as a place to escape the ubiquity of resource extraction. It became for them a site of "natural conscience"—meaning a space uncontaminated by the ills of human greed and sinfulness, a place where "nature" was an altogether different realm of existence, altogether pure.[3] Joe describes it as a spiritual connection: "I know the Hoback mountains and the Hoback mountains know me." He continues, "You know, if you go into the woods and you sit down and be quiet, you start to hear things. You start to see things ... it's just a beautiful, spiritual kind of experience." Linking these spiritual experiences to his family legacy, "started as far back as I can remember. We would always go camping and fishing up in the Hoback area. We didn't use just one spot exclusively, we went all over. Every summer my grandfather would take me and my brother for a two weeks."

These spiritual experiences in the Hoback were in stark contrast to the maladies and corruption he sees in his local community of Rock Springs. Joe explains that he loves spending time in the Hoback because it is a break from the obsession with technology, busy traffic, drug dealers, felons, and other ailments he experiences in modern society: "I don't even let my kids ride their bikes outside of our backyard, because there's too much traffic, people don't pay attention, and the child molesters, you know." He reflects for a moment, and says with shame for his generation, "Had a guy come down from the mountains who had been there for 30 years, into society now, he would probably turn right back around and run into the mountains!" Thus, the purity of the Hoback was, for Joe's family, measured relative to their experiences of modernity as a polluted space from which they sought to escape.

Of course, Joe's grandfather and father were not literally handing down the publicly owned Hoback mountains, but there is something deeply personal about this symbolic act that those outside Joe's family may never fully grasp. Like sentimental pieces of family jewelry, artwork, or memorabilia given as inheritance, the Hoback represented, in the same way, a gift from one generation to the next. To those receiving it, this was a *gift* rich with intrinsic value.

The meaning behind such a gift is what ultimately inspired Joe to get involved in the Citizens movement. In discussing his eventual participation in the movement, Joe proudly points to this incredible gift that was given to him, and that he has now given to his children:

What motivated me to get involved was that I grew up going to the Hoback, and my father handed it down to me. Those mountains was the first thing he ever give me that meant anything to me. I felt so empowered and so alive and important in my father's eyes, for him to say "these are my mountains I'm going to give them to you, take care of them." You can go through any city

3 For an extended analysis of the idea of "natural conscience," see Bell (1994).

anywhere in the country, or the world and ask a kid if their father has ever given them mountains, you know. It just doesn't happen. These mountains are just part of me. It's something deep in my heart.

The ritual act of passing down familial place attachment to the Hoback also came with the responsibility to protect it. "We were taught to respect the Hoback because it's the only thing we had," says Joe. But this gift was not only about protecting the purity of natural resources; it was at the same time as much about protecting the purity of the family legacy. Joe uses old-west frames of ownership and human dominion to talk about his environmental ethic ("the mountains are my mountains," "giving to me," "going to be mine someday," "watch over our mountains"). Thus, in one sense the Hoback is "owned" by the patriarch of the family, and then a symbolic deed is passed down, in the same way that a farmer or rancher might pass down his or or her privately owned fields. Nevertheless, within this old-west logic exists, in a deep sense, a land ethic with a responsibility to safeguard the intrinsic value of the land and the familial bond to it.

All of this provided a cultural backdrop upon which Joe interpreted the news about plans to drill the Hoback. On hearing the news, Joe reacted with a deep sense of moral outrage: "When I found out that PXP was bringing this plan to the table, I was like holy shit! ... that's really shady, and I need to do something about it if I'm going to be able to pass that down to my children like my father did for me." After hearing the news, Joe read more about the issue online and planned to attend the local town hall policy meeting about the issue. He proudly recounts this meeting: "You know, I drove to that meeting, stood up and told them exactly how I felt about everything." Joe's speech about his "family legacy being up in them mountains," and his family ritual of passing down this legacy, caught the attention of quite a few people, including Dan Smitherman.

After hearing Joe's speech, Smitherman approached him and told him about Citizens, describing it as a group of Wyomingites who share similar values. Joe recounts this, saying "Dan Smitherman was there, and he must have liked what I said, because he talked to me and we started a relationship from there ... They asked if I would be willing to help." It was a no-brainer for Joe, who was looking for a more permanent outlet to channel his moral indignation. Joe continues, "I have always believed that if a person doesn't stand up for something they believe in, then they might as well not stand for anything at all." Joe certainly stood, and he had a unique platform upon which to stand. Since that meeting, Joe has been heavily involved in the movement, being the de facto spokesperson for locals in the mining community who believed that drilling the Hoback crossed the line. From local meetings and rallies, to making his first trip across the country to Washington D.C., Joe spread his message of cultural meaning and moral outrage, recounting, "That's what motivated me, you know. I just couldn't see taking my children to this spot and overlooking oil pads and a compressor station. The beauty would be gone, and it's not the legacy I want to leave to my children.

Figure 5.14: Larry Smith in a video produced by Citizens of the Wyoming Range.

And I'll tell you something else, it made me a firm believer of standing up, making your voice heard, because it does matter."

LARRY SMITH AND LABOR ON THE LAND

"My use of the land is my connection to it. In ranching, you develop an appreciation for it, and almost a sense of ownership of it. It's your backyard, and if you spend as many hours moving and grazing cattle, and just enjoying that, it becomes part of who you are. And to see roads, and oil rigs, and stuff on it, you know, it just affects you, and naturally you would rather not have it happen." As Larry Smith (Figure 5.14), a 61-year-old rancher from Bondurant, WY, described to me in this conversation about his participation in Citizens, he links attachment to natural resources in and around the Hoback to his lifetime of labor on the land. Larry's intrinsic value of the Hoback is generated by an extrinsic, or instrumental, use of the area for subsistence. This process can involve family heritage and place attachment (like Joe Batista's), but here it is more about how the practices of old-west extraction industries can, for some people, cultivate a relationship to the land that goes well beyond simple economic dependence. Ritual labor practices, such as farming a field or herding cattle, create deeper affective bonds to places and spaces. Of course, as we have seen throughout the history of the GYE and the American West (Chapter 1), not everyone attaches sentimental meaning to such extractive labor. Like Joe's mining career, such practices can simply be seen as a way to put food on the table, rather than being a source of intrinsic value. But, for people like Larry, this sort of labor on the land creates positive place attachment and intrinsic value, and it becomes part of a person's cultural identity, shaping moral visions about how land should (or should not) be used.

Similar to Joe, Larry's ancestral connection to the area is an important part of his positive place attachment. Both of Larry's grandparents were among the first white European settlers to Jackson Hole. The nature of work for early settlers meant that Larry was born and bred a rancher on the land that his family homesteaded in the late 1800s. Larry reflected on the early years of his life, immersed in the culture of ranching, "Oh, gosh, you know. I just grew up in a subsistence type lifestyle on the ranch. We ran cattle and we had our own gardens, chickens, pigs, and you know … we had our daily routines on the ranch. You had your responsibilities before you went to school and rodeo practice." As Larry grew older, it was important to him and his family that they reproduced this culture—or in his words, "carried on that ranching lifestyle." In contrast to some exploitative old-west extraction practices (such as the early hunters and trappers to the GYE), Larry stressed that the day-to-day labor on the land, which was part and parcel of ranching culture, instilled in him ethical principles to live by: "You know it's interesting living off of the land. I guess the biggest thing we learned was that waste was not allowed. If you caught a fish, you knew it was for the table. The same with wildlife, because elk and deer were pretty important to your well-being. *So you appreciated it, even though you used it as a resource. This was a big part of our life.*" Larry applied these ethical principles to the Hoback issue, because, in his view, the PXP plan crossed the moral line between responsibly subsisting on the land and overusing or denigrating it.

While Larry may not use as effusive or romantic language as Joe to talk about his positive place attachment, it nevertheless pushed him to take environmental action. He admits that his participation in the opposition to PXP involved "some emotion, but it's more about the highest and best use of that property." While he talks in a more subdued and practical Wyoming way, Larry would often stop and reflect about how his activism is tied to "the heart, in addition to the head." Larry cherishes the work of ranching, reflecting with passion about the meaning of this work in the Hoback area, saying that "there is nothing I enjoy more than taking my saddle horse and working cattle out there. Or just going to check on cattle, you know, and riding the range and seeing the wildlife interact with all the cattle. I guess it's therapeutic to me."

He had always had this special feeling for the Hoback area, but it wasn't until the Hoback was threatened that he became active in the cause to slow energy development. He explained how his opinion about oil and gas extraction in the area began to change: "You know I've been involved in different land issues for quite a long while, and I don't know at what point you come to realize that Wyoming is such a pretty young state … so it kind of gives you pause if you step back and look at the scope of the development that's already occurred, and you come to realize that there is not much of this [Hoback] country left that isn't developed … Yes, this is what definitely caught my interest." Larry may not wear his emotion on his sleeve, but it is clear that he has been influenced by his intense physical connection to the landscape—a connection that is deeply rooted in his proud ancestral history in the area. This cultural orientation made Larry more and more uncomfortable as natural gas development crept closer to the Hoback area, leading him to take action.

Like Joe was for the mining industry, Larry became the de facto mouthpiece for the ranching community. Larry participated in the opposition from the beginning. Most notably, Larry took part in multiple meetings with PXP in Salt Lake City and Denver. As a rancher, Larry admits that this activism was new territory for him, and he was, at times, "in over my head with the negotiations, and whatnot. PXP's people were very good at what they were doing, as far as public relations... That sort of thing would intimidate you, if you let it." Because of his intimate knowledge of the land, along with his interest in protecting ranching as a way of life, he brought a unique perspective to the meetings. While, in his words, he "lacked the technical expertise" of some of the other participants, he relied on his generations of experience about wildlife in the area to raise legitimate concerns about PXP's site plan. Larry was sure that the plan would be harmful over the long term, noting that while "PXP's plan looked good on the scientific surface, I just knew that it would not have been beneficial to the local wildlife." He raised such concerns to the company and to the public. As a rancher, his voice was critical for attributing legitimacy to the movement, both in these private PXP meetings and in the public activism of Citizens. After PXP finally agreed not to drill, Larry was featured in a video produced by Citizens, where he celebrated the victory and emphasized again his physical attachment to the land, its intrinsic value, and the importance of setting it aside: "My great-grandparents were homesteaders in Jackson Hole. The family tradition of outdoors, wildlife, and livestock is basically my life... This [victory] will allow me to show this landscape to my grandchildren, pretty much intact, the way that I saw it the first time on my saddle horse."

MIKE BAIRD AND WILDERNESS EXPERIENCE

It all comes from my love for the outdoors—childhood camping, backpacking experiences in the wild, and family trips to the remote Hoback backcountry. I look at the Hoback, and think, this is an incredible place. No not here, you can't destroy this. I'm not the type of person who feels like I can just replicate what I have here someplace else. Sure, there's other places with nice trees in Montana or Washington or Oregon or California; but this also means something to me because of my relatives having been here. It's a special place, and it has a pull and a feeling that goes beyond words. It has my love and my respect. This is why I guard this land. If I can't put up a fight, and give all that I have to protect it, then who will? If it isn't me, with the legacy that I have here, with the love that I have for it, for all the experiences that I've had in the out-of-doors, all the nights I've spent under the stars—is it going to be a politician? Is it going

Figure 5.15: Mike with his fishing gear and pole, beside a river in the Hoback. Featured in a video produced by Citizens of the Wyoming Range.

to be an executive at an extraction company that's suddenly going to have a change of heart, and decide that this shouldn't happen? I doubt it. I tried to rally neighbors and friends, and a lot of people answered the calling.

Mike Baird's use of the Hoback is very different from Larry Smith's, but it nonetheless cultivated in him a similarly profound sense of place attachment that ultimately led him to become an environmental activist. Over the years, Mike has developed what he calls "an absolutely spiritual or religious connection" to the Hoback area, generated from intense and isolating experiences in landscapes that "are so wild, so open, that at night it can make you feel like you are at the edge of the earth... it's simply incredible." In the same way that ranching can be deeply meaningful for some people, recreation in wilderness can also be an important source of positive place attachment, intrinsic value, and moral boundary formation.

Mike is a 56-year-old sheet-metal fabricator from Orange County, California (Figure 5.15). While his ancestors were among the first homesteaders to Jackson Hole, Mike is not native to the area. In some ways, he is the stereotypical GYE new-westerner (see Chapter 2): transplant, of ample means, built a second home, seasonal resident, and came for the aesthetic and recreational opportunities. Mike acquired his love for the outdoors—especially hiking—during childhood trips to the Sierra Nevada mountain range and "places throughout the western United States—you name it, we hiked it." But despite being a well-traveled backpacker and outdoor aficionado, Mike developed an intense and long-lasting attachment to the Hoback area, characteristic of an old-westerner. His new-west attributes, along with his old-west ancestry and connection to the area, blur the lines between these two ideal types. In one conversation, Mike narrated the genesis of this unique relationship:

> Our relatives were homesteaders here long ago, and ran the sawmill in the valley and also had the trapping rights. When I was still young, in my early twenties, my relative bought a place here on the upper Hoback. I started coming here in 1982, to spend time with my friends in the wild. I just fell in love with the place and just started coming as often as I could. When I got married I started bringing my wife along, and then my kids. Eventually my relatives decided to start building two homes on 80 acres, one of which was a fantastic house overlooking the Hoback River.

Mike talked at length about how his connection to the Hoback runs much deeper and is more authentic than stereotypical new-west transplants, who have a superficial and fleeting attachment to the area, considering it no different from any other pretty area providing leisure opportunities. It is evident from talking with Mike that his connection does in fact run much deeper than the typical new-western transplant. Aside from his ancestral connection to the place, it was his "religious, or perhaps, spiritual" experiences in the Hoback backcountry that changed him—as if he found, after all of his travels around the United States, the *one* landscape that was *uniquely special*. Mike describes the point in time when he started to realize that he had become profoundly attached to this place:

> When I was younger we didn't own a piece of the Hoback. When we would visit, and it was time to leave, I would stand at the back fence at the cabin we would stay in, and I would look at the Wyoming Range and I would cry. I would weep. My wife asked me why, and I said its because I'm never sure when I leave here if I'll get to come back. I'm always worried that I won't make it back, and that's how special the place is to me. I mean, I can't say that I've ever felt that way about any other places I've been.

Mike and his family made their connection to the area more permanent by constructing a home near the Hoback River. For 30 years now, Mike has been "lured into the remoteness and rawness of the Hoback wilderness" for "natural experiences." As it is for Joe Batista, the Hoback is an escape from the stressors of modern society. It is a place to connect with something deeper, and more meaningful—a site of spiritual renewal. In a video produced by Citizens', Mike makes a direct link between these feelings for the Hoback and the responsibility to protect it: "This is a place where [my family] escapes from the rigors of work life. Its a place we recreate with beautiful scenery and unspoiled wilderness. I've been a lot of places, and there aren't too many places that compare... [and] we're hoping that we can rally those people who have shown concern... to bring together fundraising to help pay to close this chapter of a very scary time on the upper Hoback."

Because of his deep commitment to the Hoback, Mike played a critical role in the success of the movement. For years he traveled around the state of Wyoming, and to Washington D.C., to meet with various stakeholders. He devoted himself to understanding the technical aspects of the issue, poring over scientific and economic reports. As a long-time leader in Citizens, Mike admits that he "gets a little teary-eyed when I begin to think about the travels Dan [Smitherman] and I have made on this long trip together. And, I mean, there were times that I was really worried we weren't going to make it... but I'm not a quitter." Mike also played a critical role in organizing local support. He contributed time and money to these efforts, and became the face of local landowners who especially value the area's recreational amenities. He would routinely make the case to fellow landowners that "the spectacular nature of the Hoback is all going to change with the intrusion of development for oil or gas." Indeed, he found that "some neighbors, more than others, shared this same religious connection, if you will. The same spiritual connection to the land here." It is this unique spiritual connection; this ineffable "pull and feeling that goes beyond words," that made the Hoback "too special to drill," demarcating a clear moral boundary between it and other lands in Sublette County—and ultimately propelled Mike, and many others like him, to take part in their first environmental movement.

Moral Boundary Work and the Meaning of Activism

In what remains, I want to briefly shift attention away from place attachment, and the related moral and spiritual reasons for activism, toward the *cultural meaning of activism itself.* The puzzle here has to do with how old-westerners make sense of their newfound environmental activism—including collaboration with environmentalists—in light of their cultural narratives and way of life. *In other words, how do people who tend to oppose environmental regulation, subsist on natural resource extraction, sneer at most environmentalist groups, and have little experience in the political process understand and talk about their behavior, which on the face of it is inconsistent, and even self-defeating to their way of life?* I found that, because environmental activism in the GYE is so morally charged, old-west activists sought to reframe their activism in ways that reinforce their old-west ideals and make clear that their activism is consistent with their cultural narratives (e.g., pragmatism, antifederalism, private property rights, and individualism), as opposed to what they perceive to be more extreme, "tree-hugger" activism.

This is a process of moral "boundary work," whereby groups make implicit and explicit cultural distinctions to separate themselves from another group, in order to instill feelings of community and superiority. Moral boundaries are often centered "around such qualities as honesty, work ethic, personal integrity, sexuality, religiosity, solidarity and consideration for others. One draws moral boundaries when one feels superior to people who have low moral standards" (Lamont et al., 1996, p. 34). In this case, the qualities that are especially important to old-west moral boundaries—over and against those of tree-huggers—are practicality, reasonableness, regard for old-west extraction culture, and a general adherence to old-west "Wyoming values." In this concluding section I show how old-westerners draw these symbolic boundaries between their activism and a stereotypical form of tree-hugger activism that does not cohere with their own moral sensibilities, despite the fact that they share the same policy goals. Most important, I found that these symbolic boundaries affected how old-westerners talked about their activism, the frequency with which they asserted their identity over and against tree-huggers, the environmental groups they chose to collaborate with, the strategies they used for collaborating with such groups, and explanations about why the Citizens movement was successful. This process of moral boundary making suggests that deep cultural cleavages still loom large in the GYE, despite the collaboration in this case of unlikely old-west environmentalism.

OLD-WEST ACTIVISM AND MORAL BOUNDARY WORK

"These people normally turn up their noses at anything that smells of tree-hugging," Dan Smitherman said, "[but] these mountains are the love of my life. I will take care of them in any capacity I can" (Pioli, 2010). There was a strong sense among old-west activists in Citizens that the movement, and its participants, were not like typical environmentalists—referred to disparagingly as "tree-huggers." Unlike tree-huggers, participants in Citizens were, as Smitherman described it, more "in touch with Wyoming values." The cultural stereotype of a tree-hugger was indeed a useful straw person against which old-westerners could assert their cultural identity. Many old-west activists felt compelled to assert their identity to compensate for the fact that they were now participating in an environmental movement—an act carrying considerable symbolic weight (especially in the GYE), which many of them never thought they would do. For example, even Smitherman often said that he is the "farthest thing from a tree-hugger," was uncomfortable with being described as an "environmentalist," and instead preferred the more general title of "activist" or "organizer." One activist I spoke with even denied that Citizens is an environmental movement, responding to my question, "No, I don't think I would call it an environmental movement. I think it was more of a *community movement*, you know, a mix of people that recognized that there was some value in those natural resources." The irony here, of course, is that this was indeed an environmental movement in every sense, and despite their cultural allergies to these stereotypes, Citizens' activists sought environmental goals and collaborated with other environmental groups.

This process of boundary drawing between their own culture and the culture of traditional environmental activism also had a real effect on which environmental groups they were willing to collaborate with. Smitherman stressed that they were very careful about working with "practical" groups that shared their "Wyoming values." They collaborated with the Wyoming Outdoor Council and the Wyoming Wilderness Society, because Smitherman "found these groups to be very pragmatic, very mainstream." For example, many old-westerners were attracted to the practical approach taken by Citizens to stop the drilling. This process, more than any other, typifies the old-west qualities of rugged individualism and antifederalism. Instead of pursuing aggressive legal or political measures, the leaders of the group recognized and respected PXP's property rights to drill and came up with what one Citizens' activist called a "private solution befitting of Wyoming ideals," whereby more than 1,000 private citizens contributed $8.75 million to purchase PXP's leases fair and square.

Some old-westerners, like Susan Whitfield, a landowner near Bondurant, WY, felt that "organizations like the Sierra Club are just not my thing. I learned more about the Wyoming Wilderness Society, how they operate, and it just made a lot of practical sense to me." Most often, however, activists talked less about the positive qualities of the groups with which they collaborated and more about their objections to all other environmental groups. Two consistent moral boundaries stood out: First, that environmental groups had become too greedy; and second, that environmental groups are too emotional, loud, and polarizing.

In explaining why they chose to participate in Citizens—and thus attempting to reinforce to me that their behavior is still consistent with their old-west values—they contrasted their collaboration with "practical" groups to greedy "money-making" groups, such as the Sierra Club, or more regional, but still "economically hungry," organizations in Jackson Hole (see Chapter 2 for more about the differences between types of environmental groups in the GYE). Old-westerners like Pat Lilly complained that compared to Citizens, "other special interest environmental groups start out with good intentions, and then they become a business." Another activist explained, in a more complex way, how greed can undercut the legitimacy of these groups, thus asserting the moral superiority of Citizens:

> People that drive the environmental community have made it into an eco-
> nomic process. This is my opinion, but they manufacture issues to draw public
> attention to increased membership and funding. I see that as destroying their
> credibility, and in certain cases it diminishes their effect. And you know, I
> just feel like their good will to accomplish their mission is not there. It's more
> economical and financially oriented than actual love of the cause.

The second moral boundary is that, in contrast to Wyoming values, and compared to the way old-west folks should comport themselves, other environmental groups were too hot-tempered and emotional. As a movement of ranchers, miners, steelworkers, and other no-nonsense folks, Citizens prided itself on being "down-to-earth," "practical," and, as one activist put it, "not too emotional, or short-sighted." Another first-time activist from Jackson, who wanted to get involved after hearing about the plan to drill the Hoback chose to join Citizens because it is "kind of low profile, and has a lot of regard for real people, whereas, you know, some of the other boisterous groups don't." In their engagement with PXP and the public, Citizens took a very measured approach, acknowledging PXP's rights and trying to forge a deal that would be in the fair interest of both parties. Thus, Citizens only partnered with the two environmental groups that "have more credibility" because they were not viewed, as several activists described them, as being "too idealistic," "melodramatic," or "extreme in their views."

While old-westerners were clear that their activism was motivated by an emotional attachment to the Hoback, there was the feeling among its participants that Citizens was successful only because it channeled this emotion in morally appropriate ways—namely, it relied on old-west practicality and avoided collaboration with morally questionable (greedy, overly emotional) environmental groups. Not only would the local community have been less likely to support the movement, it was thought, but, moreover, PXP would have been less likely to negotiate with such polarizing tree-huggers. As rancher Larry Smith put it, "I know that if it had been challenged by environmental groups alone, I don't think it would have been successful. The buyout wouldn't have happened." One reason is because "some of the more emotional groups create polarization . . . and you know, the real problems never get brought to attention." In response to my question about why the movement was so successful, another rancher asserted,

> Well, I think the only reason that it was successful, or got traction the way it did, and got the attention of policy setters, was the fact that you had just basic, common, users of the land. A lot of those people worked in the oil and gas industry. So I think that's what gave it merit, and you know, had it only been the more radical environmentalists, it wouldn't have been successful like it was.

Indeed, many old-westerners went to great lengths to link the moral qualities of Citizens (e.g., Wyoming values, reasonableness, practicality, modesty) to the success of the movement, overtly differentiating themselves from less effective, and less virtuous environmental groups.

These moral boundaries also shaped *how* Citizens collaborated with environmental groups. Some old-west activists still held contempt for environmentalists because of other controversial issues in the GYE, such as wolves, buffalo, grizzly bears, restricting oil/gas development elsewhere, and snowmobiling. Their strategy, then, was to agree to put these issues aside and only discuss fracking in the Hoback. One long-time Citizens activist said that there was an implicit agreement that "we're not here to debate these other issues. We're here to resolve *this* issue on common ground." Indeed, as I describe in this chapter, they had established the ever-elusive common moral ground that is so difficult to find in GYE politics and culture, and it was held in the balance as they worked together on this issue, despite the apparent gulf that existed between stakeholders on other issues. Mike Baird says that the odds were long, but they were able to

> bring together a broad-based coalition of people that come from all different interests, to focus on one issue. We had a better chance if we focused on this one issue. I think that is so important… [because] the people involved were able to set their egos and personal agendas aside, and work together. It was a very difficult thing to accomplish. It may be very difficult to duplicate in another situation, if you wanted to fight against wolves, or snowmobiling in Yellowstone, or some other issue.

Another old-west activist reiterated this point, calling attention to the importance of how traditional environmental groups and participants in Citizens "were able to set [other issues] aside and focus on [Hoback] gas development. Some people were hunters, some were not. Some people like wolves, some people don't. Some people like motorized vehicles, some people don't." The fact that Citizens clearly outlined the moral boundaries between old-west "values" and other stereotypical environmentalists, and between the Hoback issue and other contentious GYE policy issues, meant that the terms of collaboration were very clear—ultimately helping them to dodge any unexpected cultural and political land mines that may have poisoned the movement.

Conclusion

The bigger-picture aim of this chapter was to explain why a group of old-westerners would organize an environmental movement to oppose drilling in the Hoback. This question becomes even more important in light of their own interests and way of life, given the historical significance of energy extraction in Wyoming and Sublette County. Republican Wyoming senator John Barrasso is certainly right that, as America's energy capital, Wyoming has "never been a state that has said 'Not in my back yard'." This was especially true in Sublette County. But the reaction by many locals was radically different in the wake of PXP's proposal to drill the Hoback. I investigated alternative explanations for this unusual, and unexpected, opposition to the PXP plan, but found that this was not a simple case of NIMBY, and previous economic and organizational theories did not account for the cultural complexity on the ground, nor could they explain why people care about the Hoback in the first place. The fullest account for the surprising moral outrage, and subsequent activism, has to do with old-westerners' cultural, moral, and spiritual place attachment to the Hoback area (i.e., family heritage, labor on the land, wilderness experience). The PXP plan violated powerful moral boundaries drawn from old-westerners' profound sense of attachment this area. These, I argue, are the deeper cultural forces that led to the unlikely eruption of old-west environmental activism in this case, but not against the other 30,000 gas wells, 10,600 oil wells, or 9 of the nation's 10 largest coal mines. The Hoback was simply "too special to drill" because, for many old-westerners, it had become too intrinsically valuable. This surprising backlash against energy development led to a rare collaboration between old-westerners and environmental groups, because in ascribing intrinsic value to this landscape, these two sides now had a common moral currency, and a common moral ground, upon which to base cooperation. And while many participants were not entirely comfortable with their newfound environmental activism, and needed considerable moral "boundary work," they nonetheless could not imagine the thought of even a small-scale drilling operation defiling the natural and symbolic purity of a land that had become, in one activist's words, "part of our soul."

Conclusion

Popular and scholarly attention to environmental problems has increased dramatically in recent decades, with more and more technical resources devoted to understanding the ecological, economic, legal, and political aspects of humanity's relationship with the natural environment. Indeed, this flurry of biological research, economic valuation, policy programming, legal scrutiny, attitudinal surveys, cost-benefit analyses, and the like, is indispensable for understanding modern environmental conflict. But it also has important limitations. How do we understand cases, where scientific mastery is not lacking, where there is a concerted attempt at cooperative administration, where organizational resources abound, where there is no shortage of legal expertise, and yet toxic polarization and conflict continue? Why, despite massive efforts to realize a resolution, do even the smallest issues still erupt into malignant and impassioned policy problems?

In studying this empirical problem it became apparent that the Yellowstone conflict would benefit from a scientific analysis of a different kind. The first step was to shift the analytical lens through which to view the conflict, recognizing that it is not ultimately about scientific true and false, but about moral right and wrong. Thus, I sought to focus more fundamentally on the sources of moral-environmental beliefs and sentiments, and on the lived experiences of different cultures that structure moral orders, informing people who they are, why they are, what they want, what a "good life" looks like, and why it all matters in the end. This is, of course, easier said than done. To a sociologist, it requires sorting through complex social systems made up of a messy mixture of fact (what is) and value (what ought to be)—a process that at times can feel like grasping around in the dark, in search of the elusive boundaries that form different moral orders.

Of course, we might explain this problem using other sociological theories, whether by well-worn Marxist approaches to conflict about the use of nature in material and economic competition or through traditional social movement theories about resource mobilization and political opportunities. We could also explain conflict as simply a clash between technical experts and an ill-informed public. I have shown throughout this book that these approaches, while useful, do little to reduce the fog that continues to cloud the Yellowstone conflict. Although this is indeed a conflict about material things (e.g., mountains, trees, animals, rocks, water), it is at base a moral-symbolic competition over incommensurate meanings that have real economic, political, and material consequences.

Thus, my analysis focused on uncovering these moral and spiritual bases of conflict that tended to be ignored, muted, and misunderstood. Central in this are the larger narratives, institutions, and structures in which actors are embedded, shaping for them what is sacred and worth defending. I first examined the historical process of moralization in Yellowstone, whereby material and instrumental nature came to acquire new moral and spiritual meaning. I continued this sociohistorical approach, demonstrating how dramatic social change in the GYE ushered in the new-west—a structural change that resulted in the moral "devaluation" of old-westerners, ramping up competing moral commitments, strengthening old-west identity, and creating a culture ripe for conflict. Narrowing my focus, I then considered in more depth how morality and spirituality actually matter in the day-to-day conflicts that are shrouded in surface-level technorational disagreement. I showed how the Buffalo Field Campaign successfully brought to the fore the deeper religious disagreements that fuel long-standing, and ostensibly scientific, controversy over the Yellowstone bison herd. Next, I examined toxic polarization in the Yellowstone wolf conflict, demonstrating how, despite claims about economic and scientific certainty, the wolf conflict is ultimately about incommensurable cultural commitments that are knowingly and unknowingly pushed beneath the surface of rational policy debate by opposing sides. Finally, I considered a counterexample, where in an unusual turn of events, a group of old-westerners launched a successful environmental movement against natural gas drilling (despite favoring gas development nearly everywhere else), prompted and sustained by their unique moral and spiritual attachment to a particular landscape. But they were quick to draw moral boundaries separating their environmental work from that of more emotional or impractical groups, in an attempt to reinforce their old-west ideals.

These findings raise supplementary questions that might be investigated in future studies about morality, technorationality, and policy conflict. Furthermore, while I believe that this project has important practical implications for resolving intractable policy conflict, it is not my aim here to provide concrete policy prescriptions. Nevertheless, the following three questions provide a good place to start for researchers and policymakers alike.

First, given my argument about the importance of morality and culture in conflicts like these, what then is the role of science and technical expertise? I stated clearly in the introduction that it is *not* my aim to set up a false dichotomy between morality and technorationality, or between science and religion, or any other overly simplistic dichotomy. Instead, what I have done is to show—in multimethod detail—how fact and value are deeply intertwined. Interesting questions arise, then, about the role of different epistemological approaches. How does our science influence our moral assumptions? And, conversely, how do our moral assumptions guide us toward certain scientific findings, but not others? In other words, does science shape us, or do we use science to defend our vision of what is "good" and right? This cuts to the heart of the issue, and in Yellowstone it works in both directions. This is, of course, a thorny paradox in science and technology studies that extends well beyond the study of the environment, and is a fertile area for future sociological research.

Second, does it make a practical difference to stakeholders if they become more aware of their moral assumptions? For example, would anti-wolf activists' views and behavior change if they had a robust understanding about how their worldview is embedded within old-west narratives and social structures? If all sides had a better understanding of their underlying moral assumptions, would they get together and work them out with mutual respect, or would such knowledge simply become another basis for accusation and disagreement?

Last, this study raises questions about the relative power of some moral arguments over others. How do we assess whether some moral arguments are more compelling than others? Does power rest in the logical cogency of an argument, as some moral philosophers might contend? My inclination is that logical framing matters up to a point, but that more important in predicting the power of a moral argument is the cultural and institutional context in which the argument is made. Indeed, moral arguments are important on their own terms, but as I demonstrate in this book, they should be considered in relation to larger factors like demographic change, the government's power to regulate, or activist's ability to organize. Of course, morality cannot be reduced to these larger institutional factors because they are heavily influenced by moralization and have their own moral logic: demographic change in the new-west is related to Americans' desire for aesthetic amenities and natural purity; government regulation is tied to moralization and the growth of spiritual and biocentric concerns for preservation. Thus, in assessing why some moral arguments are more powerful or compelling than others, we should focus on their internal moral and cultural logic, as well as their relation to pertinent power structures.

This study also has broader theoretical implications for sociology. Here I want to focus less on the problem of intractable policy conflict itself, and more on the central theoretical contributions related to the study of environment, culture, and religion. We have much to gain by applying important questions in sociology of culture and sociology of religion to fields where they have not received serious consideration—in this case, environmental sociology. This is a young, still evolving field that has largely remained isolated from big questions about human motivation, rationality, economic valuation, habits of talk, and moral boundary work. Acknowledged or not, these questions influence our work as sociologists and shape our research about the larger patterns structuring human life. Moving culture, and even what Durkheim called a "science of morality," to the center of social scientific analyses of the environment will no doubt improve our understanding of the human–environment nexus, will better integrate the subdiscipline into long-standing currents in sociology, and will provide an alternative and fresh perspective to a field that has favored material-based theories at the expense of deeper cultural and moral approaches.

Of course, one side-effect of working across the oft-confined silos of different fields is that a theoretical contribution in one field may be established knowledge in another. Since the early days of Durkheim and Weber, the sociology of culture and sociology of religion, have well understood that moral and religious dimensions of social life matter a great deal (albeit, of course, in drastically different ways with different effects). What then, might we learn, more generally, about culture, morality, and religion from this study?

I believe that our understanding of religious culture will suffer if we do not devote more consideration to how (and if) religion "happens" in contexts and institutions that are highly modern, rational, bureaucratic, and, by all accounts, "secular." As Courtney Bender (2010) and Nancy Ammerman (2006) both suggest, the sociological study of religion would do well to move beyond the comfortable tendencies to search for religion where we most expect to find it—in mosques, churches, denominations, and other religious organizations. This is not to say that we cannot still learn from this rich tradition of research, both theoretically and methodologically, but as the field moves ahead, we must be more sensitive to the eruptions of the sacred in "secular" contexts where we may *least* expect it. For example, I showed how the spiritual is deeply intertwined with natural science, as pro-wolf advocates almost always used spiritual arguments *in conjunction* with ecological ones in their policy pleas to the USFWS. In shifting my analysis of spirituality away from the traditional settings scholars have studied, I have attempted to open up further possibilities to examine how "religion" does, and does not, happen in institutionally diverse settings. This study is one example of what this sort of research might look like, by uncovering the spiritual dimensions of what has long been understood to be a conflict about bureaucratic disagreement, scientific dissent, and economic competition.

My much broader theoretical goal in this project, however, has been to reveal the ways that moral culture itself is always and everywhere entangled in our modern lives. This led to some interesting insights about how culture is used in motivation and justification of human action. For example, I found that habits of talk about morality and spirituality can come under the influence of larger cultural currents in American life, leading religiously motivated activists to "mute" morally or religiously laden post hoc justifications of their action. It also led to insights about how groups draw moral distinctions in order to instill feelings of community and superiority, and to align their actions with their cultural standards. For example, old-west environmental activists engaged in moral boundary work to protect their sacred ideals and collective identity, distinguishing themselves from less virtuous "tree-hugging" extremists with whom they (ironically) collaborated. In sum, by keeping our ear to the ground, we might stumble upon explosions of morality and culture that challenge our tendency toward tunnel vision and complicate the cleavages we keep between the profane and the sacred, between secularization and modernity, between the political and the religious, and between the scientific and the ostensibly irrational.

This may also require new tools. With the explosion of interest in morality across the fields of psychology, law, philosophy, and neuroscience, we have new empirical and theoretical models at our disposal, especially in the brain sciences. In charting the "new" sociology of morality, Hitlin and Vaisey (2010, p.11) argue that sociologists' main contribution in this interdisciplinary resurgence will be to investigate case studies of moral phenomena "in the wild." Likewise, Porpora and colleagues' (2013) recent analysis of morality laments the current deficiency of studies of morality "as it is actually lived," outside of the fMRI brain experiment laboratories, abstract philosophies, and large scale attitudinal surveys. I agree that we need more grounded analyses of morality in the wild, as demonstrated by my use of ethnographic fieldwork in the case studies of buffalo, wolf, and fracking conflicts.

But with that said, I believe new tools are emerging that will further strengthen the study of environment, morality, culture, and religion. Examples of this type of research are included in chapters 3 and 4, where I conduct computational content analysis on very large corpora of public letters. These large-scale text data work in conjunction with my fieldwork (and other quantitative data) to provide an additional angle with which to understand the latent moral and spiritual aspects of environmental conflict. Indeed, the rise of "big data," and associated methods like machine learning and large-scale network analysis, provide new avenues for uncovering these latent meanings. I attempted to provide two basic examples about how these emerging computational methods might be useful to estimate the frequency of moral and spiritual meanings in written discourse, as well as to graph the network of linkages between them.

But of course these advanced methods are just one more example in the long line of human endeavors to comprehend morality. Since the ancient pursuit of thinkers like Socrates, we humans have wrestled—philosophically, empirically, religiously—with right and wrong, and with big questions about goodness and justice: what does a "good" person look like, and how might one go about living a "good" life? These, I argue, are inescapable questions of moral worth and value that are fundamental building blocks upon which human cultures are built. Thus, in our pressing attempt to understand environmental destruction, environmental wonder, or environmental justice, we must begin at the root of it all, by investigating what people care about in the first place—namely, the deep and complicated relationship between moral meanings and our material environment. This relationship is based on moral orders and sentiments that are historically situated and culturally constructed. In some cases, such as with the battle for Yellowstone, they become tangled up in, and exert considerable influence on, conflicts that appear to be about rational, economic, scientific, and secular life.

Appendix: Methodological Notes

Introduction

Here I provide more information about my methodological decision making, as well as additional technical information about the computational content analysis. While I provide specific information about my data and analysis in each chapter, some additional details are better saved for a short appendix.

For example, with all of the conflicts raging over Yellowstone, why did I choose the case studies that I did? My main aim was to find three case studies that would illustrate the conflict from very different angles. I considered a host of other case studies (e.g., snowmobiling, grizzly bears, construction in the park) but settled on what I believe to be the three most representative. These cases included all sets of stakeholders outlined in the chapter on the rise of the new-west. Furthermore, these are some of the most scientifically intense and technocentric issues in the area. Thus, we would seemingly not expect cultural, moral, and spiritual dynamics to be at play in such issues. In other words, I was careful not to select on the dependent variable. Let me say a bit more on the reasoning behind each case. First, the bison issue provided an opportunity to dig beneath the surface of conflicts over loss of biodiversity—a major issue in nearly all ecological systems. My approach to this conflict required a deeper ethnographic strategy, in addition to using other sources of data described in the chapter. I chose to study the BFC because it is the only group solely dedicated to bison, and it is the most public group pushing for change.

Second, the wolf issue is perhaps the most long-lasting and widely recognized of all Yellowstone conflicts. I was especially interested in this case because it involved the broader American (and global) public in ways that my other case studies did not. It is truly a national conflict in terms of the political actors—despite the fact that wolves were introduced in only the three states surrounding Yellowstone. Furthermore, humans have a long and tenuous relationship with wolves that has changed dramatically in recent decades. Exploring this moral change was important. Last, the case study of fracking in the Hoback was an excellent counterexample to the bison and wolf case studies because in a radically different turn of events, it was old-westerners who organized an environmental movement. This, in itself, is fascinating. It provided a much different angle from which to understand the cultural dimensions of environmental issues in the region and offered more nuance to the old-west and new-west dichotomy.

Using interviews, observation, and content analysis, I was able to explore in greater depth how old-west and new-west individuals are culturally, morally, and spiritually attached to the GYE landscape—and how these sorts of attachments are related to the emergence of collective action. In addition to examining the link between place attachment and collective action, it provided an important opportunity to consider how people erect and protect moral boundaries.

How did I obtain access to such a wide variety of individuals and groups in the GYE? Authenticity and trust are everything in the area, and establishing these bonds was perhaps the most important first step to research. There are especially strong insider/outsider dynamics among old-westerners and long-time residents. One of the first questions people ask when they meet someone is, "Where are you from?"—with the explicit aim of categorizing you as (1) a tourist, (2) a transplant, or (3) a person with actual roots in the area. Strong moral boundaries and expectations exist around these three categories. Fortunately for me, my own life experience includes all three of these categories, which provided me with a unique perspective from which to do research. But I also occupied a fourth category: that of scholar/researcher. Thus, during the years I was researching, I was engaged in a constant balancing act, depending on the individual, group, or research setting. Establishing trust meant being honest, but it also meant selectively emphasizing my genuine sympathy for a wide variety of interests in the area—from concern over the decline of old-westerners' way of life to concerns over the tourism, land development, or extraction industries. In some contexts I emphasized my outsider role as a researcher, but in gaining access and establishing trust, I emphasized my native roots in the area, knowledge of the issues, and long-term practical concern for improving social relations, cultural preservation, and environmental health.

Interview Guide

I describe in detail at the end of the introduction the different sources of data for each chapter. In addition to the profusion of discourse texts (e.g., public letters, newsletters, video transcriptions) and ethnographic observation, I also conducted over 100 formal and informal interviews. Here I present the semistructured interview guide that I used for the interviews. When interviewing about a specific issue (bison, wolves, fracking), I incorporated issue-specific questions in addition to these broader questions below.

Background Information

To start, I just want to quickly gather some background data: In what year were you born?

Are you married? (if Yes, what is your spouse's occupation?)

What is your occupation?

What was the highest year you completed in school? (if college, where, and what was your major?)

For the tape, you live in (name of town or county, and state).

Family History and Practices

To begin then, I have a couple of basic questions about your experiences growing up

What did your parents do for a living?

Did you live in a rural area, or in town?

What did you do for recreation? Other hobbies?

Growing up, what family traditions were most meaningful to you? Are they still practiced? Have new ones?

How would you describe yourself in terms of your religion or spirituality? a. A particular denomination? If not, would you consider yourself evangelical, mainline/liberal, or none of these? b. How often do you attend religious services?

Is there an enduring piece of advice or wisdom that has been passed down from generation to generation in your family?

In general what do you think are the most important things in life? Why those?

Occupational Practices

I am especially interested in hearing people's stories about how they got involved in the line of work they are in, whether that means their work, or homemaking, or what they used to do if they are retired. Could you tell me your story, maybe starting with when you were young? How did you get into what you wound up doing? Were there any other influences or events that shaped the kind of work you would end up doing?

What would you say are the most important skills or habits for the work you do? Where did you learn these skills?

In your work, what does a typical day look like? For instance, what are the main things you do and spend your time on?

How has your work been changing lately? For instance, is it being affected by changes in the economy or by changes in your community?

Given the recent economic downturn, have times been better for you financially in the past than they are now, or how would you describe it? What are some of the main factors that keep your finances from being better than they are now?

Old-West and New-West Change

If someone had lived in this community 25 or 30 years ago and came back today, what would be the main changes they would notice? a. What about 5 or 10 years?

b. What are some of the main reasons for these changes? c. Have these changes been good for the community, or not so good?

Now, are you the first in your family to have lived in this community [community name/Greater Yellowstone Area], or did earlier generations live here as well? a. (If Yes earlier generations:) So, tell me the story. Which of your family came here first? Where did they come from? When did they come? And why did they settle here? b. (If No earlier generation:) Tell me the story of how you came to live here? When did you come? Where had you been before? And why did you come here?

What are some of the things you really like about living in the Greater Yellowstone area? What about things specific to your community? a. Can you give me an example—something that would illustrate what is really nice about living here? b. Why is that special to you?

And what are some of the things you don't especially like about living here? Or maybe something you would change if you could? Can you give me an example about that?

Here is another question. Is the federal government generally helping to make things better in your community, or making them worse? a. Why is it making things [better/worse]? b. Local government?

Meanings and Practices about Nature

I often hear people in the West say they have a special feeling about the land. That the land is very meaningful to them. Do you hear people saying that the land is especially meaningful, or how do they talk about it?

I've heard others say that there a difference between a local's knowledge of the land and an "outsider's." How would you describe this difference?

What qualities makes one an "outsider" in your community? Not naming names, can you give me an example?

How did your parents/grandparents/guardians teach you how you ought to behave with regard to the land (abstract teaching or visceral practices, working with hands, showing how, etc.)?

Are those practices/values still being taught by members of your community? What about in the GYE as a whole?

What comes to mind when I say the phrase "old-west"?

Does the cowboy way of life still exist? Describe it for me.

Science and Rationality

How do people use science (ecology, biology) for solving environmental problems in the GYE? a. Probe about the importance of science (environmental impact statements (EISs), lawsuits). b. Probe: why is science so effective?

How do people use economic evidence to solve environmental problems?

What other rational forms of evidence are used to solve environmental problems?

Suppose you couldn't appeal to "rational" evidence (ecology, economics) in debates over issues in the GYE. How would you argue? What would you appeal to, or what evidence (aesthetic, people's values, emotions, history) would you use to convince people that preserving GYE natural resources is important?

Some people have spiritual and religious reasons to support or oppose environmental issues in the GYE. When debating issues in public, should people only use a nonreligious way of talking, or can they use their spiritual or religious arguments to influence environmental policy?

Morality

How do you normally decide or know what is good and bad, right and wrong in life? In general, is it easy or hard for you to decide between right and wrong? a. What about when it comes to the environment. Do you have more or less confidence about what's right or wrong? b. What has influenced your beliefs about what's right and wrong?

What do you think it is that makes something right or wrong? Is it rules or laws? God's will? How it feels: What kinds of "feelings" do you mean? Where do those feelings come from, in your view? Consequences: What kinds of "consequences"? How black and white is right and wrong?

Some people say that there really are no final rights and wrongs in life, that everything is relative, that morality is simply what people make for themselves or their culture. a. Do you agree or disagree? Why? b. If Yes, should people be able to treat the environment in the ways that they see fit? What if they own the property? Should they be able to treat their land any way they please as long as they don't push these views on others?

How do you determine what is right or wrong for the environment?

In your opinion, what types of people are best suited to decide what is right and wrong with regard to the environment?

In your opinion, are some areas of the natural environment more valuable and important than others? a. Which ones? b. Why? What qualities make it more valuable? How did you come to these beliefs? High restrictions: Tetons/YNP; Low restrictions: oil fields in central Wyoming.

Does the level of beauty in a landscape affect our determination of right and wrong? a. What are some examples? (e.g., Drilling for oil in central Wyoming versus in Teton national park) b. But some people find flat land just as beautiful. How do we decide?

In your own opinion, is it easier or harder for you to discern right and wrong with regard to the environment in a place like Yellowstone?

Dominionism

In your opinion, do humans have the right to modify the natural environment to suit their needs?

In your opinion, do plants and animals have as much right to exist as humans do? Are these rights the same ones that extend to humans?

In your opinion, are humans meant to rule over the rest of nature?

Antifederalism

In your opinion, does the federal government do too much or too little to protect the environment?

Most of the land in the GYE is owned by the federal government. Do you think it would be better or worse off if it were owned by individuals?

Sacredness

In your view, is nature "sacred"? a. If Yes, What makes something sacred, or not? (God, it just "is"—intrinsic value) Does sacredness make it more important to protect? b. How do we learn that it is sacred?

Is there something about YNP that makes it more sacred than other places?

In your opinion, do you think we can put a price tag on nature? Millions of dollars are spent on conservation issues in the GYE. Is there a limit to how much we should spend to protect the GYE? Limits or no limits?

Wilderness Experience

Early environmental thinkers emphasized the deep emotional experiences they would have in nature. Have you had similar experiences out in nature? a. If Yes, can you tell me a story about one of these experiences? What was it like? What did you do? How did you feel? b. Many environmental thinkers often described them as "spiritual." Does this term describe your experience? What was spiritual about it? c. How important were these to getting you involved in environmental work?

In your opinion, is wilderness a purer place than human society—a peaceful escape from society and the pollution of materialism, selfishness, and other negativities of human society?

On a scale of 1 to 10, how pure is YNP? a. What would make it more pure? Devoid of all human influence? No roads, no management? b. If No, what is the ideal goal for conservationists in GYE?

Others have not described wilderness in such romantic ways. Instead of highlighting its beauty and the peace many feel in wilderness, they highlight the darker side of wilderness—as a place full of pain and struggle, of terror and unpredictability. What are your thoughts about this, or how would you put it?

Computational Content Analysis

The rise of the Internet, digital archives, and social media in recent years has been accompanied by an explosion in the volume of available text-based data. As the interest in "big data" continues to spread across all scientific fields, researchers in the social sciences are beginning to wade into this data gold mine.[1] These new methods and this abundance of novel data provide an opportunity for sociologists to examine important theoretical questions anew. I believe that cultural sociologists in particular have a lot to gain from such approaches because they provide new methodological avenues for moving, in new ways, above the micro level to more confidently uncover networks of meaning with greater rigor, structure, and representativeness.

The computer-assisted content analysis I use in this study involves five main steps: (1) acquire all the text, (2) clean and prepare the text for analysis (e.g., removing duplicates, geocoding, stemming), (3) develop reliable and valid computer instructions to classify meaningful categories, (4) conduct the analyses, (5) interpret the findings.

Grimmer and Stewart (2013) note that a lexicon approach is especially useful and reliable if the categories of meaning are clearly identifiable and known beforehand, as they are in this mixed-methods research design (in contrast to an unsupervised machine-learning approach, where categories are often not known a priori). Thus, following recent research examining the affective and semantic content of social media (Golder and Macy 2011), I measure cultural meaning through the words and phrases of stakeholders, which I group into larger categories of meaning. I created the larger categories of moral and scientific meaning retroductively (Sayer 2010), by which I mean I began with general patterns derived from extensive fieldwork, observation, and historical study, and then worked back from these patterns to uncover the deeper cultural beliefs, commitments, and desires that I argue produce them. This was an iterative process conducted in correspondence with prior theoretical work on environmental values and morality, to best ensure reliability and validity.[2]

The most important step, then, is to develop lexicons containing words and phrases that are valid and reliable indicators of these larger categories (presented in the tables in each chapter). Developing the lexicon is an extensive process, requiring multiple iterations and continuous modification by testing their validity on random samples of letters. I use a dictionary and thesaurus algorithm to suggest terms to help continually increase the precision of the lexicon as they

1 Adams and Roscigno (2005); Bail (2014); Giles (2012); Golder and Macy (2011); King (2011a).
2 Bengston et al. (2004); Kellert (1996); Kempton et al. (1996).

are applied to more sample letters. Throughout this iterative process, it scores the precision of phrases and categories and suggests related phrases, inflected forms, synonyms, and antonyms to apply. After building up a comprehensive lexicon of all possible words indicating the categories of meaning, I began the process of increasing the validity of the measures by trimming words that do not reliably measure the specific categories in at least 80 percent of sampled cases the widely accepted threshold in content analysis.[3] Based on a final examination of the categories on a random sample of 500 letters, the threshold of 80 percent reliability was reached for all categories.

It will be useful to say a bit more about the data itself. In Chapter 4, the texts I analyze include thousands of BFC's written documents, full texts of every newsletter and press release, selected video transcriptions, and thousands of written public comments from everyday citizens, organizations, and political institutions, as well as legal documents, transcriptions of field hearings in Montana, and United States congressional hearings about the issue. I aquired these data through Web-scraping and through extensive communication with environmental organizations and government agencies described in chapter 3.

For Chapter 5, I collected thousands of public comment letters written to the USFWS concerning the 2011 wolf proposal. Members of the public were invited to submit comments for 100 days between October 5, 2011, and January 13, 2012, and then again for another 15 more days between May 1, 2012, and May 16, 2012. The majority of letters that were received were duplicate form letters submitted by environmental organizations. For example, Defenders of Wildlife collected 14,563 form letter signatures, Sierra Club 17,200, and the National Resource Defense Council 62,215 signed letters. All of these comments are form-letter duplicates, and were treated as such after they were submitted to the USFWS. I restrict my analysis to individual, unique comments alone. Most unique comments were submitted online through the Regulations.gov website, although some were hand-written and mailed directly to the USFWS. I requested and received this population of unique (nonform, nonduplicate) letters from the USFWS offices in Washington D.C. I received 10,902 in total. However, I found that even this "official" collection of unique letters contained thousands of duplicates. I therefore used an assortment of automated scripts to identify duplicate sentences and paragraphs, carefully removing every public letter than contained any verbatim repeated elements, leaving a total of 5,478 unique letters for analysis. The majority of these letters are pro-wolf, which, given the intent of the USFWS proposal to delist the wolf, is not surprising. Pro-wolf advocates were responding to what they viewed as a frightening proposal that threatened to ruin decades of progress. An analysis of a random sample of 500 letters revealed that only 4.5 percent of the letters are anti-wolf (i.e., supporting the policy proposed).

3 Krippendorff (2012).

BIBLIOGRAPHY

Adams, Josh, and Vincent J Roscigno. 2005. "White Supremacists, Oppositional Culture and the World Wide Web." *Social Forces* 84:759–778.

Albanese, Catherine L. 1991. *Nature Religion in America: From the Algonkian Indians to the New Age*. University of Chicago Press.

Alexander, J.C. 2003. *The Meanings of Social Life: A Cultural Sociology*. Oxford University Press.

Ammerman, Nancy T. 2006. *Everyday Religion: Observing Modern Religious Lives*. Oxford University Press.

Bail, Chris. 2014. "The Cultural Environment: Measuring Culture with Big Data." *Theory and Society* 43:465–482.

Barringer, Mark Daniel. 2002. *Selling Yellowstone: Capitalism and the Construction of Nature*. University Press of Kansas.

Barron, James. 1988. "Louis L'Amour, Writer, Is Dead; Famed Chronicler of West Was 80." *New York Times*, June 13.

Bath, Alistair J. 1989. "The Public and Wolf Reintroduction in Yellowstone National Park." *Society & Natural Resources* 2:297–306.

Beck, Ulrich. 1992. *Risk Society: Towards a New Modernity*. SAGE Publications.

Beisel, Nicola Kay. 1997. *Imperiled Innocents: Anthony Comstock and Family Reproduction in Victorian America*. Princeton University Press.

Bell, Michael Mayerfeld. 1994. *Childerley: Nature and Morality in a Country Village*. University of Chicago Press.

Bellah, Robert, Richard Madsen, William Sullivan, Ann Swidler, and Steven Tipton. 2008. *Habits of the Heart: Individualism and Commitment in American Life*. 3rd edition University of California Press.

Bender, Courtney. 2010. *The New Metaphysicals: Spirituality and the American Religious Imagination*. University of Chicago Press.

Bengston, David N., T. J. Webb, and David P. Fan. 2004. "Shifting Forest Value Orientations in the United States, 1980–2001: A Computer Content Analysis." *Environmental Values* 13:373–392.

Berger, Joel, and Jon P. Beckmann. 2010. "Sexual Predators, Energy Development, and Conservation in Greater Yellowstone." *Conservation Biology* 24:891–896.

Berger, Peter, and Thomas Luckmann. 1966. *The Social Construction of Reality: A Treatise in the Sociology of Knowledge*. Anchor Books.

Beyers, W. B. 1999. "Employment Growth in the Rural West from 1985 to 1995 Outpaced the Nation." *Rural Development Perspectives* 14.

Blumer, Herbert. 1969. *Symbolic Interactionism: Perspective and Method.* Prentice-Hall.

Boltanski, Luc, and Laurent Thévenot. 2006. *On Justification: Economies of Worth.* Princeton University Press.

Booth, Douglas E. 2006. "Spatial Patterns in the Economic Development of the Mountain West." *Growth and Change* 30:384–405.

Brister, Daniel. 2013. *In the Presence of Buffalo: Working to Stop the Yellowstone Slaughter.* Westwinds Press.

Brown, Matthew. 2011. "Northern Yellowstone Elk Herd Suffers Major Decline." *Huffington Post.*

Brulle, Robert J. 2008. "The U.S. Environmental Movement." In *20 Lessons in Environmental Sociology*, edited by Kenneth A Gould and Tammy L Lewis, pp. 211–227. Roxbury Press.

Bruner, Jon. 2011. "How to Build an Interactive Map with Open-Source Tools." http://jebruner.com/2011/11/how-to-build-an-interactive-map-with-open-source:tools, accessed September 1, 2013.

Buffalo Field Campaign. 1998. "Six Bison Killed: Two Wearing Radio Collars." Press release, January 29.

Bullard, Robert D. 2008. *Dumping in Dixie: Race, Class, and Environmental Quality.* Westview Press.

Bureau of Economic Analysis. 2012. "Regional Economic Data Tables." U.S. Department of Commerce.

Burns, Ken. 2009. *The National Parks: America's Best Idea.* Public Broadcasting Service Film.

Campbell, C. 2006. "Do Today's Sociologists Really Appreciate Weber's Essay. 'The Protestant Ethic and the Spirit of Capitalism'?" *Sociological Review* 54:207–223.

Cannon, K. P. 1993. "Paleoindian Use of Obsidian in the Greater Yellowstone Area." *Yellowstone Science* 1:6–9.

Carson, Rachel. 1962. *Silent Spring.* Houghton Mifflin Harcourt.

Cawley, R. McGreggor. 1996. *Federal Land, Western Anger: The Sagebrush Rebellion and Environmental Politics.* University Press of Kansas.

Cerulo, Karen A. 2010. "Mining the Intersections of Cognitive Sociology and Neuroscience." *Poetics* 38:115–132.

Chambers Noble, Ann. 2011. "The Jonah Field and Pinedale Anticline: A Natural-Gas Success Story." http://wyohistory.org/essays/jonah-field-and-pindale-anticline-natural-gas-success-story/, accessed November 1, 2013.

Cherney, David N. 2011. "Environmental Saviors." University of Colorado, unpublished dissertation, pp. 1–241.

Clark, Susan G. 2008. *Ensuring Greater Yellowstone's Future: Choices for Leaders and Citizens.* Yale University Press.

Coleman, Jon T. 2004. *Vicious: Wolves and Men in America*. Yale University Press.

Collins, Randall. 2005. *Interaction Ritual Chains*. Princeton University Press.

Damasio, Antonio. 1994. *Descartes' Error: Emotion, Reason, and the Human Brain*. Penguin Books.

Daniels, Tom. 1999. *When City and Country Collide: Managing Growth in the Metropolitan Fringe*. Island Press.

Daugherty, John. 1999. *A Place Called Jackson Hole: A Historic Resource Study of Grand Teton National Park*. Grand Teton Natural History Association.

Dax, Michael. 2013. "Weep for Dead Wolves, but Not as 'human.'" *Cody Enterprise*, April 10.

Deno, K. T. Duffy. 1998. "The Effect of Federal Wilderness on County Growth in the Intermountain Western United States." *Journal of Regional Science* 38: 109–136.

Dickens, Peter. 2002. *Reconstructing Nature: Alienation, Emancipation and the Division of Labour*. Routledge.

Dietz, T., P. C. Stern, and G. A. Guagnano. 1998. "Social Structural and Social Psychological Bases of Environmental Concern." *Environment and Behavior* 30:450–471.

Dobbin, F. 1999. "Book Review: The Struggle for Water: Politics, Rationality, and Identity in the American Southwest." *American Journal of Sociology* 105: 237–238.

Douglas, Mary. 1966. *Purity and Danger: An Analysis of Concepts of Pollution and Taboo*. New York: Routledge.

Duffield, John, C. J. Neher, and D. A. Patterson. 2006. "Wolves and People in Yellowstone: Impacts on the Regional Economy." University of Montana, Final Report for Yellowstone Park Foundation.

Duncan, O. D. 1959. "Human Ecology and Population Studies." In *The Study of Population*, edited by P. Hauser and O. D. Duncan. University of Chicago Press.

Dunlap, Riley E., K. D. Van Liere, A. G. Mertig, and R. E. Jones. 2000. "Measuring Endorsement of the New Ecological Paradigm: A Revised NEP Scale." *Journal of Social Issues* 56:425–442.

Dunlap, Riley E., C. Xiao, and Araon M. McCright. 2001. "Politics and Environment in America: Partisan and Ideological Cleavages in Public Support for Environmentalism." *Environmental Politics* 10:23–48.

Dunlap, T. R. 2005. "Faith in Nature: Environmentalism as Religious Quest." University of Washington Press.

Durkheim, Emile. 1973. *Moral Education: A Study in the Theory and Application of the Sociology of Education*. Simon and Schuster.

Durkheim, Emile. 1997. *The Division of Labor in Society*. Simon and Schuster.

Durkheim, Emile. 2001. *The Elementary Forms of Religious Life*. Oxford University Press.

EASI. 2012. "EASI Culture Index." Easy Analytic Software, Inc.

Effler, Erika Summers. 2010. *Laughing Saints and Righteous Heroes: Emotional Rhythms in Social Movement Groups*. University of Chicago Press.

Ehrlich, Paul R. 1968. *The Population Bomb*. Sierra Club/Ballantine Books.

Emerson, Alfred. 1946. "The Biological Basis of Social Cooperation." *Transactions of the Illinois Academy of Science* pp. 9–18.

Espeland, Wendy Nelson. 1998. *The Struggle for Water: Politics, Rationality, and Identity in the American Southwest*. University of Chicago Press.

Feinberg, M., and R. Willer. 2013. "The Moral Roots of Environmental Attitudes." *Psychological Science* 24:56–62.

Finley, Michael V. 1999. "Yellowstone's Northern Range: Where Nature Takes Its Course." *National Park Service Newsletter* pp. 1–4.

Fischer, Hank. 1995. *Wolf Wars: The Remarkable Inside Story of the Restoration of Wolves to Yellowstone*. Falcon Press Publishing.

Fourcade, Marion. 2011. "Cents and Sensibility: Economic Valuation and the Nature of 'Nature.'" *American Journal of Sociology* 116:1721–77.

Frentz, Irene C., Frank L. Farmer, James M. Guldin, and Kimberly Smith. 2004. "Public Lands and Population growth." *Society and Natural Resources* 17: 57–68.

Fuller, A. 2007. "Boomtown Blues: How Natural Gas Changed the Way of Life in Sublette County." *The New Yorker*, February 5.

Galloway, G. B. 1959. "Development of the Committee System in the House of Representatives." *American Historical Review* 65:17–30.

Geertz, Clifford. 1973. *The Interpretation of Cultures: Selected Essays*. Basic Books.

General Accounting Office. 1979. "Learning to Look Ahead: The Need for a National Materials Policy and Planning Process." Technical report.

Ghaziani, Amin, and D. Baldassarri. 2011. "Cultural Anchors and the Organization of Differences: A Multi-Method Analysis of LGBT Marches on Washington." *American Sociological Review* 76:179–206.

Giles, Jim. 2012. "Computational Social Science: Making the Links." *Science* 488:448–450.

Goffman, Erving. 1959. *The Presentation of Self in Everyday Life*. Doubleday Anchor.

Golder, S. A., and Michael Macy. 2011. "Diurnal and Seasonal Mood Vary with Work, Sleep, and Daylength across Diverse Cultures." *Science* 333:1878–1881.

Gosnell, Hannah, Julia Hobson Haggerty, and Patrick A. Byorth. 2007. "Ranch Ownership Change and New Approaches to Water Resource Management in Southwestern Montana: Implications for Fisheries." *Journal of the American Water Resources Association* 43:990–1003.

Gosnell, Hannah, Julia Hobson Haggerty, and William R. Travis. 2006. "Ranchland Ownership Change in the Greater Yellowstone Ecosystem, 1990–2001: Implications for Conservation." *Society & Natural Resources* 19: 743–758.

Gould, Kenneth A., and Tammy L. Lewis. 2009. *Twenty Lessons in Environmental Sociology*. Oxford University Press.

Grimmer, Justin, and B. M. Stewart. 2013. "Text as Data: The Promise and Pitfalls of Automatic Content Analysis Methods for Political Texts." *Political Analysis* 21:267–297.

Gude, Patricia H., Andrew J. Hansen, Ray Rasker, and Bruce Maxwell. 2006. "Rates and Drivers of Rural Residential Development in the Greater Yellowstone." *Landscape and Urban Planning* 77:131–151.

Gusfield, Joseph R. 1963. *Symbolic Crusade: Status Politics and the American Temperance Movement*. University of Illinois Press.

GYC. 2013. "Greater Yellowstone Coalition." http://greateryellowstone.org.

Haidt, Jonathan. 2001. "The Emotional Dog and Its Rational Tail: A Social Intuitionist Approach to Moral Judgment." *Psychological Review* 108:814.

Haines, Aubrey L. 1977. *The Yellowstone Story: a History of Our First National Park*. Yellowstone Library and Museum Association and Colorado Associated University Press.

Hansen, Andrew J., Ray Rasker, Bruce Maxwell, J. J. Rotella, Jerry Johnson, A. W. Parmenter, U. Langner, W. B. Cohen, R. L. Lawrence, and M. P. V. Kraska. 2002. "Ecological Causes and Consequences of Demographic Change in the New West." *BioScience* 52:151–162.

Hardin, Garrett. 1968. "Tragedy of the Commons." *Science* 162:1243–1248.

Hays, S. P. 1989. *Beauty, Health, and Permanence: Environmental Politics in the United States, 1955–1985*. Cambridge University Press.

Healy, Kieran. 2006. *Last Best Gifts: Altruism and the Market for Human Blood and Organs*. University of Chicago Press.

Hine, Robert V., and John Mack Faragher. 2000. *The American West: A New Interpretive History*. Yale University Press.

Hitlin, Steven, and Stephen Vaisey. 2010. *Handbook of the Sociology of Morality*. Springer.

Holmes, F. Patrick, and Walter E. Hecox. 2004. "Does Wilderness Impoverish Rural Regions?" *International Journal of Wilderness* 10.

Hout, Michael, and Claude S. Fischer. 2002. "Why More Americans Have No Religious Preference: Politics and Generations." *American Sociological Review* 67:165–190.

Hunter, James Davison. 1991. *Culture Wars: The Struggle to Control the Family, Art, Education, Law, and Politics in America*. Basic Books.

Hunter, Lori M., Jason D. Boardman, and Jarron Saint Onge. 2005. "The Association between Natural Amenities, Rural Population Growth, and Long-Term Residents' Economic Well-Being." *Rural Sociology*.

Inglehart, Ronald F. 1971. "The Silent Revolution in Europe: Intergenerational Change in Post-industrial Societies." *American Political Science Review* 65:991–1017.

Inglehart, Ronald F. 2008. "Changing Values among Western Publics from 1970 to 2006." *West European Politics* 31:130–146.

Jasper, James M. 1997. *The Art of Moral Protest: Culture, Biography, and Creativity in Social Movements*. University of Chicago Press.

Jasper, James M., and Jane D. Poulsen. 1995. "Recruiting Strangers and Friends: Moral Shocks and Social Networks in Animal Rights and Anti-Nuclear Protests." *Social Problems* 42(4): 493–512.

Johnson, Jerry. 2004. "Impacts of Tourism-Related In-Migration: The Greater Yellowstone Region." In *Environmental Impacts of Ecotourism: Case Studies of Ecotourism*, edited by Ralf Buckley. CABI Publishing, pp. 25–40.

Johnson, K. M. 1998. "Renewed Population Growth in Rural America." *Research in Rural Sociology and Development* 7:23–45.

Jones, R. E., J. M. Fly, J. Talley, and H. K. Cordell. 2003. "Green Migration into Rural America: The New Frontier of Environmentalism?" *Society & Natural Resources* 16:221–238.

Kay, Charles E. 1994. "Aboriginal Overkill." *Human Nature* 5:359–398.

Keiter, R. B. and Mark S. Boyce. 1994. *The Greater Yellowstone Ecosystem: Redefining America's Wilderness Heritage*. Yale University Press.

Kellert, Stephen. 1996. *The Value of Life: Biological Diversity and Human Society*. Island Press.

Kempton, W. M., J. S. Boster, and J. A. Hartley. 1996. *Environmental Values in American Culture*. MIT Press.

King, Gary. 2011a. "Ensuring the Data-Rich Future of the Social Sciences." *Science* 331:719–721.

King, Jeffrey D. 2011b. *Crying Wolf*. Broken Hints Media Film.

Klemz, Patric. 2008. "Time to Cut a Deal." *Missoula Independent*.

Knapp, T. A., and P. E. Gravest. 2006. "On the Role of Amenities in Models of Migration and Regional Development." *Journal of Regional Science* 29: 71–87.

Koshmrl, Mike. 2012. "Crowd Heralds Noble Deal." *Jackson Hole News & Guide*.

Krannich, R. S., A. E. Luloff, and Donald R. Field. 2011. *People, Places and Landscapes: Social Change in High Amenity Rural Areas*. Springer Verlag.

Krippendorff, Klaus H. 2012. *Content Analysis: An Introduction to Its Methodology*. SAGE Publications.

Lakoff, George, and Mark Johnson. 1999. *Philosophy in the Flesh: The Embodied Mind and Its Challenge to Western Thought*. Basic Books.

Lamont, Michèle, John Schmalzbauer, M. Waller, and D. Weber. 1996. "Cultural and Moral Boundaries in the United States: Structural Position, Geographic Location, and Lifestyle Explanations." *Poetics* 24:31–56.

Leopold, Aldo. 1986. *A Sand County Almanac*. Ballantine Books.

Limerick, Patricia Nelson. 2011. *The Legacy of Conquest: The Unbroken Past of the American West*. W. W. Norton.

Looking Horse, Chief Arvol. 1997. "Statement on Massacre of the Buffalo at Yellowstone National Park." Spiritual Gathering, Rapid City, SD, April 4.

Lorah, Paul, and Rob Southwick. 2003. "Environmental Protection, Population Change, and Economic Development in the Rural Western United States." *Population & Environment* 24:255–272.

Luckmann, Thomas. 1967. *The Invisible Religion: The Problem of Religion in Modern Society*. MacMillan.

Luhmann, Niklas. 1989. *Ecological Communication*. University of Chicago Press.

Luker, Kristin. 1984. *Abortion and the Politics of Motherhood*. University of California Press.

Lynds, Ranie. 2013. "Wyoming's Oil and Gas Resources." Technical report. State of Wyoming Geological Survey.

MacArthur, R. H., and E. O. Wilson. 1967. *The Theory of Island Biogeography*. Princeton University Press.

MacIntyre, Alasdair C. 1981. *After Virtue: A Study in Moral Theory*. University of Notre Dame.

MacIntyre, Alasdair C. 1988. *Whose Justice? Which Rationality?* University of Notre Dame Press.

MacIntyre, Alasdair C. 1990. *Three Rival Versions of Moral Enquiry: Encyclopaedia, Genealogy, and Tradition: Being Gifford Lectures Delivered in the University of Edinburgh in 1988*. University of Notre Dame Press.

Madonna, Kevin J. 1994. "Wolf in North America: Defining International Ecosystems vs. Defining International Boundaries." *Journal of Land Use & Environmental Law*. 10:305.

Malthus, Thomas. 1798. *An Essay on the Principle of Population*. Oxford University Press.

McAdam, Doug. 1982. *Political Process and the Development of Black Insurgency, 1930–1970*. University of Chicago Press.

McBeth, M. K., and Elizabeth Shanahan. 2004. "Public Opinion for Sale: The Role of Policy Marketers in Greater Yellowstone Policy Conflict." *Policy Sciences* 37:319–338.

McCarthy, John D., and Mayer N. Zald. 1977. "Resource Mobilization and Social Movements: A Partial Theory." *American Journal of Sociology* 82:1212–1241.

McVeigh, Rory. 2009. *The Rise of the Ku Klux Klan: Right-Wing Movements and National Politics*. University of Minnesota Press.

Meagher, Mary, and Margaret E. Meyer. 1994. "On the Origin of Brucellosis in Bison of Yellowstone National Park: A Review." *Conservation Biology* 8: 645–653.

Mech, L. David. 2012. "Is Science in Danger of Sanctifying the Wolf?" *Biological Conservation* 150:143–149.

Meyer, David S., and Debra C. Minkoff. 2004. "Conceptualizing Political Opportunity." *Social Forces* 82:1457–1492.

Mills, C. Wright. 1940. "Situated Actions and Vocabularies of Motive." *American Sociological Review* 5:904.

Mills, C. Wright. 1959. *The Sociological Imagination.* Oxford University Press.

Muir, John. 1898. "The Yellowstone National Park." *Atlantic Monthly*, pp. 509–523.

Nagle, John. 2005. "The Spiritual Values of Wilderness." *Environmental Law* 36.

Narvaez, Darcia, and Tonia Bock. 2002. "Moral Schemas and Tacit Judgement or How the Defining Issues Test Is Supported by Cognitive Science." *Journal of Moral Education* 31:297–314.

Nash, Roderick. 1989. *The Rights of Nature: A History of Environmental Ethics.* University of Wisconsin Press.

Nash, Roderick. 2001. *Wilderness and the American Mind.* 4th edition. Yale University Press.

National Park Service. 2011. "Legislative History of Yellowstone National Park." National Park Service.

National Park Service. 2013. *Yellowstone History: Windows into Wonderland.* NPS.gov.

Nie, Martin. 2003. *Beyond Wolves: The Politics of Wolf Recovery and Management.* University of Minnesota Press.

Northern Rockies Conservation Cooperative. 2012. "Greater Yellowstone Conservation Directory."

Ostlind, Emilene. 2010. "The Supposedly Protected Wyoming Range Faces New Energy Development." *High Country News*, December 8.

Park, R. E. 1952. *Human Communities: The City and Human Ecology.* The Free Press.

Pepper, David. 1993. *Eco-Socialism: From Deep Ecology to Social Justice.* Routledge.

Pioli, Katherine. 2010. "Not Your Average Tree Huggers." *Jackson Hole News & Guide.*

Plumb, Glenn, and R. Sucec. 2006. "A Bison Conservation History in the US National Parks." *Journal of the West* 45(2):22–28.

Polletta, Francesca. 2009. *It Was Like a Fever: Storytelling in Protest and Politics.* University of Chicago Press.

Porpora, Douglas V., Alexander Nikolaev, Julia Hagemann May, and Alexander Jenkins. 2013. *Post-Ethical Society: The Iraq War, Abu Ghraib, and the Moral Failure of the Secular.* University of Chicago Press.

Power, T. M. 1991. "Ecosystem Preservation and the Economy in the Greater Yellowstone Area." *Conservation Biology* 5:395–404.

Power, Thomas Michael, and Richard N. Barrett. 2001. *Post-Cowboy Economics.* Island Press.

Pritchard, James A. 1999. *Preserving Yellowstone's Natural Conditions: Science and the Perception of Nature.* University of Nebraska Press.

Pyne, Stephen Joseph. 1982. *Fire in America: A Cultural History of Wildland and Rural Fire.* Princeton University Press.

Rasker, Ray, and Ben Alexander. 2003. *Getting Ahead in Greater Yellowstone*. Sonora Institute and Yellowstone Business Partnership.

Rasker, Ray, Patricia H. Gude, and Mark Delorey. 2012. "The Effect of Protected Federal Lands on Economic Prosperity in the Non-Metropolitan West." Working paper submitted to the Journal of Regional Analysis and Policy, pp. 1–20.

Rasker, Ray, and Andrew J. Hansen. 2000. "Natural Amenities and Population Growth in the Greater Yellowstone Region." *Human Ecology Review* 7:30–40.

Reading, R. P., T. W. Clark, and Stephen Kellert. 1994. "Attitudes and Knowledge of People Living in the Greater Yellowstone Ecosystem." *Society & Natural Resources* 7:349–365.

Rengert, Kristopher M., and Robert E. Lang. 2001. "Cowboys and Cappuccino: The Emerging Diversity of the Rural West." *Fannie Mae Foundation Census Notes and Data Series*.

Ricoeur, Paul. 1984. *Time and Narrative*. Volume 1. University of Chicago Press.

Riebsame, William E., and James J. Robb. 1997. *Atlas of the New West: Portrait of a Changing Nation*. University of Colorado Center for the American West.

Rittel, H. W. J., and M. M. Webber. 1973. "Dilemmas in a General Theory of Planning." *Policy Sciences* 4:155–169.

Robbins, Jim. 2013. "On the Montana Range, Efforts to Restore Bison Meet Resistance." *New York Times*, April 1.

Robbins, P., K. Meehan, Hannah Gosnell, and S. J. Gilbertz. 2009. "Writing the New West: A Critical Review." *Rural Sociology* 74:356–382.

Roberts, Phil. 2012. *New History of Wyoming*. University of Wyoming, Department of History, uwyo.edu/robertshistory/.

Roof, Wade Clark. 1999. *Spiritual Marketplace: Baby Boomers and the Remaking of American Religion*. Princeton University Press.

Rorty, Richard. 2009. *Philosophy and the Mirror of Nature*. Princeton University Press.

Rozin, Paul. 1999. "The Process of Moralization." *Psychological Science* 10: 218–221.

Rozin, Paul, and Leher Singh. 1999. "The Moralization of Cigarette Smoking in the United States." *Journal of Consumer Psychology* 8:321–337.

Rudzitis, Gundars, and Harley E. Johansen. 1991. "How Important Is Wilderness? Results from a United States Survey." *Environmental Management* 15: 227–233.

Runte, Alfred. 1987. *National Parks: The American Experience*. University of Nebraska Press.

Russell, Sharman Apt. 1993. *Kill the Cowboy: A Battle of Mythology in the New West*. University of Nebraska.

Sayer. Andrew. 2010. *Methods in Social Sciences*. Routleg Press.

Schnaiberg, Allan. 1980. *The Environment, from Surplus to Scarcity*. Oxford University Press.

Schullery, Paul. 2004. "Searching for Yellowstone: Ecology and Wonder in the Last Wilderness." Montana Historical Society.

Schullery, Paul, and Lee H. Whittlesey. 2003. *Myth and History in the Creation of Yellowstone National Park.* University of Nebraska Press.

Shanahan, Elizabeth, M. K. McBeth, Linda E. Tigert, and P. L. Hathaway. 2010. "From Protests to Litigation to YouTube: A Longitudinal Case Study of Strategic Lobby Tactic Choice for the Buffalo Field Campaign." *Social Science Journal* 47:137–150.

Shields, Jon A. 2009. *The Democratic Virtues of the Christian Right.* Princeton University Press.

Shumway, J. Matthew, and Samuel M. Otterstrom. 2001. "Spatial Patterns of Migration and Income Change in the Mountain West: The Dominance of Service-Based, Amenity-Rich Counties." *Professional Geographer* 53:492–502.

Shweder, Richard A. 2003. *Why Do Men Barbecue? Recipes for Cultural Psychology.* Harvard University Press.

Smith, Christian. 2003. *Moral, Believing Animals.* Oxford University Press.

Smith, Duane A. 2008. *Rocky Mountain Heartland: Colorado, Montana, and Wyoming in the Twentieth Century.* University of Arizona Press.

Smith, M. D., and R. S. Krannich. 2000. "'Culture Clash' Revisited: Newcomer and Longer-Term Residents' Attitudes toward Land Use, Development, and Environmental Issues in Rural Communities in the Rocky Mountain West." *Rural Sociology* 65:396–421.

Snepenger, D. J., and Jerry Johnson. 1995. "Travel-Stimulated Entrepreneurial Migration." *Journal of Travel Research* 34:40–44.

Spaargaren, Gert, and Arthur P. J. Mol. 1992. "Sociology, Environment, and Modernity: Ecological Modernization as a Theory of Social Change." *Society & Natural Resources* 5:323–344.

Spence, Mark David. 2000. *Dispossessing the Wilderness: Indian Removal and the Making of the National Parks.* Oxford University Press.

Spinrad, Leonard. 1979. *Speaker's Lifetime Library.* Parker Publishing Company.

Stern, Paul C. 2000. "Toward a Coherent Theory of Environmentally Significant Behavior." *Journal of Social Issues* 56(3):407–424.

Stets, Jan E., and Michael J. Carter. 2012. "A Theory of the Self for the Sociology of Morality." *American Sociological Review* 77:120–140.

Strauss, Claudia. 2005. "Analyzing Discourse for Cultural Complexity." In *Finding Culture in Talk*, edited by Naomi Quinn. Palgrave Macmillan, pp. 203–242.

Swidler, Ann. 1986. "Culture in Action: Symbols and Strategies." *American Sociological Review* 51:273–286.

Swidler, Ann. 1995. *Cultural Power and Social Movements.* University of Minnesota Press.

Swidler, Ann. 2001. *Talk of Love: How Culture Matters.* University of Chicago Press.

Taylor, Charles. 1989. *Sources of the Self.* Harvard University Press.

Tepper, Steven J. 2011. *Not Here, Not Now, Not That! Protest over Art and Culture in America*. University of Chicago Press.

Thompson, Michael, Richard J. Ellis, and Aaron B. Wildavsky. 1990. *Cultural Theory*. Westview Press.

Travis, W. R. 2007. *New Geographies of the American West: Land Use and the Changing Patterns of Place*. Island Press.

Travis, William R., Julia Hobson, Hannah Gosnell Schneider, James Ferriday, Thomas Dickinson, and Geneva Mixon. 2002. "Ranchland Dynamics in the Greater Yellowstone Ecosystem." *Center of the American West*, pp. 1–32.

Trentelman, Carla Koons. 2009. "Place Attachment and Community Attachment: A Primer Grounded in the Lived Experience of a Community Sociologist." *Society & Natural Resources* 22:191–210.

Tucker, Mary Evelyn, and John Grim. 2013. *Ecology and Religion*. Island Press.

Turner, Ernest Sackville. 1964. *All Heaven in a Rage*. St. Martin's Press.

Turner, Jack. 2009. *Travels in the Greater Yellowstone*. St. Martin's Griffin.

Urbigkit, Cat. 2008. *Yellowstone Wolves: A Chronicle of the Animal, the People, and the Politics*. McDonald & Woodward.

U.S. Census Bureau. 2010. *United States Dicennial Census*.

U.S. Congress. 1964. *Wilderness Act*. 88th Congress.

U.S. Congress. 1969. *National Environmental Policy Act of 1969* (P.L.91-190). United States Committee on Interior and Insular Affairs.

U.S. Congress Senate Library. 1979. *Cumulative Index of Congressional Committee Hearings (not Confidential in Character)*. From Seventy-Fourth Congress (January 3, 1935) Through Eighty-Fifth Congress (January 3, 1959) in the United States Senate Library. "Preface," p.V.

U.S. Department of the Interior. 1873. *Annual Report of the Department of the Interior*.

USDA. 1968. *USDA Census of Agriculture*.

USDA. 1997. *USDA Census of Agriculture*.

USFWS. 1994. "The Reintroduction of Gray Wolves to Yellowstone National Park and Central Idaho: Final Environmental Impact Statement." Technical report.

Vaisey, Stephen. 2009. "Motivation and Justification: A Dual-Process Model of Culture in Action." *American Journal of Sociology* 114:1675–1715.

Van Koppen, C. S. A. 2000. "Resource, Arcadia, Lifeworld: Nature Concepts in Environmental Sociology." *Sociologia Ruralis* 40:300–318.

Wagner, Frederic H., Ronald Foresta, Richard Bruce Gill, Dale Richard McCullough, Michael R. Pelton, William F. Porter, and Hal Salwasser. 1995. *Wildlife Policies in the U.S. National Parks*. Island Press.

Weber, Max. 2009. *From Max Weber: Essays in Sociology*. Routledge.

Weixelman, Joseph Owen. 1992. "The Power to Evoke Wonder." M.A. thesis. Montana State University.

White, P. J., Rick L. Wallen, Chris Geremia, John J. Treanor, and Douglas W. Blanton. 2011. "Management of Yellowstone Bison and Brucellosis Transmission Risk: Implications for Conservation and Restoration." *Biological Conservation* 144:1322–1334.

White, Richard. 1993. *It's Your Misfortune and None of My Own: A New History of the American West*. University of Oklahoma Press.

Wilson, M. A. 1997. "The Wolf in Yellowstone: Science, Symbol, or Politics? Deconstructing the Conflict between Environmentalism and Wise Use." *Society & Natural Resources* 10:453–468.

Winkler, R., D. R. Field, A. E. Luloff, R. S. Krannich, and T. Williams. 2007. "Social Landscapes of the Inter-Mountain West: A Comparison of 'Old West' and 'New West' Communities." *Rural Sociology* 72:478–501.

Wuthnow, Robert. 1989. *Meaning and Moral Order: Explorations in Cultural Analysis*. University of California Press.

Wuthnow, Robert. 2010. *Remaking the Heartland: Middle America since the 1950s*. Princeton University Press.

Yellowstone Park Foundation. 2013. "About Yellowstone."

Yochim, Michael J. 2009. *Yellowstone and the Snowmobile: Locking Horns over National Park Use*. University Press of Kansas.

Yuskavage, R. E. 2007. "Converting Historical Industry Time Series Data from SIC to NAICS." U.S. Department of Commerce Bureau of Economic Analysis.

Zelizer, Viviana A. Rotman. 1979. *Morals and Markets: The Development of Life Insurance in the United States*. Columbia University Press.

Zelizer, Viviana A. Rotman. 1985. *Pricing the Priceless Child*. Princeton University Press.

Zelizer, Viviana A. Rotman. 2010. *Economic Lives: How Culture Shapes the Economy*. Princeton University Press.

INDEX

286 | Index

Princeton Studies in Cultural Sociology

Paul J. DiMaggio, Michèle Lamont, Robert J. Wuthnow
and Viviana A. Zelizer, Series Editors

Partisan Publics: Communication and Contention across Brazilian Youth Activist Networks by Ann Mische

Disrupting Science: Social Movements, American Scientists, and the Politics of the Military, 1945–1975 by Kelly Moore

Weaving Self-Evidence: A Sociology of Logic by Claude Rosental, translated by Catherine Porter

The Taylorized Beauty of the Mechanical: Scientific Management and the Rise of Modernist Architecture by Mauro F. Guillén

Impossible Engineering: Technology and Territoriality on the Canal du Midi by Chandra Mukerji

Economists and Societies: Discipline and Profession in the United States, Britain, and France, 1890s to 1990s by Marion Fourcade

Reds, Whites, and Blues: Social Movements, Folk Music, and Race in the United States by William G. Roy

Privilege: The Making of an Adolescent Elite at St. Paul's School by Shamus Rahman Khan

Making Volunteers: Civic Life after Welfare's End by Nina Eliasoph

Becoming Right: How Campuses Shape Young Conservatives by Amy J. Binder and Kate Wood

The Moral Background: An Inquiry into the History of Business Ethics by Gabriel Abend

There Goes the Gayborhood by Amin Ghaziani

The Battle for Yellowstone: Morality and the Sacred Roots of Environmental Conflict by Justin Farrell

CPSIA information can be obtained
at www.ICGtesting.com
Printed in the USA
LVHW01s2213100518
576716LV00005B/995/P

9 780691 176307